Barbara Denny

The Playmaster of Blankenburg
– the story of Friedrich Froebel
(1782–1852)

Autolycus Publications
14 Barlby Road, London W10 6AR

'The last word of my theory I shall carry to my grave: the time is not ripe for it. If three hundred years after my death my system of education is completely and according to its real principle carried out through Europe, I shall rejoice in heaven. If only the seed be cast abroad its springing up will not fail, nor the fruit be wanting.'—Friedrich Froebel.

AUTHOR'S NOTE

The Playmaster of Blankenburg is not a novel in the normal sense. It is the factual story of Friedrich Froebel, based on his own short autobiography, his writings and letters. It has been carefully researched (see page 224) and is supported by later material on his life and work, but with some fictional embellishments of a minor nature.

What I have attempted to do is to put flesh on the bones, to give life and personality to a man who probably did more for progressive education than any other one individual but who has been entirely neglected outside narrow academic circles to the extent that students have been known to ask '*What* is Froebel?' not '*Who* was Froebel?'

The Playmaster will not add one iota to the academic knowledge of this great man, but I hope it will bring him to the hearts, minds and imagination of many who have benefited from his inspired and dedicated life.

Published in association with the Friends of Ibstock Place School

ISBN 0 903413 52 3

Printed by Edgcott Press Ltd.

© 1982 Autolycus Publications

CHAPTER ONE

One raindrop ran into another, like glass beads on a string, until swelling with its weight one big drop ran down the window-pane and splashed on to the sill below.

The little boy watched them... another... and another... and another.

It was one of the many delights he treasured. Yesterday he had seen a fly. The fly was really rather small and ugly but viewed conversely through the pane of glass it appeared brave and beautiful, its wings sparkling and many-coloured, its hairy legs performing amazing acrobatics to smooth its gleaming sides, and its little protruding eyes glowing like jewels.

The window was almost hidden from the room by its heavy curtains, and the inside sill was wide enough to form a window-seat. This was the place that Friedrich called his 'magic window.' It was quiet and secret, and he could sit there for hours without anyone disturbing him, or even knowing that he was there.

The window was on the third floor of the ugly old house, with its secluded garden. It stood just outside the village of Oberweissbach, in the Thuringen Forest in Central Germany, in the year 1786. The garden was surrounded by a high wall: so high that even from these upper windows the little boy could only see the tops of the trees and the steep, forest-clad slopes of the hills which rose almost immediately behind the house.

The garden, too, was overgrown, with trees which made the house even more gloomy than its dark decorations and heavy furniture. Friedrich's father, the Pastor Froebel, had resisted all efforts of his wife and sons to have some of the trees felled. An austere Lutheran minister, he had a compelling love of nature, the only softening influence in his otherwise stern character, and although the trees threatened the success of his much-loved garden, he would not have them harmed. 'They give shade in summer and nesting places for the birds,' he said, 'Let them stay.'

The Pastor Froebel's garden was his one concession to material pleasures. He was as strict with himself as with his family, and even the four-year-old Friedrich did not escape his righteous wrath and strict codes of behaviour. Improvements to the house, new clothes, new furnishings, he regarded as temptations of the Devil. All spare money (and there was little enough of it), all effort, must be devoted to the church, the great gloomy building adjoining the manse and dominating it.

'Vain glorification,' he would thunder at the breakfast table when one of his growing sons appeared in a new cravat or necktie, and there would follow an impromptu sermon on the sins of vanity.

With this austerity and solemnity, even beyond his fifty years, the Pastor had little to offer his older sons, born of his first wife, who had died nine months after the birth of Friedrich. Even this he bore with little sign of outward emotion, suffering it as a chastisement of the vengeful deity which inspired his religious fervour. Like an ox under the yoke, he bent his shoulders beneath the burden of his bereavement, becoming only a little more austere, stricter, and less approachable.

A year previously, however, he had married again, a young woman member of his congregation, a spinster in her early thirties. She had long ago given up the idea of a good marriage, and overwhelmed both herself and her family by her good fortune in being selected for such an honourable role as the much respected minister's second wife and mother to his orphan sons. She was a pleasant-looking woman with a gentler approach to her religion than her husband, but even her presence in the manse had not changed its outward dreariness; vanity was still vanity, and the furnishings of fifty years ago were still serviceable.

Friedrich sat watching the raindrops for an hour or more before he was disturbed by his brother's voice.

'Are you here *again*?'

Traugott, the youngest of his brothers, was a sturdy twelve-year-old, with fair hair and a ruddy complexion still bearing the traces of its summer sunburn. He was Friedrich's favourite, although he loved them all, and they him, in the rough manner of older boys with a child.

Traugott was the only one not too old yet for a game, not too occupied with his studies to find time for telling a story. Traugott even took the blame for him when their father's displeasure came down on them, which was often, (although his punishment was more severe, as befitting one older and therefore more responsible, than it would be for little Friedrich, who was still regarded as the baby).

'What are you doing now?'

'Watching the rain,' said Friedrich.

'Yesterday it was a fly!'

'It was a *lovely* fly... It had hairy legs!'

Traugott laughed: 'If you had been Noah you would have had flies in the Ark.'

'Of course I would...'

'Father's writing a sermon on the Flood,' confided Traugott, with the air of someone who has special knowledge of high affairs. 'He believes there might even be *another* Flood... it has rained so hard and so long, and the world is so sinful...'

The sinful world had no concern for Friedrich. He was thinking of the Ark. His small face flushed with pleasure at the thought of all those beasts and birds with him in a boat.

'When shall we build the Ark?' he asked Traugott eagerly.

'I'm only joking, silly,' said Traugott, suddenly the older brother. 'Come on, we'll be late for supper...' He held out his hand to the little boy to jump down.

The boys walked together downstairs to the room they used as a sort of nursery study. Sitting by the fire, working on an embroidered sheet-hem, part of her belated trousseau, was their stepmother. She was a small, neat woman, not unpretty, but too plump, her figure already spreading into waistlessness, due no doubt to her love of sweets and pastries. (The Pastor disapproved of this, another small vanity, and she was therefore forced to confine most of her indulgence to these nursery suppers served in the early part of the evening.)

Christoph, Christian and August, her other stepsons, were lounging by the fire. Christoph, the eldest, tall and dark, had his dead mother's gentle nature. He was to follow his father into the church, but his devotions were more those of the poet and mystic than the disciplinarian. What his father called vanity, he preferred to regard as beauty.

Christoph was the only brother able to avert their father's anger from Friedrich in his childish misdemeanours. Traugott would take the blame and the punishment, Christoph would involve the Pastor in argument over the offence, and the purpose of the reprimand would be forgotten.

Christian was a pleasant, delicate-looking boy who had never quite got over the rigours of illness in his youth, when he had been stricken with diphtheria and his life despaired of.

August was equally tall, but fair as Traugott, another sturdy lad with a love of activity and the open air. He fretted in the gloom of the manse, and was impatient to be independent and away.

'Hurry up,' said Sofia. 'We're all waiting for you... Friedrich, you've been dreaming again at that window! Come here, liebling, you're quite cold.' She chaffed the little boy's hands between her own.

The maid had already brought in the food, and was drawing the curtains against the darkening sky outside.

'The Pastor will be having his refreshment in his study,' Sofia told her. 'He has not finished his sermon and doesn't wish to be disturbed.'

Friedrich sat on his little stool. This was the custom in recent months of nursery suppers. His stepmother put jam on his bread and handed it to him, then she poured the thick, sweet chocolate into his mug.

Friedrich was warm and happy, he bit hungrily into his bread and jam. Life had changed at the manse in the last months. Now there was someone other than the maids to help him dress and do his hair. The peasant girls were kind, but their touch was rough and they had so much work to do in the cumbersome great house that they were often hurried and impatient.

Sofia's touch was gentle, and her leisure considerable in a house which, despite its modest income, could still afford a number of servants. As she tied the tapes on Friedrich's numerous small garments, she told him stories and sang little rhymes. She fancied herself as the minister's wife, and even more so as the mother of his motherless children.

The nursery suppers, when she could be together with her new family of sons, were just one of the many welcome innovations which she had introduced since she had become Frau Froebel. Once the older boys had eaten together, their father preferring to dine in his study alone. Little Friedrich had usually taken his meals in the kitchen with the servants. He did not mind this; the kitchen was warm and full of exciting sights and sounds. Sometimes the cook gave him the sugar which filled the hollows in the candied fruits she made from peaches and apricots; and there were bubblings and hissings from the big boiling saucepans and pots which he liked to pretend were the cauldrons of witches.

The black beetles lived in the kitchen, too, and Friedrich's affection for black beetles was a source of horrified amazement to the maids, who were terrified of them. The most terrible moment of his short life had been the time when one girl, dismayed at the sight of the little boy sitting on the floor among the beetles, trying to touch their shining backs with his finger, had brought her wooden shoe down on a score or more.

'Dirty, beastly things!' she raged. 'You'll die of plague if you touch them!'

Friedrich's fear of the plague was nothing compared to the horror of the dark, blooded mass that lay beneath her foot. He was very sick and cried all night, comforted by no-one, not even the gentle Christoph.

The kitchen meals were no more, although Friedrich was always a welcome visitor to the lower rooms of the house, and assured of tasties and sweetmeats from the cook and maids. Now he ate with his stepmother in her sitting room, or in the nursery study ... and there was always something special, such as jam made from the wild cherries or bilberries that grew on the slopes of the hill.

The hill dominated the house. The timber from its trees had made its beams, the old wood burned on its fires, and so steeply did it mount from the garden boundary, that even in summer the sun never rose above its crest until well after breakfast time, and its shadow engulfed even the top of the pointed tower of the church. The house, already gloomy with its long, narrow passages and heavily over-furnished rooms, was made darker and gloomier by the dominating presence of the hill.

Friedrich was too young to have climbed to its peak, over 2000 feet of ambling, wooded paths, never severely steep but arduous. Sometimes he and Traugott walked together on the lower slopes, where the ash trees were bright with red berries in the autumn. Sometimes he heard a deer rustling through the undergrowth, or caught a glimpse of its antlers in the sunlight which filtered through the leaves.

One day last autumn the boys had been shocked to silence by the blood-chilling scream of two rutting stags and heard their antlers clashing in combat.

Friedrich loved the forest, not the least because it frightened him just a little, like the bad bits in the fairy tales he loved, the places where the witches cackled and the giants roared.

The forest also was the place of all magic, the charcoal-burners, grimed like blackamoors, and the wood-cutters, all familiar characters of romance.

There were wolves in the forest, too... although they seldom were seen or heard anywhere near the village. Fearsome tales were told, nevertheless, of travellers who had been attacked on winter nights as they made their way over the hills to Erfurt or Saale. The presence of the wolves lent enchantment to the woods...

As Friedrich sat eating his bread and jam by the fire, he was dreaming of the wolves... the 'grey shadows' Traugott called them. How would they fit into the life of the Ark when the Flood came...?

'Mama,' he said (it had been agreed that he should call Sofia 'Mama,' although the older boys called her 'Aunt'). 'Didn't God say that the wolf and the lamb shall dwell together...?'

'Yes, dear, He did.'

'Then it will be alright in the Ark?'

'In the Ark, dear?'

'Yes, Mama, when the Flood comes...'

'The Flood?' Sofia looked at Traugott.

'Traugott! What have you been telling him now?'

'I'm sorry, Aunt,' said Traugott. 'I told him that Father was writing a sermon about the Flood.'

'He's too little to frighten with such things. Traugott, it was naughty of you...'

'I wasn't frightened' said Friedrich indignantly, eager to defend his adored Traugott. 'I *want* there to be a Flood. I *want* to live in the Ark with all the animals...'

7

Sofia laughed. 'There's not going to be a flood, liebling...'

Seeing Friedrich's lip trembling, near to tears, Traugott ruffled his hair. 'You're my little man, aren't you, Friedling? Tomorrow we'll go hunting together and I'll show you the wren's nest I found yesterday...'

Friedrich bit deeper into his cake. The world was very warm and safe and splendid...

*   *   *

On his fifth birthday Sofia had a surprise for Friedrich.

'You are going to have a baby brother or sister,' she said.

Friedrich could not have had a better birthday present. During the weeks that followed he thought of nothing else. Here was the playfellow for whom he had always longed, who would fill the long hours when Traugott was studying with his tutor and could not come out to play with him in the garden or in the woods. In his childish mind, Friedrich imagined the baby would immediately be a little boy or girl, strong and sturdy enough to walk in the woods with him as he did now with Traugott.

He was bitterly disappointed therefore when, the following August, he was led on tiptoe into his step-mother's bedroom to be shown the new baby, a crumpled scrap with a little, red, frenzied face peering from the folds of a voluminous shawl.

The shock was too much for him. He burst into a storm of noisy tempestuous weeping.

His father was furious.

'You wretched boy!' he stormed as he dragged the sobbing child out of the room. 'Your wilful ways will be punished by God if not by your father... You are no longer the baby in this house. Remember that!'

Friedrich crept miserably away to his window. He buried his face in the folds of its curtains, smelling their dust with a sort of self-torture which offset his misery of mind, and wept, not the least because he had been banned from nursery suppers with his brothers.

The days before the baby's birth had been thunderous and sultry. Last night, when lights had burned late at the manse and the doctor had ridden up the drive after midnight to join the midwife who delivered the village women. Friedrich had been awake listening, not knowing why, but sensing some atmosphere of urgency and importance. Somewhere in the half-light of early dawn he had heard a cry strangely like the sound he had once heard in the woods.

'A snared rabbit,' Traugott had said then, but there were no snares in the manse garden, he knew that. Half asleep, he did not associate the sound with the baby, although his brother Christoph had told him that his little brother or sister would be with them very soon now. Soon after this he had sunk into a hot restless sleep in which babies and rabbits had played with him in the wood... the dream turning into a nightmare where his playfellows had turned into wolves. He had awakened gasping and beating his pillow.

He shivered in the window-seat as he recalled his terror.

Now the storm had passed, and the garden was drenched and glistening in the late afternoon sunshine from a sky that was still yellow and leaden from the thunder. A blackbird was singing on the branch of the mulberry tree, which almost touched the window-pane. Through the boy's tears it appeared distorted and nightmarish too.

Friedrich's outburst at the sight of the new baby was soon forgotten in the general hustle and excitement of the new arrival. The starchy nurse who had been employed to care for Sofia and her son was also to look after Friedrich. Her attentions were even less welcome than had been those of the maids. She was even more hurried and less patient, and Friedrich had his hair tweaked and his tapes pulled too tight by her hasty hands. What is more, she had a passion for cleanliness, and scrubbed his neck and knees until they were sore every time she washed him. He was very glad when at last she packed her black bag and bustled away in the hired carriage to officiate at another confinement in a neighbouring village.

The nurse's departure, however, was succeeded by a more permanent and even less welcome visitor. Sofia's spinster sister, made homeless by the recent death of her mother, came to assist her sister with the new arrival in the nursery. She had not even Sofia's mild good looks, and to Friedrich she presented a formidable appearance in her black, tight bodices, her hair pulled severely away from her face, and a habit of pursing her lips which gave her an air of disapproval of the world as a whole, and Friedrich in particular. What is more, she seemed to have unlimited time to interfere with his life, and a most uncanny way of appearing at the most inopportune moments, when he was either exceptionally dirty or untidy from his games in the garden, or engaged in some secret, childish pursuit, harmless enough in itself, but sufficient to merit a scolding.

After the long lying-in of childbirth, Sofia came downstairs paler and thinner (both of which qualities became her better than her late, round rosiness). Little Karl was settled in his wicker cradle in the corner of the nursery study, which had now been furnished more to meet his needs than those of the older members of the family.

At first, Friedrich had been delighted to see his stepmother again, but soon he realised that she had changed more than in her appearance. Whereas she had always petted him, jammed his bread or toast, tied on his pinafore, she left this to her sister (who cared little for the tasks) or his brothers, while her attentions were devoted to the baby.

It was Traugott who gave Friedrich his plate and mug, and when he got too excited and laughed too much at one of Christian's jokes, Sofia scolded him that he would wake Karl.

After his first disappointment, Friedrich had forgiven the baby for its ugliness and for being so small. Christoph, sensing the little boy's sadness, had sat by his bed one night soon after his first scolding, and taking him in his arms had stilled his fierce sobbing.

He told him that the baby would grow, quite quickly. ('Think how puppies and kittens grow,' he said. 'Remember how blind and helpless they are'). Soon, Karl would be big and strong enough to do all the things that Friedrich wanted him to do.

'You must help him,' said Christoph. 'He will need you. You must care for him every day.'

He made Friedrich a little sword and belt to hold it, and told him to guard the baby, just as soldiers guarded a king.

This appealed to Friedrich, who had only seen soldiers once when they came to the village to recruit. He wore an old, feathered hat of Christoph's which fell ludicrously over his ears, and stood guard outside the baby's room so long and so silently that the maids began to whisper that he was touched.

Although he felt his stepmother's change of interest keenly, Friedrich was not as cast down as he might have been had it not been for the company of a new friend, the potting-shed boy, Redau. Redau was already devoted to the dark haired little Friedrich, who followed him around as he went about the garden weeding and pricking out. It was Redau who showed him the first tiny leaves of the seedlings, unfolding like little loops from the brown earth. He put an acorn in a pot for him, so that he could watch it grow, and he had an amazing knowledge of all the creeping, crawling things that lived under stones and between the cracks in the walls. He shared Friedrich's love of spiders. 'Them's good for the garden,' he would say, and together they would admire the dew-dropped webs hanging from the vines on the early autumn mornings.

Traugott was having to spend more and more of his time at his studies. He had announced his desire to study medicine and was under the instruction of a tutor, who spent long hours with him in the school-room at the back of the house. Friedrich could see him through the window, his head in his hands, bowed over his books.

Having therefore lost one companion, at least during the day, Freidrich was naturally anxious to accept the friendship of the gardener's boy.

No one paid much attention to this rather unusual friendship, for in many ways Friedrich had been relegated to his previous situation in the house... something between a pet dog and a duty, occasionally petted, occasionally 'done to.' Like a dog, his food was put before him and he ate it. Sofia still attended to some of his needs, although he was now able to do much more for himself, but she was less patient, and scolded more often.

'Stand still!' she would snap as he stood to have his back-tapes tied on his little chemise shirt, or 'keep quiet... you'll wake baby.'

The Pastor's only concession to pleasure was his garden. Although employing a man and Red to tend it, he spent many hours there himself pruning the roses and training the vines which grew along the south side of the house. These gardening times were the only intimate contact that Friedrich had with his father. The Pastor conducted family prayers every morning, and each night before bed, Friedrich was taken solemnly to kiss his father goodnight. Otherwise his father was the tall, black-clad figure who presided at the dining table (so distant at the far end that he seemed to live in another world from that at the other end of the table, where Friedrich was slowly ladling boiled fish and milk pudding into his mouth).

It was the same on Sundays, when Friedrich sat in church with his stepmother and brothers in the special pew reserved for the Pastor's family. Because he was so small, even sitting on a cushion specially provided for him to make him taller, and the fronts of the pews so high, all Friedrich could see of his father as he preached was his head. At these times his father and God became confused, as a disembodied face, black-bearded, stern and admonishing, seeing all as it looked down from above, sky or pulpit, watching his many misdeeds, even anticipating them.

But in the garden his father was almost a human being. He still wore black, but a shabbier suit than the one he normally wore about the house, and old heavy boots. Friedrich would carry the gardening basket, with the shears and pruning scissors, the bundles of bass for tying back the rose tendrils, and the little twists of wire that the Pastor used to train the vines.

'Why do you do that...?' he asked his father.

The Pastor replied: 'If I did not, the garden would be wild, like a jungle, and you would not be able to play in it. Plants, like little children, have to be shown the right way to go...' As he said this, his hands busy with his task, the Pastor sounded almost gentle. He was always ready to explain what he was doing to the little boy, often adding a reference to biblical agriculture, to give his instruction a dual purpose.

One day, warmed by the confidence of the garden, Friedrich dared to ask his father about Hell. The Pastor did not tone his reply to his son's years. The fiery torment, he said, awaited all who broke the Lord's Commandments. Friedrich knew the Commandments, though he did not understand all of them, but he suffered considerably over the one which said, 'Thou shalt not steal...' Was it stealing to take an apricot when there were so many?

Hell became more real to him than Heaven. Heaven was beyond his imagination. Hell was the great kitchen magnified and multiplied, or the furnaces of the charcoal-burners, and the souls in torment he imagined as the logs twisted and blackened in the flames. But any fear he felt, which was slight, was no more than that he felt in the fairy tales. It was less real than his nightmares of wolves, and his terror of the dark end of the corridor, beyond his bedroom, and the cupboard under the stairs, where the servants kept the brooms.

Another day, when they were in the garden together, Friedrich asked his father a question which had burned in his mind for weeks.

'Father... when Karl is older, can he play with me?'

'Of course, when you have time.'

'But I have all day to play, Father.'

'That is what I mean... it is time you began lessons. Soon you will be six, and boys of six must learn to read and write and to know their numbers. I was talking to your mother yesterday, and she tells me you are too often idle, and that you spend too much time with that gardener's boy. You will be learning rough ways unfitting to your station as a Pastor's son. That dog of his is unhealthy...you might even catch the plague. In future you will come to my study every morning for instruction.'

Therefore, as the autumn of 1787 paled into winter, Friedrich spent less and less time in the garden. Every morning he would sit on a small stool in his father's study, its heavy curtains drawn against the December sun (too much light strained the eyes, his father believed). The late birds singing in the trees on the cold, crisp mornings, mocked his halting efforts to make sense from the black shapes before him. In the small sunlight that filtered into the room, the letters looked like ants dancing before his eyes.

All the passages he had to read were from the scriptures.

'God is love,' said his father, and Friedrich would chant after him 'God is love,' following his finger on the copy, but when later the Pastor pointed to the same phrase he could not remember it. Sometimes he would guess frantically, and transcribe some other passage learnt parrot-fashion. The old Gothic characters, with their loops and furbishings, looked all alike. There were no pictures to help, only his father's long, relentless finger pointing and admonishing, and his patient, but despairing prompting.

Writing was no easier. Laboriously copying his father's copyplate hand, Friedrich would scrape on his slate...

'In the beginning was the Word.' or 'The wages of sin is death.' (Mostly texts of the latter type, for the Pastor lost no opportunity to sermonise).

As Friedrich, tight-fisted, tried to shape the words of 'the wages of sin is death,' he had in his mind's eye an old man who attended his father's church and who doubled the duties of village carpenter with those of undertaker and gravedigger. A wizened and blackened old man, he had never heard that cleanliness was next to Godliness, the blackness was grimed into his skin and hung about him like soot on a chimney sweep.

To Friedrich, who felt a shiver of almost delicious horror as he wrote, the black old man was sin, whose wages were death. Did he not, after all, bury dead people? But who would pay him? God perhaps? That remote, bodyless, bearded face extending a hand from the clouds to hand down his terrible reward from above.

These day-dreamings did little to help Friedrich's reading and writing progress, and his father, who had successfully taught all his other sons, despaired of him.

'That boy is backward, I fear,' he told Sofia.

'I am not surprised,' said his wife. 'He was neglected until you married me, the companion of servants, living in the kitchen. Even now he spends too much of his time with that wretched gardener's boy.'

'Another thing,' said Sofia. 'I do not like the way Friedrich behaves to little Karl. I am sure he is jealous of the poor little mite, and if you say he is backward, there is no knowing what might happen if we leave them together, I shall not have a moment's peace.'

'I don't think you need be anxious in that respect, my dear,' said the Pastor, 'Friedrich may be slow at his studies, but he is a loving, sensitive child... and naturally he must feel a little envious of the attentions you have to pay to little Karl. It is our duty to ensure that this tendency is not encouraged.' Nevertheless, he had already decided that something must be done about his difficult little son.

Eventually, the best solution that could be found was that Friedrich should attend the village school. The Pastor took a great interest in this institution, of which he was Superintendent. It was arranged, therefore, that because of his age (he was just seven), and the roughness of some of the village boys, he should join the girls' class.

His first Monday at school dawned fine and sunny. The hill rose darkly against the bright blue sky with little puffs of clouds, and there was a mist over the tree-tops, indicating a hot day to come. As it was to be always, the momentous days in Friedrich's life invariably occurred in high summer.

He was dressed in his Sunday suit, black, with tight little trousers which irritated the skin of his thighs as it grew hot. He would have been a complete miniature of his father, had it not been for the latter's black beard, as together they set out on the short walk through the woods from the manse to the village. The grass-hoppers were chirping and the air was full of the humming of bees in the lime blossoms: The path was sandy, and as the little boy tried to match his steps to the larger ones of the man, little black spiders scurried in panic before them. The hedge-rows were thick with roses, and fox-gloves formed banks of purple down the slopes of the hill, which ran into the meadowlands below.

As they made their way down, Friedrich could hear the school bell coming and going on the breeze. He was not frightened, only excited...

It had been arranged that they should arrive a little after the school assembly so that the governess could set the other children to their lessons and give more attention to Friedrich.

She met them at the gate, the tall bearded man and the little boy, an oddly assorted pair in their black garb. A stern, but not unkindly looking woman, she took Friedrich by the hand and bobbed a curtsy to the Pastor, for whom she had great admiration.

'Can you read yet, Friedrich?'

'Not very well, ma'am.'

'Or write?'

'Not very well, ma'am'

'Never mind, you will learn... but you must work hard, and just because you are to be in the girls' class, do not think that you can be idle.'

As they passed in through the door of the school, Friedrich caught his first breath of the musty smell which pervaded the whole building. For ever after he associated with this, his first school, the lingering fumes of the old coke stove which burned in the centre of the room from late September to early April, and left its memory around for the rest of the year.

When the class door opened, he heard the chanting of the little girls' voices, reciting in unison the text they had been told to learn from his father's sermon the previous day. There were about fifteen little girls, aged from Friedrich's own age, or a little younger, to one or two nearing twelve. As the three entered, one or two heads lifted from their bowed position over the high desks, and bright eyes peered from between folded fingers.

Friedrich had never seen so many children before, but it was not the sight but the sound that captivated him and remained with him as a vivid memory all the rest of his life. The fresh, girlish voices were chanting, 'Seek ye first the Kingdom of God'. Unlike some of his father's texts of the God of wrath and thunder, this gentle instruction had fired Friedrich's imagination. The kingdom of God, he felt, would be something like his beloved forest, only more perfect, where snares were never set; where there were no cries of pain in the dusk; where it would be always spring or summer, and the flowers would always bloom.

The kingdom of God, thought Friedrich, was worth seeking.

Much to his father's surprise and relief, Friedrich settled down well at the village school. He suffered a few taunts from the bigger boys when he came out into the schoolyard with his girl companions after lessons, but his status as the Pastor's son prevented any serious bullying. In any case, there was something about the little boy's grim independence, despite his rather frail appearance, that even the roughest of his male schoolfellows respected.

On one occasion, when one of the bolder boys shouted
'Here comes Fritzy with the girls... Where's your petticoat, Fritzy...?,' Friedrich flew at him with such ferocity that the governess had to be called to separate them. The incident never reached the Pastor's ears for fear he should consider the school lacking in supervision and discipline.

The teaching was not much different to that which Friedrich had already experienced with his father, but he made steady if slow progress. The formula was still one of constant repetition. The children chanted in unison, after the governess, the fundamental rules of the three 'Rs.' The only occasional variation was when, instead of repeating after their teacher, they laboriously copied out long passages on their slates with squeaky pencils, wiping away their efforts, before renewing them, with damp and smelly little rags.

Once a day, before school began, they sang a short and simple hymn. This Friedrich enjoyed, and he took much trouble to learn the tune and the words, so that he could sing it later at home to Karl, or on his way to school.

Twice a week the Pastor visited the school to give religious instruction, a slightly milder version of his Sunday sermons, but still with a liberal dressing of fire and brimstone, thumping the desk in front of him with his clenched fist, and glowering at the little girls and Friedrich from beneath fierce, bushy eyebrows. At these times Friedrich was proud of his father.

At first one of the maids took Friedrich to school by the wood path, but after a while he was allowed to make the short journey alone, and this became the most treasured part of his day. He grew to know every inch of the way, and all its charms and secrets. When the winter came he eagerly followed the tracks in the snow which he had learned to recognise. The pug-marks of the badgers, the narrowly lined-up prints of the foxes, the minute pin-prick steps of the mice, and fine tracery of birds' feet. Earlier, in the autumn, he had watched the squirrels garnering the nuts, chattering busily at each other and scolding him for his intrusion. He collected blackberries in his hat and ate them as he walked, arriving at school with his lips and tongue stained purple.

Christmas came and passed, and one day the snow was spiked with the first green of the snowdrops. When the thaw set in, and the snow shrank to a few transparent icy patches on the grass, the yellow coltsfoots burned like Easter candles, leafless and vulnerable in the March wind.

If Friedrich's progress in class was slow, his knowledge of the woods and its wildlife was quick and infinite. Never a day passed but he added to his store of information: the flash of a wing which distinguished one bird from another; the flowers, and the fruits and berries that followed; the shape of the trees in summer, when they were green and heavy with leaves, or in the winter, when their black bones glared out of the snow. To all this he added his intimate knowledge of the wild creatures: the banks where the badgers played; the meadow paths where the hares started from their forms with such suddenness, and so close that they made him jump, and he would laugh with delight to see them leaping away into the hedge.

The Kingdom of God was obviously here, in the woods all around him.

At first the little girls in his class regarded Friedrich as a sort of curiosity; but they soon came to regard him as a normal part of their school life. He was neither clever enough to shame them nor stupid enough to annoy the governess, and thus bring her wrath down on them all. The big girls were inclined to spoil him, calling him 'little birdie' for his habit of putting the pheasant feathers he found in his cap, and giving him sweetmeats from their lunch packets. The littler girls found him an eager companion in their games of make-believe, played in the short recreation time in the middle of the day.

Among these little girls was Lotte, daughter of one of the Pastor's church elders, and the same age as Friedrich, though not so tall. Friedrich had smiled at her as they passed in the churchyard path on Sundays on the way to service.

Lotte was a plump little girl with fair plaits which were too short to hang down gracefully; instead they stuck out on either side of her round little face like two small horns. She was always ready to smile, though naturally solemn in expression, and eager to join any game, or perform any task that might win her the approval of either her schoolfellows or the governess. Because she was a girl it was not considered right for Lotte to come to school on her own, and she was usually brought by an older sister.

One day in the early spring, when there was still snow on the ground, Lotte's mother called at the manse early in the morning, bringing Lotte with her. It seemed that Lotte's sister had an irritating cough and a slight fever, and her mother did not think it wise for her to come out in the cold. The family lived not far from the manse, and the solution to the problem seemed obvious.

'You are to take Lotte to school with you today,' Friedrich was told by Sofia. 'Be sure you take great care of her, and don't lead her into any mischief, or let her get her boots dirty.'

The children set off together through the snow. Friedrich showed Lotte the black patches of the rooks' nests in the skeletons of the trees, and the place where a few days ago he had found the remains of a pheasant caught by a marauding fox. The ground was still blood-stained with untidy heaps of feathers scattered around on the snow. Lotte's hand tightened in his and her round grey eyes grew even rounder. He felt very brave and grown-up.

Meanwhile, life at the manse went on much as before. Karl grew from a sturdy toddler into a cheerful little boy, but Sofia never quite recovered her earlier affection for Friedrich. It was as if that plump bosom had only enough affection for one child, and that was her own, her adored little Karl.

When Karl was nearly four, Friedrich had a wonderful idea. He was fond of his little stepbrother, and not often disturbed by the lack of affection from Sofia, which he had in any case enjoyed for such a brief spell that it was almost forgotten. What is more, he had learned by experience that the way to his stepmother's heart was through that of her young son; anything that pleased Karl pleased her too, and even earned a brief show of affection.

For some time Friedrich had been trying to think of some gift, some surprise that he could give Karl on his birthday. It was a hopeless task for even had he any money, which he had not, there was no shop in Oberweissbach but the general store, which had little in it to please a small boy.

The solution to his problem was given to him, but unwittingly, by Redau, when the two were engaged in one of their illicit potting-shed conversations (for the Pastor still disapproved of his son's intimacy with the servants, and particularly Red). Red was the illegitimate son of one of the village girls. The girl had been sent away into service, and her boy brought up by his grandmother. The Pastor was certain that the mother's sin still dwelt in her luckless son, and as such he was no fit companion for young Friedrich.

Red was a friendless boy himself. Never having been to school, he knew none of the boys of the village, who considered him simple. He had worked since he was eight—long hours in all weathers in the Pastor's garden, and in the potting shed under the stern eye of the gardener, a sour old man who shared his master's belief that the sins of the mother would surely be visited upon the son, and gave Red no chance to forget it.

When Friedrich confided in Red that he intended to give little Karl a birthday present, Red laughed.

'You're a queer one,' he said. 'They say you're jealous of the baby, yet all you do is to take him presents. I saw you give him that peach I picked for you the other day.'

'I'm not jealous,' said Friedrich. 'I love Karl. Very soon now he'll be big enough to play with me, just as I used to play once with Traugott.'

'Say they don't let him play with thee.?' said Red slowly with the sad wisdom of one who has learned the ways of the world.

'They *will*, Red... but they *will*. He's my little brother. I can show him the woods, the badgers' holes, the rooks' nests, all the wonderful things that Traugott used to show me.'

'Mayhap,' said Redau, shrugging his shoulders and ruffling the little boy's hair. 'But don't say I didn't warn thee not to get excited, thou'll only be disappointed.'

'I tell thee what...' he added, seeing the little boy's lower lip trembling, and regretting his frankness, 'I'll show thee a secret...!'

'A secret!' Friedrich was speechless with excitement his momentary sadness forgotten. 'Show me... Show me!'

The bigger boy hesitated. Even now he was not certain that he should share his secret, even with Friedrich, but seeing the child's bright face beginning to cloud again into disappointment, he relented.

'Not now... but later. When its getting dark, just before your bed-time, if you can come out here then, I'll show thee the secret.'

The time between the afternoon and dusk never passed more slowly. When at last the west was reddening, and the trees were black against the hillsides, Friedrich (who had been too excited to eat his bread and jam, and had nearly been sent to bed with a suspected fever owing to his bright eyes and burning cheeks) crept into the garden.

Red was there to meet him, and led him down to the end of the garden, where there was an old hut used to store seed-boxes and flower-pots. He opened the creaking door, which made an alarmingly loud noise, and they crept in. Red had brought a taper and a tinder to light it. As the flame guttered in the dark hut, Friedrich caught a glimpse of something moving on the floor in the far corner. A bright eye flashed in the light and a tiny snarl made him start. Lying on an old sack between a pile of boxes were two fox-cubs.

Friedrich was enchanted. He had seen the flash of a fox in the snow, or the start of a red brush in the undergrowth, but this was the first time that he had had a close up view of cubs. They snapped and snarled at each other with baby ferocity as they fought each other for possession of a rabbit's foot.

Red bent down and picked up one by the scruff. It waved its little paws with fierce ineffectuality, and went on snarling furiously. When Red took it in his arms and offered it a scrap of meat from his pocket, it took it. The snarling changed to a soft growl and it allowed him to stroke its head.

'Can I?' whispered Friedrich.

'Yes' said Red, 'but be careful. His teeth may be small, but they're sharp.'

Friedrich gingerly touched the little bright brown head; the fur was short and springy, but soft. It was wonderful. The cub even rose against his caress, pushing its little face against his hand while still growling softly to itself.

Leaving the cubs fed and curled asleep in each other's arms, the boys crept back through the dusky garden, where the scent of tobacco plants and stocks was already heavy on the evening air. Friedrich lay awake long into the night thinking of the cubs, and before he fell into a restless, excited sleep he knew what he would do for Karl's birthday.

The birthday dawned bright and clear. Sofia dressed Karl in his best clothes, and there were presents for him from all his brothers, although all Friedrich could offer was one of his old toys shabbily restored. It seemed to please Karl well enough, although he had already been playing with it for months, because it had been newly wrapped in paper and therefore took on the guise of a surprise.

After breakfast, Friedrich and Karl were left alone together in the nursery. School had finished for the summer as it was harvest-time, and many of the children were needed at home on the farms and in the vineyards.

'Shall I tell you a secret, Karl?'

The little boy was as eager as Friedrich himself had been.

'Can I take Karl into the garden, Mama?' Friedrich asked a little later.

'If you don't let him run too much,' said Sofia. 'The sun is very hot... and make sure he wears his sunbonnet.'

The sun *was* hot in the garden, and the children gladly reached the shade of the trees.

'Now I'll show you my secret,' said Friedrich. 'It can be your birthday secret.'

He looked a little anxiously about him. He did not want to see Red at that moment; he was not so sure that Red wanted to share their secret with anyone.

'Secret! Secret!' chanted Karl, dancing beside Friedrich, until he had to be scolded a little for fear they would be discovered.

'Is it a fairy, Friedling?'

'Sort of...'

They reached the old shed, and Karl hung back when Friedrich beckoned him in.

'It's dark...,' he said, his lip dropping. Karl had always been afraid of the dark.

'It's not *really*,' said Friedrich, 'not when you come inside. See?'
Karl came, hesitatingly.
'The secret's here,' said Friedrich. 'You won't see it unless you come in...'
The reminder of the secret revived Karl's flagging courage and he crept in after Friedrich.
There were the cubs, lying fast asleep, fat and replete with the mauled half-carcass of a rabbit beside them.
'Look!'
Karl bent down to peer delightedly at the tangled ball of red-brown fur, the two cubs locked in an embrace for warmth, a small brush curled across one face, a lazy paw across the other. Before Friedrich could stop him Karl put his hand down and touched one...
With a sharp snarl the cub was awake. Karl jumped back with a shriek, but not before the sharp teeth of the vixen cub had sunk into his chubby arm just above the wrist.
He turned and fled, shrieking and screaming down the garden path.
Sofia, hearing the commotion as she sat with her sewing in the shade of the porch, came running out to him.
The little boy flung himself at her, blood pouring from his arm and screaming louder than ever.
'Devil! Devil!' he screamed between his sobs. 'Friedrich took me into the shed in the dark and a devil bit me!'
Sofia hustled the child indoors, almost hysterical herself. With the aid of one of the older maids and her sister she applied various medicaments to the wound, which was not as bad as the blood and screams had at first indicated.
Friedrich, momentarily spared the coming wrath by the need of the moment, was stunned. His wonderful surprise had not only failed but had turned to disaster.
The commotion that had alerted Sofia had also brought Red running from the potting shed, where he had been pricking out next spring's wallflowers.
'What's the littl'un done?'
Friedrich could not speak. He looked at Red and his face was bright with embarrassment.
'What happened to make him scream so?' Red asked again.
'I showed him your fox-cubs,' said Friedrich.
The older boy was as pale as Friedrich was flushed.
'You shouldn't have done that' was all he said, and he walked away.
Whatever punishment was to come, and come it must, it could not be worse for Friedrich than this cold disapproval from his adored Red. He would have run after him, desperate for forgiveness, if he had not heard his father calling

him from the house.

Miserably, he answered the summons.

Because he never lied to his father, Friedrich told the truth, about the hut and the cubs, and his intention to give Karl a lovely surprise on his birthday. Sofia's weeping, added to Karl's screaming, had already shattered the Pastor's peaceful morning, and he was in no mood for fancies.

When he had soundly beaten Friedrich and sent him to bed, although it was scarely mid-day, he turned his attention to the garden hut... but Red had forestalled him, the cubs had gone.

Red's own punishment came later from the gardener, whose ancient body belied the strength of his arm, but Red was used to beatings and did not care much. At least his cubs were safe.

Karl, bandaged and cosseted, sat up in bed eating raspberries and cream. 'You're my little wounded soldier,' said Sofia.

In his room, Friedrich had nothing until one of the maids brought him bread and water just before bed-time.

The next morning he was allowed to come down to breakfast, but told he must not go in the garden. This intensified his misery, for he was desperate to know if his folly had brought harm on the little foxes. Instead he had to sit with his father in the study writing out, over and over again, the terrible old text. 'The wages of sin is death.'

When he came up to nursery supper at the end of the day, Sofia eyed him coldly.

'You will have no jam to-day,' she said. The sting was not in that small deprivation but in the fact that she used the impersonal third person, reserved for the servants, instead of the affectionate 'thou' of the family circle.

The words fell on a silent room. Traugott looked up from the book he was reading, but Sofia made no correction; when she spoke again it was still in the impersonal.

Friedrich was nine. She never addressed him in any other way again.

CHAPTER TWO

The Pastor had failed in his efforts to teach Friedrich to read and write, but Christoph, his elder brother, had no difficulty in teaching the little boy to ride—an essential ability in the wide countryside, with its scattered communities and hundreds of square miles of forest. Horseback was the only form of transport apart from a few mail-coaches. This pursuit was the happiest in Friedrich's childhood, being a repetition and an extension of the early happy days in the woods with Traugott.

The Pastor had bought Friedrich a pony, the only really important present he had ever received, and although the purpose of it was utilitarian it did not lessen his delight. It was a far from aristocratic animal. The family finances did not run to any extravagance, and it had been acquired at a nominal sum from a parishioner, due to its rather inelegant appearance. It had a slightly sway back and its facial markings gave it an air of being rather surprised at everything it saw around it. All this made it all the more acceptable to Friedrich, for what it lacked in beauty it gained in an affectionate disposition, and to Friedrich, a sentimental boy with few outlets for his affection, the pony became an adored companion. He found in the animal's very oddness something akin to his own loneliness, and lavished attention on it, to which it responded with equal devotion. This gave his riding lessons added ease and attraction.

There was a little paddock at one side of the manse, and here Christoph patiently taught his brother the rudiments of horsemanship until he was able enough to go for little rides in the woods on the lower slopes of the hill.

These rides widened his knowledge of the countryside as the scope of their journeys became wider. They also brought him into closer and more intimate contact with his oldest and most favourite brother.

All through his young days Christoph stood between Friedrich and the harshness of life. Now approaching the time of his ordination into the church, and though by nature a gentle young man, he was far from meek, and held fierce convictions which, as he grew older, clashed more and more with those of his father. These occasions stood out in the calm day-to-day life of the manse like a black cloud on a sunny day, a sudden noise in quiet. Once, when he was younger, and some remark of his father's moved him to disagreement, Christoph would flush but remain quiet, now he was less able to let such moments pass unchallenged.

On one occasion, when the Pastor had given vent to a particularly harsh doctrine, Christoph could no longer contain his feelings and bluntly contradicted his father. For a moment there was shocked silence in the family, but the Pastor, recognising his oldest son's growing years, retaliated after the first moment of surprise, and there followed an argument which resembled a storm in the hills in its frightening intensity. The older man and his son, their relationship forgotten, hot in their own convictions, clashed in a thunder of words which left Friedrich shivering in his corner. Christoph was flushed, the Pastor pale with concentration, and neither of them giving way, so that the argument eventually rolled into silence like a storm that can return at the changing of the wind.

The Pastor's censure was not always reserved for the members of his family, many times the door of his study muffled only faintly his voice raised in condemnation against one of his flock. Friedrich, attracted as children always are by things of which they are faintly afraid, would linger on the stairs when these interviews were taking place. More often than not they concerned the matrimonial problems, or extra-marital adventures, of some lusty farm-worker whose activities had been reported to the Pastor by his wife or a village busybody. The Pastor was at his best on these admonishing occasions, and his voice rose in chastisement so it could easily be heard by the little boy crouching outside the door in a frenzy of curiosity. What he heard on some occasions upset him considerably.

As usual it was Christoph who first noticed his distress.

'What's the matter?' he asked him.

'Nothing...'

'Come, there must be something,' said Christoph patiently, 'you look so gloomy'.

'I was thinking.'

'What about?'

'I was thinking that when I grow up I will never have a wife.'

'Isn't it rather soon to decide?' laughed Christoph.

'You may change your mind when you are older.'

'I *won't*,' said Friedrich hotly. 'I think it must be horrid to have a wife. I think its all *horrid*.'

Christoph looked at the little boy thoughtfully. He did not say any more, for he had an idea what had upset him. He knew the Pastor's voice was loud, and his study sessions with his parishioners had a fascination for Friedrich.

When they were out together a few days later, Friedrich pointed out the purple fringes on the hazel catkins to Christoph.

'Look... aren't they pretty... why are they all fluffy like that?'

Christoph showed him that some catkins were yellow, not purple...

'Yes.' said Friedrich—'Why?'

'Because some are male flowers and others female... both are beautiful, but only together can they create new hazel trees. That is how nature works.'

Friedrich looked at the hazel catkins. Both *were* beautiful. Christoph was right, it was much nicer than the things he heard his father say.

Even at ten Friedrich was fascinated by the miracles of nature. Each spring of his short life he would touch the opening buds with wondering fingers, amazed that they should spring, as if by magic, from the blackened wood of winter. The acorn he held in his hand was equally a magic token; it was impossible to believe that all the great oaks of the forest had been born of such a minute beginning. Seeds, fine as pepper dust, made the flowers, and the hours he had spent with Redau had added to his knowledge.

Christoph shared his little brother's delight in such things, and fostered his interest during their forest rides.

It was at Christoph's suggestion that Pastor Froebel even gave the little boy a garden of his own—a tiny plot in a remote corner, made unpromising by the near proximity of the trees, but nevertheless satisfying to Friedrich. Here he planted more acorns, and sprinkled any seeds that his father or Christoph gave him. Through spring into summer he would dash out every morning to peer for signs of growth, and was frequently amazed to find after a night of warm rain that things actually *had* come up while he slept.

Not all his gardening ventures were as satisfying. Impatient for a flower bud to open on a cherished plant, he gently unfolded its closed petals; but they were not as he hoped—red and lovely, as they would have been when the flower was in full bloom, but small, green and shrunken. What is more, the bud then withered and died. Nature, Friedrich discovered then, was not to be hurried, even by impatient little boys.

The garden, the rides with Christoph, the short interludes with his schoolfellows, were Friedrich's only small pleasures. He was still much alone, still far from the favour of his stepmother, and even further from that of his aunt. Karl too had not proved to be the hoped-for playmate. He was a likeable, but stolid little boy who clung to the skirts of his mother or aunt, and had a woman governess to teach him. By the time Friedrich had finished his lessons, Karl was on the way to bed, and they only had much of each other's company in school holidays.

A few weeks after Friedrich's eleventh birthday there was great excitement at the manse. The Pastor's late wife's brother, Hoffmann, an archdeacon at Stadt Ilm, some twenty miles away, was coming on a visit.

Visitors were rare enough at Oberweissbach and this one had a special attraction for Friedrich, who had never known his mother but had built up an imaginary picture of her, based on the locket cherished by Christoph and the stories told to him by the other brothers in the family. He was impatient to meet Uncle Hoffmann, whom he had not seen since he was a very little boy, for though the distance from Stadt Ilm was not great, it was an arduous ride over the hills for an elderly man, and the Pastor and his brother-in-law had little in common beyond their religious calling.

Certainly they were physical opposites: while Pastor Froebel was tall, dark and thin, the Archdeacon was short and fat, nearly bald, with just a fringe of white hair round his brows. His beard grew only on the sides of his cheeks, giving them the appearance of being blown-out, as if he was out of breath (which he often was). His face was round and as rosy as a ripe apple ('from the beer he drinks' said the Pastor, although actually he partook very moderately, and then only for his 'digestion').

As soon as Friedrich saw Uncle Hoffman, he took an instant liking to him, and the affection was as spontaneously returned. Always wishing that he had been blessed with a son of his own, the Archdeacon could see in this already tall, dark-haired boy the child that might have been his, had not his wife died young and left him childless.

Friedrich's young features were already moulding into maturity, his high cheek-bones and a thin, almost aquiline, nose emerging from childhood's chubbiness. 'He's got character,' the Archdeacon said to himself as he studied him. After the usual greetings and courtesies had been exchanged, Uncle Hoffman, refreshed from his journey, asked if Friedrich might be allowed to show him the garden.

The Archdeacon and his nephew were soon alone in the wooded walk which ran almost the entire length of the boundary wall.

'You know, you are remarkably like your dear mother, God rest her soul'. The Archdeacon looked kindly at the boy beside him.

Friedrich could not have been paid a nicer compliment. He flushed with pleasure.

'Am I, Sir?'

'Yes, you have her eyes, and there is something about your voice that reminds me of my "liebe rose," as I called her when she was a little girl.'

They walked in silence for a while.

'There is a wonderful view here, Sir.' Friedrich stopped at a break in the trees, pointing to a natural avenue between the pines beyond the garden which revealed vistas of the hillside, purple with foxgloves.

'You love the forest?' asked Uncle Hoffman.

'Yes Sir, very much.'

'So did your mother. She knew every plant by name and all the birds by their calls.'

'That is my school down there.' Friedrich pointed to the red roof of the school house, with its bell tower just visible beyond the treetops.

'Are you progressing well with your studies?'

'Quite well, Sir.'

Uncle Hoffman put his hand on the boy's shoulder. He seemed happy enough, but was there a slight shadow in his face, the kind old man wondered? Something not easily definable as yet, but something that worried him a little. The boy was obviously intelligent, friendly, but too subdued, too withdrawn, even mature, for an eleven-year-old.

Later, when Friedrich was in bed, Uncle Hoffman sat with the Pastor in his study. They exchanged news of ecclesiastical acquaintances and enquired after each other's health and the health of each other's families—the trivial conversation of men who are brought together by relationship but have nothing really in common.

Then Hoffman asked in turn about his nephews: Christoph, already destined for the church; Christian, well on the way to becoming a weaver and dyer; August, the business man of the family; and Traugott, in the early stages of the study of medicine.

'They are good sons' said the Pastor.

'And what of young Friedrich?' Hoffman tried to conceal the anxiety in his voice.

'Friedrich?' the Pastor shrugged. 'Friedrich, I am afraid, is a disappointment to me. He is the cross I must bear.'

'But my dear brother-in-law, I have met the boy, spoken to him. He is intelligent, polite, a nice boy, I thought, and so like his dear mother, a credit to you. Why do you say this about him?'

'He is a dreamer and wilful... oh, I suppose it was partially my fault; after Rose died I had no heart for the child. I suppose I neglected him, although he never lacked comforts. For years he was backward in his studies, though lately he has improved. What concerns me now is his fondness for servants and peasants. Sofia does not consider him a good influence on little Karl.'

Archdeacon Hoffman felt he might have the key of the problem in his hand. He *knew* he had it the next day when Sofia, off guard, addressed Friedrich, as was her habit now, by the formal 'Sie'. She had never done otherwise since the incident with the fox-cubs. Christoph did his best to make light of this on occasions when he saw Friedrich to be particularly embarrassed, by calling his young brother 'Herr Froebel' and bowing to him with mock formality, as if this was a family joke instead of a perpetual reprimand.

Hoffman, however, was quick to notice Friedrich flush at this treatment in front of a visitor. He had spoken to the boy again since their first meeting, and liked him greatly. He was amazed, too, and delighted by his interest and considerable knowledge of the natural history of the wild and lovely countryside around him.

Later in the day, when Hoffman and Froebel were alone again, the Archdeacon, drawing on his pipe (of which the Pastor heartily disapproved), once more raised the subject of his sister's youngest child.

'Johann, I hope you won't mind me mentioning this,' he said, daring to use his brother-in-law's Christian name, by which he rarely addressed him. 'But I could not help noticing that Sofia treats Friedrich very strangely, even coldly. Has he done something to displease her?'

'Many things, I fear,' said the Pastor with the air of a man resigned to an impossible situation. 'As I told you, the boy is wilful and difficult. He must be sternly treated, although it distresses me to do so; otherwise he takes advantage. It is our duty to discipline him or the world will have worse punishment for him when he is older.'

'He progresses at school?'

'Yes, but now I am at a loss as to his education. After this year he will be too old for the village school.'

This was Hoffman's opportunity. God-given and unexpected. In his usual custom he did not wait to consider the practicalities.

'There is a good grammar school in Stadt Ilm. Let him come to me. My mother-in-law will welcome a young face about the house again, and he will be a great joy to me in my old age.'

The Pastor could not help being relieved by this excellent solution to his problems, but he felt it fit to hesitate somewhat, for fear his brother-in-law should consider him too hasty or shirking in his responsibility towards a difficult son.

'I will ask Sofia,' he said. 'It is kind of you, Hoffman, and it certainly would be a great opportunity for Friedrich.'

Sofia was as relieved as her husband, and not nearly as reticent in showing her relief. 'Of course he must go,' she said, without hesitation.

So it was arranged that Friedrich should travel to Stadt Ilm to live with his Uncle Hoffman and to continue his education at the grammar school.

Hoffman, a widower, lived with his late wife's old mother in a pleasant house on the banks of the River Ilm, on the outskirts of the town. The old lady, as he expected, was delighted at the prospect of a 'son in the house' and immediately set about making preparations for his arrival, which was fixed for the late days of July, so that he might enjoy some summer time settling in his new home before school began again in the autumn.

Christoph accompanied Friedrich on the journey—the first he had ever made away from home. They had risen early and set out along the hill-road before the sun had heightened in the sky, their horses' breath like puffs of steam ahead of them in the cold air of the morning. As the day wore on, the sun's warmth increased and they were glad to shed their cloaks. Now the clouds from the horses' nostrils changed to steam from their gleaming flanks, for the road was steep and stoney.

Friedrich was delighted that it was Christoph who was to accompany him on his first long journey from home, and such a momentous one. They rode in silence, both savouring the sweet, fresh air, the song of the larks rising from the meadows below, and the peerless views of the rolling hills, black with regiments of pines, and beyond them the mountains.

As they passed one of the peaks, Christoph drew Friedrich's attention to a great bird circling in the far distance above its crags.

'An eagle!'

Even at this distance they got some impression of its size by comparison to other birds, much nearer, yet much smaller to the eye.

At another turn of the track they startled a herd of deer. Their leader, a fine eight-pointed stag, paused a moment, pawing the ground with his front hooves, head raised, nostrils wide. Travellers were rare, and he was not unduly alarmed by the intrusion...mainly curious. After regarding them for a minute, he decided that caution was advisable and led his herd crashing into the bracken. As they passed where the deer had been, Friedrich and Christoph caught a waft of their musty odour still lingering on the air.

Friedrich's only regret at leaving Oberweissbach, was the parting with his brothers, and in particular with Christoph, who had become his champion and friend—more a father to him, for all their comparative nearness in years, than the Pastor. It had been Christoph who had made enquiries after the unfortunate incident with the fox cubs; had persuaded their father that the whole thing had been of the best intentions, and had only ended in disaster by misfortune. What is more, although he could not avert Red's beating from the gardener, he ensured that the cubs were moved to a safe new hiding place.

This was only one of the many kindnesses and confidences which bound the young boy to his older brother, and as they rode together on their last journey for many years they had never felt closer.

They met Uncle Hoffman at the Inn where they had agreed to pass the night, about two thirds of the way towards Stadt Ilm. The long summer day was fading, and the sun turning to a ball of fire behind the pines. Hoffman was standing in the courtyard waiting for them, his good-natured face beaming, pulling on his pipe.

They dined together before a cheerful log fire, as the evenings and mornings were cold even after a hot day in the mountains. The food was good, a tender Rostbraten, ribs of beef fried with onion, and plenty of sweet vegetables, crisp bread, new butter, followed by wild raspberries and cream, and washed down by the cold, dark beer of the district from the inn's deep cellars.

Friedrich drank, too... and felt a man among men.

His brother Christoph and Uncle Hoffman were already good friends and included the little boy in their conversation. When the clock struck ten, Friedrich began to feel his eyelids drooping with the fatigue and excitement of the day, the warmth of the food and the beer. Upstairs, in the inn's smallest bedroom, he fell asleep between cool sheets with owls calling in the pines outside, and a new moon shining on his pillow.

In the morning he had to say goodbye to Christoph, who was returning to Oberweissbach. This was a moment of sadness for Friedrich, but Uncle Hoffman allowed no time for brooding and soon Uncle and nephew were away themselves along the rough track which wound through the valley to Stadt Ilm.

It was a happy journey, as the earlier one had been from Oberweissbach with Christoph. The Archdeacon had various calls to make at villages along the way, at each of which he was received with joyful ceremony, so that the comparatively short journey took all day. But although he was saddle-sore and stiff from the long ride, Friedrich was fresh in spirit when at last the roofs of Stadt Ilm came into view around a bend in the river which ran beside the road.

Hoffman's old mother-in-law was at the gate to greet them, having heard their horses' hooves on the road. She embraced her son-in-law and Friedrich, who realised at that moment that this was the first time he had been kissed since he was a little boy.

'You must be tired, liebling,' she said. 'Some milk and an egg perhaps? Then straight to bed. There'll be plenty of time for talk tomorrow.'

Friedrich ate his supper while Hoffman and the old lady exchanged news of the journey. He was too sleepy to pay much attention to anything but the pleasure of the food to his hungry stomach and the comfort of his surroundings.

When he tucked down into the depth of the feather-mattressed four-poster in a bedroom which overlooked the rose-filled garden, the old lady crept in.

'She is like the good fairy,' he thought to himself, 'who comes disguised as an old woman picking sticks.' In his sleepiness he felt the weight of his eleven years had fallen from him and his mind wandered back to babyhood.

'I've come to say goodnight, Friedrich. Have you said your prayers?'

'Yes, ma'am.'

She tucked the bedclothes about him.

'You mustn't call me ma'am' she smiled. 'I shall be your "grossmutter". I have never been called that before, but I should like it very much.'

She bent and kissed the drowsy boy on the forehead.

'Goodnight, grossmutter,' said Friedrich, and buried his head in the lavender-scented pillow. He had never been so happy. He was crying, and he did not want the old lady to see.

*   *   *

During the first month of his stay at Stadt Ilm there had been no lessons. Instead, Friedrich spent the time exploring the town and the surrounding countryside. His Uncle was immensely proud of the wonderful new Gothic church, built only twelve years or so earlier, and spent hours with Friedrich both inside and out, explaining its architecture and pointing out its many beauties.

Other leisure was often spent by the river, which ran at the bottom of the garden of his Uncle's house. The Archdeacon was a keen fisherman, but much to Friedrich's relief his interest was in the sport rather than the prize and he seldom kept what he caught. Neither of them liked the sight of the gasping fish panting for life on the bank; only when Grossmutter demanded something for the pot did they put the poor creature out of its misery and bring it home in the basket. At other times the creel intended for fish was more likely to be filled with wild raspberries or damsons, or a posy of wild flowers picked on the river-bank.

It was the happiest summer of Friedrich's life.

The school at Stadt Ilm was much larger than the village school house at Oberweissbach and Friedrich's years with the girls had ended. At Stadt Ilm he had forty lusty schoolfellows, all male, and mostly around his own age.

He was introduced to his classmates by Uncle Hoffman, who was obviously popular with the boys, and therefore started his school life at considerable advantage. Although his knowledge and ability at set games was lamentable he had a natural agility learned from his outdoor life. He rode well, could climb trees and hold his own in a rough-and-tumble. Added to this his unusual gifts of making whistles from hollow twigs, plaiting whips and making berry-guns appealed to the town boys, and he never lacked companionship.

What a change from the solitary life of the manse! Where he had been one alone he was now one of many. Even lessons took on a new attraction. The methods of the village school had been much the same as his father's, a matter of constant repetition, but at Stadt Ilm there were at least some tutors who approached learning from a more imaginative angle.

Herr Schmidt, who took mathematics, was such a teacher. He encouraged the boys in simple experiments (water flooded the classroom floor when he was demonstrating displacement by volume) and his problems were set in practical terms of the countryside, the buying and selling of sheep and oxen, the contents of barns or cellars, the areas of fields, so that the boys felt they had a connection with the real life they knew.

On the other hand, Herr Strauss, who taught geography, believed that lessons, like physic, should taste nasty to be any good. Friedrich, who loved the land, who studied the map lines of mountains and rivers with an imaginative eye which brought them to life, found that even such exciting realities became dry as dust when listed in laborious statistics by Herr Strauss, who droned like a drowsy bee through the late September afternoons, to no avail, not even his own.

When school ended at four on winter days, Friedrich, his schoolbooks under his arm, would walk home through the narrow streets of the town with the lamps shining in the windows of the shops. Unused to town life, he found the sight enchanting and could spend longer than his time allowed gazing at their fascinating displays, especially as Christmas approached: the sweetshop, with its iced gingerbread men, the jars of twisted and coloured sugarsticks; the grocer's, with its rows of spice pots and the exciting smell of bacon, hams and cheeses. The only shop he didn't like at all was the butcher's, with its stiff carcasses and the butcher with his bloody apron. Worse still, he knew too that behind the shop was the slaughter yard, and it sickened him to see the unhappy little bands of sheep or cows being hustled through the streets early in the morning to meet their end. Some of the schoolboys boasted that they had visited this horrible place, but Friedrich managed to avoid the subject without being branded a coward or a namby.

*   *   *

As the winter passed and eventually warmed into spring, Friedrich, now completely settled at his new school, found himself included in the out-of-lessons activities of his schoolfellows. These involved expeditions on the hillside gathering wild strawberries, swimming in the river, or long walks in the woods.

Beside his uncle's garden, and between it and the river, was a strip of semi-wild land which the children called the 'water garden' because of its marshy nature, threaded with streams and small pools. It was partially overgrown with shrubs and small trees, but there were clearings which made ideal centres for games of robbers or soldiers, for mock battles and exciting ambushes. In spring its grassy glades were carpeted with primroses and the streams fringed by clumps of kingcups and yellow iris.

On the long, light evenings, their lessons done, the children would gather there to play until, hot and tired, they dragged themselves home to bed, to be scolded if they were not careful, for neglecting to wash and going to bed with dirty feet.

On such occasions Grossmutter, usually gentle, would whip back the sheets from the bed when she came to say goodnight, revealing Friedrich's dusty toes.

'Blackamoor!' she would scold, and Friedrich, heavy with sleep would have to go down to the kitchen again to wash his feet in a bowl of water. Grossmutter always had gingerbread in the larder and even on such occasions Friedrich would usually be given a slice before going back to bed, cold but clean.

Sundays at Stadt Ilm followed the same pattern as at Oberweissbach but were much more cheerful. The two visits to church were a pleasure rather than a duty, owing to Uncle Hoffman's sermons, which were inspired by his love of beauty, his knowledge and appreciation of nature in all its forms, and his own gentle kindness.

Equally inspiring were the scripture lessons which were part of the curriculum at the grammar school. A devout and intelligent schoolmaster made the life of Jesus so real to his class of forty boisterous boys that a few of them, Friedrich included, were moved to embarrassing tears at the end of a lesson in which he described the betrayal and crucifixion with vivid imagination. From the meek son of an avenging father (as portrayed by the Pastor), Friedrich now saw Jesus as a man among men, the leader of the Christian soldiers, a man for whom he was not ashamed to weep. He would spend hours at this stage of his life reading the Bible, not in the rather morbid religious fervour which affects some young people in the early years of their childhood, but as other boys read an adventure story. It had the same attractions for him as his boys' books, the favourite of which was the story of Samuel Lewill. Samuel was the owner of a magic ring which warned him by its pressure when he was about to undertake some unworthy deed. Samuel threw the ring away. Friedrich, in his youthful righteousness, would dearly have loved to have found it.

Grossmutter had lotions for cuts and bruises, and a tolerance for young boys who caught their jackets on briars and split their breeches climbing fences. She would scold mildly—'Do you think I *like* mending...?'—then patiently patch and sew, her glasses slipping down her nose, as she sat by the window on summer evenings with the scent of the stocks wafting in at the window and the moths fluttering round her lamp. She seemed to enjoy, too, his tales of boyish adventures and was ready with some surprise such as an apple cake or fresh jam for tea when his friends were invited to join him for the afternoon or evening. In the cooler weather there were nuts to roast by the fire, and grandmother would join in as the young people sang.

Friedrich learned to play the mandolin. Uncle Hoffman was quite an accomplished musician and enjoyed teaching his nephew, so that soon the two could play simple duets together. Music was a new experience and a new delight for Friedrich, for the Pastor's strict doctrines had kept even church music to a minimum, considering it dangerously close to vanity.

Friedrich had been with Uncle Hoffman nearly two years when he heard from his brother Traugott that another child from Oberweissbach was to make the journey to Stadt Ilm—his little schoolfellow, Lotte, who was to continue her education there in the care of an aunt.

Grossmutter invited Lotte to visit them a few days after her arrival and Friedrich was surprised to find her vastly changed. She still had her plaits but she had grown taller and was no longer the little dumpling girl he had led by the hand to school through the woods. Grossmutter did her best in Lotte's honour: there were warm new scones, fresh-baked bread, jam and honey, and a cake made with fresh cherries.

Lotte was shy, answering politely the questions put to her by the Archdeacon and Grossmutter, fidgeting with her little lace-edged apron, often blushing, especially when spoken to by Friedrich. But when later she joined him and the other childern in the water-garden, her shyness left her and she joined in the game with boisterous enthusiasm, as noisy as any one of them, her shyness forgotten, as fast as a boy, despite her petticoats, and twice as nimble.

One of Friedrich's classmates was a lad called Willi, the son of the town's Burgomaster. He and his sisters, Gertrud, who was a little older, and Grete, a plump twelve-year-old, were regular playmates in the water-garden. Friedrich had a particular admiration for Gertrud, a clever girl, accomplished at her lessons, and able to play the harp and mandolin. Getting too old now for games, except on rare occasions when the mood took her, she would still join in the gatherings round the fire in the evenings. Lotte, too, was invited to join in these happy sessions, when the Archdeacon would lead them in the beloved old hymns or mountain songs. Even grossmutter would be persuaded to add her fine but thin voice to the harmony.

Friedrich made few return visits to Oberweissbach during his four years with Uncle Hoffmann, but on his brief stays during school holidays he found the manse considerably improved. Sofia had at last persuaded her husband that the minister's house should not be the most old-fashioned and shabby in the neighbourhood and there had been many improvements and innovations.

Even the Pastor's sacred study had not escaped her attentions. In addition to new draperies it had acquired some wall decorations, which fascinated Friedrich on the brief occasions he was allowed in there to take an approved book from the shelf his father kept specially for the children. The new pictures on the study walls were copper-plate engravings of scenes from history. The one Friedrich liked best was of Charlemagne's court, a splendid drawing full of detail and movement before which he would stand for as long as he was permitted, taking in every tiny incident. Another fascinating addition to the study was a wall-chart which showed the German alphabet in relationship to that of other tongues. Struggling with Greek, the schoolboy was amazed and delighted to see that the Greek symbols he found so difficult actually had a similarity with his own familiar Gothic characters, and he would spend hours carefully copying one letter after another. But these journeys to his old home were rare. The pattern of the seasons was that of Stadt Ilm.

When high summer brought a break from school there was time again for games and picnics in the water-garden and in the surrounding country, with its pretty woods and hilly pastures.

Every summer, Grossmutter spent hours in her kitchen making jam and preserves, potting honey and pickling cabbage and beetroots and little green cucumbers. The air was always full of rich, spicy smells and the big iron pot on the stove was always bubbling. For Friedrich there would be the skimmings from the jam to taste and the reward of ripe plums if he helped in their stoning.

The most luscious of all Grossmutter's jams was that she made from the wild cherries and strawberries that grew in profusion on the lower slopes of the surrounding hillsides. The making of the preserves became a ritual in which the children joined with enthusiasm. Ever since his arrival at Stadt Ilm, Friedrich had regarded this as the happiest time of the year. He and the Burgomaster's children, and now Lotte too, would meet on the bridge over the river early in the morning and, armed with baskets and a picnic lunch, spend the day on the hillsides picking fruit. This year was no exception and a day was fixed for a Saturday in early July when the strawberries were still plentiful on the sunny slopes.

On the day arranged, Lotte and Friedrich, Willi and Grete met at their usual place on the bridge. Each had brought a bundle containing their lunch and the boys also had their mandolins. They made a colourful picture as they set off along the road, the girls' pinafores gay with embroidery and the bright ribbons on the mandolins fluttering in the breeze.

As they walked they sang. Grete had a pretty voice and Lotte's was high and clear. With the deepening voices of the boys they made a tuneful harmony, so that farm workers they passed on the road stopped to listen and laugh and applaud them as they went.

When the road shrank to a track and began to wind upwards, at the end of the valley towards the wooded hills, they grew out of breath and had to stop singing. Hot and panting they reached a turn in the path after the first steep grassy slope and turned to look back down the valley. There was Stadt Ilm, looking like a toy-town below, the bridge where they had met crossing the river, a diminutive boat passing underneath it. There was the tower of the church, so splendidly tall below, but now dwarfed and tiny, and the old castle. Looking carefully, Friedrich could just see the outline of his Uncle's garden and the red roof of the house. Beyond the town were the farms, with their patchwork of fields gradually changing to rougher pasture until the trees began up the sides of the hills on the other side of the valley, and far into the distance the river wound like a silver ribbon until it disappeared between a curve in the hills.

Their breath recovered, they continued up the path in dappled sunshine. As the trees thickened the grass beneath them was more lush and green, and in the sunny patches here and there were the pale grey-green leaves and white spires of the helleborine orchids, like pale candles.

The first trees of the lower hill were ash and beech and when these thinned at the next bend of the way there was an open slope where no trees grew and the grass was bright with wildflowers, the big golden cups of the globe flowers, forget-me-nots and the large alpine daisies and summer gentians. The girls gathered posies and wound them in their hair and the boys stuck wild roses in the bands of their hats, so that the children themselves seemed to blend into the background of bright flowers.

Through the upland meadow a stream bubbled over a stony bed, formed by the scree which sprawled down from the upper slopes of the hill. The sound of the water was cool delight in the heat of the day. The water, spreading into the grass on either side of the stream bed, made the ground squelch under their shoes. They had to cross this strip of marshy ground to reach the lush natural strawberry beds of the hills beyond, and laughing with excitement the two girls began to pick their way from one clump of reeds to another, trying to find a foothold. The boys, in their heavy boots, did not bother but strode through the waterlogged grass ignoring the puddles that formed under their feet among the kingcups and water mints, the smell of the mint crushed by their steps adding sweetness to the already scented warm air.

Leaping from tussock to tussock, the girls, trying to keep their balance, laughing and calling to each other, fell behind a few yards. Half way across Lotte missed her footing and slipped. It was too late to save her and there she was, tears of laughter welling down her flushed cheeks, her left ankle deep in the bog. She pulled it free and it came out with a squelch, heavy with mud and decorated with a trail of water weed.

'You clodhopper!' cried Willi. 'You *always* fall in the water. Why don't you look where you are going?'

'I was looking at the sky!' said Lotte, still laughing and swinging her mud-laden foot on which the shoe was no longer visible. 'What shall I *do*? Don't all stand there laughing! Help me!'

'Head in air!' taunted Grete. 'No wonder you always fall in!'

'You *never* fall in, do you?' Now Lotte was getting a little cross, her good natured face flushing under its sunburn.

They still had half way to go across the marshy ground. Friedrich, who was ahead, came back to her as she tried to keep her balance one-legged on the tussock.

'I'll carry you,' he said.

'You *can't*! Friedrich, I'm much too heavy.'

'Come on, of course I can. What do you think I am, a weakling?'

He stooped swiftly and picked her up in his arms. She was surprisingly light, or he was surprised at his own strength. It was a strange and new sensation, this burden in his arms, warm and relaxed against him. It was his first physical contact with a girl. In his early schooldays at Oberweissbach he played with the girls in his class, pulled their hair and chased them in their games, and in the water-garden he had often caught Grete or Lotte in the fierce embrace of combat between rival 'robber bands', but he had never held a girl in his arms like this.

He noticed for the first time that Lotte had a sweet freshness about her, a mixture of the lavender in which her aunt kept her blouses and the smell of sun on skin.

'Am I *very* heavy?' she asked, and as she turned her head to speak to him Friedrich noticed the way her fair hair sprang away from her temples and the flush of sunburn on her cheeks, glowing with exertion and excitement.

Willi, not to be out done, had picked up his sister Grete, and as the ground rose and dried out the boys put down their burdens and threw themselves down on the grass laughing and panting.

'*Look* at my shoe!' said Lotte in mock dismay. 'What shall I do? Its terrible!'

It was indeed, a shapeless mess of rather smelly mud.

'Let me clean it.' Willi, the practical one, scraped away with leaves and bits of stick until he revealed at least the outline of a shoe.

'I think we should wash it' said Grete. 'It smells rather.'

She held her fingers over her little snub nose.

When they had finished the shoe was wet but clean and it was decided that after this adventure they might as well find a place to eat their lunch. The open slope was topped by a glade of birches and here they settled down on the dried leaves still lying from last autumn on the summer grass.

The food tasted as good as it always did in the open air and sunshine. The bread was crisp, the crust cracking into brown flakes as they bit it, the cheese creamy and the slices of ham sweet and tender. The fruit they had brought had grown warm in their packs and tasted all the better for it, but the milk in their leather bottles had stayed cool and they finished their meal with long draughts of it, drunk by holding the bottle to their lips and throwing back their heads so that they had to shut their eyes to keep out the dazzle of the sun.

Food and sunshine made them drowsy, and Willi and Friedrich strummed lazily on their mandolins as the girls dozed in the shade. After about an hour, Grete jumped up, shaking her skirt free of leaves.

'I'm going to pick strawberries,' she said. 'Come on, Lotte!'

Lotte's wet shoe had been drying in the sun. When she put it on her foot she uttered a cry of dismay. 'I can't get it on!' The shoe had shrunk so that only Lotte's toes were covered and her heel stuck out.

'Now you *are* stuck,' wailed Grete. 'Oh Lotte, you are a nuisance! Never mind... Willi will come and pick with me. Perhaps Friedrich can do something to your shoe. He's good at mending things. We'll start picking for you.'

Willi and Grete went off together, swinging their baskets down through the little trees to the sunny slopes where they knew the strawberries grew.

'*Can* you mend it?' Lotte asked Friedrich.

He looked at the mishapen shoe. 'I'll have to cut it.'

'Never mind,' said Lotte. 'It's ruined now, anyway.'

Friedrich took out the woodsman's knife he always carried and made a few cuts in the stiff leather.

'Try that.'

Lotte had removed her white stocking, which had been mud-soaked too. Her toes were stained with the brackish water but he noticed how white was the skin of her foot against her sunbrowned hand as she tried to ease the shoe on.

'I think it *will* fit,' she said. Certainly her heel could be squeezed in. 'It won't be very comfortable but I think I can walk in it.'

'Well, that's alright then... shall we try and catch up with the others?'

Suddenly Friedrich did not want to stay alone with her. For the first time ever in their years together he felt shy and tongue-tied, but Lotte made no effort to get up.

'No, let's wait a bit... there's plenty of time.'

Friedrich leant back against the tree-trunk and began to play a little tune they used to sing in the winter evenings by the fire with Uncle Hoffman. He shut his eyes against the bright sunlight and his eyelids were patterned with spinning colours against a scarlet background.

Down the hillside, Grete and Willi heard him playing and began to sing.

As he played Friedrich felt more at ease. Lotte was humming the tune softly and it seemed very good to be with her here in the sunshine on the quiet hillside, with the birds singing and the birch leaves whispering in the light breeze. He glowed with the recent memory of her reliance on him to carry her over the stream, to help her with her shoe.

After a while he stopped playing. Lotte was lying full length on the grass, her white pinafore pulled up over her face to shade it from the sun, her fair plaits spread on the leafy grass and her lace cap abandoned beside her. Her tight bodice stretched over her young body revealed the small shapely rising of her breasts, gently swelling into womanhood.

Friedrich, moved by something unknown to him, felt an overwhelming desire for contact with her, his playmate and confidante, his loyal and loving Lotte. He wanted to touch her small brown hand lying beside his on the grass but, suddenly afraid to do this, he gently tweaked her nose under the apron.

She sat up with a start.

'It was a magpie!' laughed Friedrich.

'You horrible boy!' she was laughing as she picked up a handful of dried leaves and tossed them up at him. They landed in his hair, turning him into a Pan with his thin, brown face, his mandolin at his side. Not to be outmatched, Friedrich siezed a handful of leaves in his turn and threw them at Lotte.

The leaf battle lasted for several minutes of scramble and laughter until Lotte cried first for peace. By now they were both smothered in the dried white leaves the birches had shed last October. Friedrich stood up and dusted himself down, Lotte was picking the little dried fragments from her hair. He stooped down to help her. When her hair was free she shook her skirt, but obstinate little bits clung to the cotton and to her lace shawl. Friedrich picked at them with her. As he did so his hand touched her bodice. In that second he could feel her heart beating fast and firm beneath her breast. It was only a momentary contact but as it happened she looked at him with her grey eyes solemn beneath black brows. It was a look he had never seen before... and his own eyes meeting hers seemed to be drowning in them.

He felt a strange stirring which was at once wonderful and terrible. His heart was beating as if he had been running and he was almost breathless. She, too, was breathing deeply, although the exertion of their romping had long past.

Friedrich's earlier feelings of tenderness when he carried her over the brook returned with greater intensity.

Now he did touch her. He put his hands on her shoulders as she lay below him and bent over her. Her lips were full and slightly parted over the tips of her little white teeth. They both knew at that instant what he would do, but in that knowing he hesitated... he could not without asking.

'Can I kiss you?...' His tongue stumbled over the unfamiliar words.

Oh why, why had he asked her? She wanted so much to say 'yes', yet in her confusion she dare not... supposing he thought her too bold, too forward, supposing he hated her for it... the thing she wanted most of all in her newly wakened dreams?

So she said 'No...' She repeated it again, almost in panic, as if convincing herself that this was what she meant. 'No, Friedrich. *No!*'

In seconds his feeling had passed and was replaced with another, half anger, half fear, turning quickly to fury because he had been moved by emotions he did not understand, and had made a fool of himself. To cover his embarrassment and distress he began to laugh...

'Ha! I caught you!... I don't want to kiss you, silly! What are you getting all fussed-up about?'

His laughter hurt her more than his anger would have done. 'I *hate* you!' The words had come from her before she could stop them, although she knew it was not him that she hated but what had happened to them.

Friedrich picked up his mandolin and, without speaking or even looking at her, plunged away into the wood.

She sprang up to follow him.

'Friedrich!' she called. But he had gone. Alone she frantically tugged on her tight shoe. The day which had begun so promisingly had turned sultry. She plunged into the glade in the direction in which he had gone, calling his name, not because she was frightened at being alone but because she was made desperate by something she did not understand and made unhappy by this sudden bitterness between them after a moment of enchantment.

In a short while she stopped, and listened. She could still hear Grete and Willi calling to each other below, but nearer than this the faint notes of a mandolin. She crept quietly towards the direction of the sound and stopped when she saw Friedrich sitting with his back to her under a tree, playing softly to himself.

She stood watching him for a moment. She could just see the outline of his face, solemn and almost sullen.

'Friedrich...' She moved towards him.

'Don't follow me,' he said roughly. 'Can't you leave me alone? Go and help Willi and Grete—I don't want a girl always trailing after me!' He got up and walked away without looking back.

Lotte wandered miserably back through the wood to their picnic place. She gathered her things together and limped in her tight shoe down the hill to where Grete and Willi were still busy picking.

Grete called out 'Come on, lazy... we've picked pounds, we thought you were never coming. Did you fall asleep or something?'

Lotte couldn't answer because of the aching lump in her throat.

'Where's Friedrich?' asked Willi.

'He's gone home... we've had a quarrel.'

Grete noticed then that Lotte was crying. Being a kind little girl she went over and put her arm round her.

'Don't worry, Lotte... he'll get over it. Boys are stupid!' She pulled a face at Willi. 'Have some strawberries,'

Lotte did not eat any strawberries, although they lay so small and sweet and luscious in the basket. By the time they got to the last turn in the path home the thunder was beginning to roll in the hills and big drops of rain were falling.

In her shrunken shoe, Lotte's heel had been rubbed raw. She limped between Willi and Grete back to her home in the Konigstrasse, uncheered by the basket of fruit they pressed on her, to be questioned by her aunt and scolded for spoiling her shoes.

It was raining hard by the time Friedrich too returned alone to Uncle Hoffman's house with no strawberries at all. Grossmutter, wise in the way of children, made no enquiries. All she said was: 'It was a shame that your lovely day should end like this. Now take off those wet things and put them by the fire to dry, then I should go straight to bed.'

Friedrich did as he was told. Upstairs in his bedroom he knelt to say his prayers but his mind strayed from the familiar words.

In bed he lay awake staring at the ceiling, listening to the rain beating on the window and the thunder still rolling in the hills. Usually this gave him a feeling of comfortable security, to be warm, safe and dry indoors while a storm raged without, but now he could only think of Lotte. In his mind he could see her still lying in the grass in the sunshine, as he had never seen her before. He hated her for it—hated her because suddenly everything had changed. But although he hated her he could not rub the picture of her out of his eyes.

It rained all night and most of the days that followed, so that none of the children were able to meet out of doors.

On the following Saturday afternoon the rain ceased, although it was still dull and sultry and the clouds hung heavily over the hills, so that the town seemed to be closed in by angry grey skies.

Lotte was pale—due, said her aunt, to lack of fresh air. She should go for a walk. Reluctantly she took her cloak and a shawl for her head and walked down to the river-garden. The rain was still dripping from the trees and the air was heavy with the smell of wet earth and the long grass brushing her skirts was cold and sodden.

As she turned down the path to the water she saw someone standing under the trees. It was Friedrich. She knew she had only come down to the river hoping to see him but now he was there she was frightened. They had not met since the day he had walked away from her on the hillside a week ago.

He had a dog with him, an odd-looking creature, wet and bedraggled. Lotte walked towards him and stood beside him. She did not speak and he did not turn his head at her approach but said, as one picking up a conversation where it had only momentarily stopped, 'Do you think he's a stray?'

'No,' she said. 'I've seen him in the town. I think he belongs to the shoemaker's. He hangs around the tanner's yard waiting for scraps...poor old thing.' She held out a hand for the dog to sniff, which it did, wagging its tail.

Friedrich still did not turn to look at her. Instead he looked down at the ground in front of him.

'I'm sorry, Lotte...I *am* sorry, really.' It took a lot of saying.

Lotte did not answer.

'I suppose it's too late now', Friedrich continued miserably, kicking the grass.

'Too late?'

'I love you so much, Lotte! You are my dearest and best friend and now you probably hate me.'

Lotte still did not speak but she did not need to. She just put out her hand and slipped it into Friedrich's; both hands were cold and wet with the rain but the contact between them was full of warmth and comfort. There was no need for words.

Both just fifteen, they looked at each other, they were no longer frightened, just wondering. He did not kiss her. They walked home through the wet garden hand in hand. He picked a syringa bloom from a bush and put it in her hair.

'You look so much better for your walk' said her aunt when she came home.

On her birthday Friedrich gave Lotte a present. He had no money, and flowers grew too plentifully on their hillside and in the gardens to be considered a gift. Laboriously he worked secretly with Uncle Hoffman's few and simple tools. Using the only material available, an old silver nail, he bent it into the shape of a ring, twisting the ends to form a little cross.

He gave it to her in the water garden.

'Happy birthday, Lotte!'

She took it and held it in the palm of her hand.

'It's not very good.' He was abashed, now that she was looking at it—it suddenly seemed very rough and insignificant, although he had been secretly rather proud of it when he surveyed it in the poorer light of Uncle Hoffman's tool shed.

To Lotte it was as precious as gold.

'It's beautiful!' Her shining eyes told him she meant it. 'Did you *really* make it yourself? You *are* clever. I'll keep it always and *always* !' She held out her hand. 'Put it on for me...'

He took her right hand and put the ring on the middle finger.

Later, when she was alone, Lotte took the ring off her right hand and put it on the left. She turned the crossed end round so that the band lay plain across her third finger.

It was unlucky, her aunt would have said.

CHAPTER THREE

After this emotional crisis the friendship between Lotte and Friedrich settled back to its old happy level. He never asked her again if he could kiss her. Even the urge to do so had lost some of its importance, although he sometimes thought about it with the curiosity of all young people about adult life.

'The Prince kissed her' he had read so often in the fairy tales of long ago. Now he was almost morbidly curious about such things. His brother Christoph had recently married. What was it like to be married, he wondered? His mind automatically shied from the subject.

Would it be wrong to kiss Lotte? Would it be different from kissing Uncle Hoffman and Grossmutter, as he did every night at bedtime? Then there were the cold kisses bestowed on him only very rarely in his childhood by his stepmother. Like a novice swimmer, the deep water of experience at once frightened and attracted him.

In the late summer evenings that followed, he and Lotte met almost every day in the water-garden, but whereas the children once spent the time in boisterous games, they were now more inclined to pair off in twos and threes, talking, always talking, and dreaming.

Other than Friedrich, Lotte had another inseparable companion, a shepherd dog belonging to her Uncle. His name was Brig and he was a large, raw-boned dog with engaging ways, and Friedrich was as much his slave as Lotte when they spent hours throwing sticks for him or combing his coat free from burrs.

One October morning, when the leaves were turning to red and gold and some of the smaller trees were already bare, Lotte came to the water-garden alone. There was no school on Saturdays and this was the day when the children always met if the weather was fine.

'Brig is ill!' she told Friedrich. 'Uncle thinks he may have been poisoned! I can't stay, I'll come later and tell you how it is with him.'

Friedrich watched miserably as she ran back up the path back to her home.

When they met later he could see that she had been crying. Her face was blotchy and her usually tidy hair was wild and lacked a ribbon. She was waiting for him under their usual tree, and when she saw him coming ran towards him, but when they came face to face could say nothing.

He did not need to ask her. Awkwardly, because it revived memories, he put his hands on her shoulders and even at that moment was moved to find how small and soft they felt.

Sensing his question she just nodded her head miserably.

'What do you want me to do?' he asked. He knew by her look that there was something.

'Don't let Tan have him;' she said. 'Uncle says Tan can burn him, like he burns the leaves. Don't let them, Friedling. I know it's only his body, Uncle says, but I don't want him *burnt!*' She was weeping openly now, but silently, the tears rolling down her cheeks.

'Friedling, animals have souls, haven't they?'

'I'm sure'

He was near to tears himself now, fighting back the ache in his throat.

'Friedling, will *you* bury him, in a proper grave?'

'Where?'

'Here, in our water-garden.'

'But Lotte, how can we? Someone might see us; they might not like it.'

'We could do it tonight, no one would know. Please Friedrich, please!'

How could he refuse her?

It was an adventurous plan. It was dark by six in the early cold twilight of the October day. Friedrich put on his high boots and a heavy coat, wrapped a dark scarf round his neck and took a spade from Uncle Hoffman's toolshed.

Fortunately his comings and goings were seldom questioned, his uncle believing that freedom was part of his education and trusting the sense that he hoped he had implanted in him and the boy's natural physical ability to look after himself.

Lotte's part was harder. She had to lie.

'I'm going to see Grete,' she told her aunt.

She was there waiting for Friedrich in the shadows of the lane at the garden gate of her house. Beside her was a shapeless, sad bundle.

'I've got him,' she said.

It had been a desperate deed, done in courage born out of love. Tan, her Uncle's gardener, had relented: her tears were more than he could withstand. 'His little maid' as he called her when she came first to Stadt Ilm. It was Tan who wrapped the old dog's body in a sack and tied it with rope and carried it to where it could be hidden in the hedge, until she could drag it out at dusk.

Between them Friedrich and Lotte carried their sad load into the darkening shadows of the trees. An owl hooted and somewhere far away a fox barked. The silver birches looked ghostly in the half-light.

They came to a clearing.

'Let's bury him here,' said Lotte.

Friedrich started to dig. The ground was hard and full of roots. He sweated and barked his knuckles on the stones.

The old dog seemed larger in death and it was nearly an hour before the hole seemed large and deep enough to hold him. Gently they lowered the bundle in, covering it with leaves.

A few late wild flowers were still growing and Lotte laid a little posy of them on the old dog's body before Friedrich began to shovel back the earth.

'Shouldn't we pray?' she said. 'It's not wicked to pray for a dog, is it?'

'What should we say?'

'When Grandpapa died they said "Take him into Thy eternal peace." I thought it sounded lovely.'

She smoothed the soft, new-dug earth with her hand.

'Friedrich, do you believe there is a heaven?'

Did he? Friedrich had never thought of heaven in connection with death. The Kingdom of his childhood, the heavenly forest, was a fairy-tale that had nothing to do with death.

Faced with the question here in the wood, with the dead dog buried at his feet, he was suddenly shaken by it. One day he would die, *must* die. He would be like Brig, under the earth, stiff and cold. Not another person, but *him!* A cold fear took him.

'I don't know' he said.

'Neither do I,' said Lotte. The declaration of their mutual uncertainty was more binding than any affection. They had admitted to each other what they had so far not even dared to admit to themselves.

They walked back through the wood in silence.

When he went to bed that night Friedrich thought again of death. His mind drawn towards the subject with a sort of horrifying fascination. His heart beat faster and his stomach turned with fear. In a short while he was sobbing.

Grossmutter heard him and crept in.

'What is it, liebling...?'

'Lotte's dog is dead,' he told her; but he did not tell her that it was not for this that he was crying.

In November, Friedrich had a letter from his father. It was not unexpected but its coming was still an unpleasant shock. His schooling at Stadt Ilm was drawing to an end and a decision had to be made regarding his future. He must return to Oberweissbach.

Grossmutter was in tears when she heard the news. Uncle Hoffman puffed harder than ever on his pipe.

'Your father will know what is best for you,' he said loyally.

In the haste of packing up and arranging his journey, Friedrich did not see Lotte for several days. On the morning before his departure he went to her home.

She came down the stairs towards him, her hair loose instead of in its accustomed plaits.

'I've come to say goodbye,' he told her. He had broken the news to Lotte almost immediately but had avoided admitting to himself the inevitability of parting. Now the words seemed woefully inadequate.

Lotte's eyes were filled with tears and her fingers played with the little ring she still wore.

He took her hand. 'May I kiss you?'

This time she did not say 'No.' There would be no other times. She held her face up to his, only a few inches above her in height, and he found that in his emotion his eyes failed to focus so that her features were blurred.

His mouth was firm on hers, the lips closed, but she could feel the hardness of his teeth behind them. It was a hard kiss, a boy's kiss, in which strength had more part than passion. The pressure of his mouth on hers became almost pain, so that she had to draw away.

They looked at each other then. His dark eyes soft with his boy's love of her, the love that bloomed in the moment of parting, surprisingly mature and tender in two so young, yet intensified by their youth and innocence.

'It will not be long...I will come back,' he promised.

He kissed her again, but this time lightly on the cheek, and was gone.

For two days she wept. She would not eat and her aunt scolded her. Friendship, yes, that was all very well, but this ridiculous emotion was too much. Lotte, in her turn, dared not wear her ring except in secret, but hid it in the folds of her handkerchiefs. She even woke in the night in a nightmare of panic in which she wondered if kissing a boy meant you could have a baby...her friend Gertrud had spoken of such things.

She wrote Friedrich a long letter and he replied almost at once. It was the first approach to a love-letter that either of them had ever written or received.

Friedrich wrote again. This time Lotte's uncle caught her reading the letter and took it from her. He liked Friedrich but was disturbed by the intensity of the relationship between two such young people. After consultation with Lotte's aunt he decided to write to Freidrich's father, and a letter conveying the situation was soon on its way to the Manse at Oberweissbach, where there were already hot scenes of controversy over Friedrich's future.

The Pastor called Friedrich to his study.

When the boy entered he saw that his father had a letter in his hand. With sinking heart Friedrich recognised the writing as his own and the letter as that he had sent to Lotte.

All the previous sermons that Friedrich had heard on sex and sin were surpassed by that which followed.

The Pastor took as his text the most lurid Biblical warning on f(and the lusts of the flesh. The facts of life as his father related then relation or resemblance to the simple truths which Friedrich had accept as part of everyday life in his closeness to the country pattern o₁ oirth of lambs in the spring, the kittens that appeared with enchanting regularity among the barnyard cats, the puppies of the labourers' bitches.

As the Pastor's private sermon developed, Friedrich felt himself blushing with shame and confusion; he felt unclean. He had never done any of these things, but was this the dreadful meaning and reason of his earlier confusion, was this why he had been so disturbed and distressed the day he picked the leaves off Lotte's dress in the woods? He recalled his confusion, even fury, as he had rushed away from her, and the swift, bitter quarrel that had followed. He remembered their last and only kiss. Was that also a sin? The shame rose hotly in him. Was it the Devil, then, that had put that exquisite—as it had seemed then—feeling of tenderness for her in his mind? His father was saying so.

'The Devil walks in many guises,' he said, 'even in that of God himself, to tempt the unwary into wickedness.'

At the end of an hour Friedrich left his father's study and walked alone into the garden. It was late autumn; the leaves had already fallen from most of the trees and the air had a sharp chill in it. The cold went deeper than Friedrich's flesh and bones, it had penetrated his heart.

The weeks that followed were no happier, he was bitterly homesick for Stadt Ilm, for Uncle Hoffman and Grossmutter and, of course, Lotte. He wanted to go back desperately, not as he was now but as he was before. He could not think of Lotte without a deep sadness and longing, but even this was mingled with shame and conscience. There were times when he felt sure that his feelings for Lotte had been as noble as they had seemed at the time. At others his father's words came back to him with chilling reality.

To all this confusion was added that of the uncertainty over his future. He had made reasonable progress at school but distinguished himself in no particular subject. He was attracted to medicine, although he doubted if his scholastic ability was equal to the years of study it would require; but particularly he wanted to join his brother Traugott, who was already at the University in Jena. The idea of University life appealed to him and next to Christoph, Traugott had always been a favourite brother. The thought of sharing a student's life with him, away from the restraining influences of home, was pleasant indeed.

Sofia, however, had no enthusiasm for Friedrich's progress to Jena University. She considered the money spent on his older brother's education was already too much. This, plus the large amount of capital the Pastor passed into the fund for the rebuilding and enlargement of his church, left little for her housekeeping and other needs.

'It would be a sheer waste of time and money' she told the Pastor. 'In any case, what would he study? Has he ever shown any aptitude at school? If he has, I have yet to hear of it.'

The Pastor had to admit that she was right, and he too was well aware of the family's financial position.

A solution presented itself when his wife reminded him of Friedrich's early passion for the open-air life and his interest in the forest, it reminded him that she had a cousin who was an official in the Thuringen State Forest. Surely it would be a good career for Friedrich to become a forester? There were many good posts to be had on the large estates in the neighbourhood, and he could easily gain an apprenticeship through the good offices of her relation.

A forester? Friedrich was not averse to the idea. If he could not go to Jena with Traugott, the prospect of an outdoor life in the forests he loved was pleasant enough. In any case he had no choice. The Pastor made the necessary arrangements and it was settled that before Christmas Friedrich would make the two-day journey to the north-east, where the warden of the forestry encampment had agreed to accept him among his apprentices.

The second time Friedrich rode away from Oberweissbach on a momentous journey he rode alone. This time, too, it was not summer but deep winter, with a fair sprinkling of snow already whitening the ground and the trees black and bare. The journey was long and lonely and he had plenty of time to think. His thoughts, divided between the past and the uncertainty of the future, were occasionally interrupted by some remarkable feature of the landscape, still lovely, even in the austerity of winter. He stopped his horse for a moment to stand in wonder at the beauty of a frozen waterfall, a sculpture in ice, as if its torrent had been turned to glass. The evening of the first day of his journey had also been one of scarlet splendour in a fiery sunset which had turned the waters of a lake to molten fire and the surrounding hills to silhouettes against the scarlet sky.

He spent the night in a village inn and went on again early the next morning—another crisp, clear day which accentuated the beauty of the scenery. He arrived at his destination just before dark and was cheered by the sight of lights burning in the huts, the smell of cooking and the sound of voices and laughter.

The Forest Warden to whom he was to be apprenticed greeted him austerely. He was a strange-looking man, tall and gloomy, and Friedrich's first impression was not one of liking. The other apprentices were more encouraging in appearance and although they surveyed Friedrich with frank curiosity their welcome was not unfriendly.

Friedrich's appearance may have given good reason for their quizzical looks, for the Pastor had not thought it necessary to equip his son with any special clothes for his new life. The boots he wore were decidedly too high for him, having been inherited from one of his brothers—and one greatly taller than he, although he was a big boy for his fifteen-and-a-half years. The boots gave him the ludicrous appearance of growing out of them like a leggy plant in too large a pot.

The other boys accepted him quickly, with a natural friendliness and much good-natured chaffing. 'Old Big Boots' they called him, but his experience of the rough and tumble of school at Stadt Ilm had taught him to regard this as a compliment, boys only making fun of those they like.

He was not so happy in his work. He loved the forest and the opportunity to explore new acres previously unknown to him. As his work brought him constantly in contact with the forest he was able to endure it, but the routine was strict, the work hard and long, and the instruction by the warden lacking in interest and imagination. He would have the boys perform the same simple tasks over and over rather than take the trouble to instruct them in new and more difficult aspects of their work. He regarded them more as a band of cheap labourers than as students and sometimes Friedrich would spend all of one cold winter day in the vicinity of the encampment loading timber on to the carts, which took it to the neighbouring village. This work was supposed to be done by the unskilled peasants employed by the Forestry Commission. For these the warden found other work, cleaning or repairing in his own quarters.

At other times Friedrich would be sent alone to clear brushwood from the seedling pines on the acres of the hillside which had been replanted with young trees. Here at least he had the company of the birds. The robins sat and watched as he worked, their round bodies puffed up against the cold, their bright eyes following his every movement. The jays shrieked their reproaches at him for violating the solitude of their paradise, and the starlings chattered to keep themselves warm as they sat in cheerful rows on the branches of the bigger trees.

The evenings were mostly spent in the hut, which served as both dormitory and living quarters for the apprentices. After a long day the boys, their cheeks burning after hours in the cold wind, were usually content to lie on their bunks reading or writing letters to their homes, or talking and, sometimes, singing. Occasionally a party of them would walk the three or four miles through the forest to the village, where the beer cellar offered both warmth and entertainment as well as refreshment.

Friedrich went on one of these expeditions feeling rather honoured at being included in the regular life of his new companions. He felt his appearance keenly, for the other boys had clothes other than those they used for work and took great pride in dressing themselves up for an evening of enjoyment. All Friedrich could do by way of smartening himself up was to decorate his hat with a few pheasants feathers, which if anything, plus the largeness of his wretched boots, added to his odd appearance, although he did not fully realise it.

In the village beer-cellar the boys, some of them a little older than Friedrich, took great delight in acting with a great deal of manly ostentation. They sung lustily in their newly deepened voices, they banged their beer mugs on the tables, and when the village girls showed suitable appreciation they were quick to pinch a plump arm or put a hand round a comely waist.

Some of the girls came to the table, and one, a pretty seventeen-year-old they called Dora, seemed particularly attracted to Friedrich as a newcomer and singled him out for her special attention.

'You're a solemn one' she said, sitting down beside him.
'Don't you like girls?'

'Yes, I mean... No.' Friedrich stammered, much to her amusement. She patted his shoulder.

'Surely you like me? I like you... *very* much,' she added, to encourage him.

Friedrich was embarrassed, glad at least that the others should see that he deserved some attention from one of the girls, but at a loss to know how to respond to it.

This girl was not like Lotte... or was she? The thought brought a bright flush to his cheeks.

'You're blushing.' the girl laughed. 'Look!' she called out to the others, 'Friedrich's blushing! That's more than most of you could do!'

We can do better than that!' laughed Jacob, a big, blond boy with a wink, pinching the cheek of the girl who was sitting on his lap drinking out of his beer mug.

Dora put an arm round Friedrich's shoulders. 'You can kiss me if you like' she said turning her pretty, plump face up to him.

As he looked at her, Friedrich saw that her low-cut bodice revealed the curves of her young breasts and the dark hollow inbetween. He flushed deeper with confusion and embarrassment, accentuated by the fact that he liked what he saw, while hating himself for liking it.

'Come on!' she persisted. 'Don't be shy... kiss me, I'll not eat you!'

Her voice jolted him out of his confusion.

'I don't kiss girls,' he said.

He got up, leaving his beer and the others laughing behind him and walked out into the night.

The cold air shocked his hot cheeks, but it smelt fresh and good after the smoky atmosphere of the beer-cellar. The snow was crisp and shining white in the moonlight. His boots squeaked and crunched in it as he walked back to the camp alone.

This is what his father had meant... perhaps it would have been the same with Lotte. She was a little girl when they played together at Stadt Ilm. Girls changed when they grew older... like that girl.

Friedrich still felt hot with embarrassment when he thought of her. The worst thing was that the memory of her still stirred him. He was ashamed and disgusted with himself, he would not go to the beer-cellar again.

When the older boys came back after midnight, singing down the snowy track, Friedrich was in his bunk pretending to be asleep. He did not feel that he could bear their banter, even if it was good natured. Whether they thought him asleep or not it did not prevent their talking about him.

'He's a queer one,' said Georg, one of the oldest boys with a reputation among the village girls. 'Fancy him going off like that!'

'Served Dora right,' said Max. 'She's too forward, that one. It gave her a shock for someone to say "No" to her.'

'She never says "No", I'll warrant!' said Fritz, a stocky, jolly boy, and his joke was taken up with a great deal of raucous laughter by the others, who were quick to pursue the subject of their amorous adventures with the comely Dora.

'Some say she had three of us in one evening...!'

'Three? That's nothing! Why, I knew a girl in Frankfurt,' boasted Jacob. 'Biggest thighs I ever saw, she had, like a farm mare... *and* knew how to use them!' He smacked his lips with exaggerated appetite. Friedrich turned his face to the wall; he felt sick and unclean.

He kept his promise to himself and did not visit the village again. His spare time, now that the Spring was coming, he spent more in the forest, where he also spent his working days. It was a wet March but the warden took no notice of the weather and kept the boys working at their usual hours, bringing them back to the camp in the evenings soaked to the skin.

One day, when it had rained even harder and longer than usual, Friedrich got back to the camp with the rain-water running down the back of his neck and squelching in his boots. He was cold and shivering as he peeled off his sodden clothes and replaced them by the few spare dry garments he had after previous soakings. Later that night he woke in his bunk with his face burning and his feet icy cold. He was shivering even more than before; his throat felt

dry and his head ached.
In the morning he told Jacob he couldn't get up.
'I feel terrible,' he said.
The warden came to look at him. He was used to boys who preferred bed to work.
'I hope you're not shamming!' he said, but one look at Friedrich told him immediately that this was not a feigned illness of convenience.
'Alright,' he said. 'You can stay here today.'
Friedrich spent the day tossing in his bunk, in which the blankets felt like sandpaper. His eyes felt dry and sore and his limbs ached.
In the evening, when the warden came in again, he looked at Friedrich rather anxiously. Two bright fever-patches burnt on the boy's cheeks and his eyes had dark circles round them.
He called Jacob. 'When you go to the village tonight ask the doctor to call in the morning...we don't want young Froebel dying on us.'
The doctor came in the middle of the next morning. After a miserable feverish night Friedrich had sunk into a hot restless sleep when the doctor let himself into the hut, all the other apprentices being at work in the forest.
The doctor put a cool hand on the boy's hot forehead, felt his hot, dry hands.
'You've been getting yourself wet and cold' he said. 'Have you boys got no changes of clothing?'
'Everything gets so wet, sir,' said Friedrich, 'and things take so long to dry.'
The old man shook his head.
'Oh well, I suppose you are mostly all tough enough... but you can't always get away with it'
He went to his pack and took out a packet. There was water by Friedrich's bunk and he shook the contents into the cup.
'Drink this.' It was mildly bittersweet, but not unpleasant. 'Now sleep...I'll call again tomorrow.'
Friedrich slept all the rest of the day and all night. In the morning he was able to drink some of the hot milk the other boys had on their oatmeal at breakfast.
The doctor came in the afternoon. Friedrich was sitting up. The flush had gone from his face, and although he still had an irritating cough and his head still ached, he felt better.
The doctor was satisfied.
'That's more like it,' he said. 'I'll leave you some more medicine and I'll tell that warden there's to be no work for you this week unless he wants to bury you under one of his trees!'

Friedrich laughed. The doctor, pleased to see the boy so much better and responding, sat down on the end of his bunk.

'Do you like your work?' he asked.

There was something about the old man that reminded Friedrich happily of Uncle Hoffman.

'Not much, sir.'

'That's bad, boy, Why? Don't you want to become a forester?'

'Well, sir, I love the forest but the work we do here is dull and hard. We don't seem to learn very much... it's all "do this" and "do that," just the same old things.' Friedrich was not sure that he should say so much for fear it got back to the warden, but the doctor seemed kind and interested.

'But you still say you love the forest.'

'I was brought up in the forest, sir, but a long way from here, at Oberweissbach. I love the trees and the birds and animals, and the wild flowers and plants.'

The doctor was delighted by the enthusiasm in the young face. He liked the intelligent features, the deep, dark eyes. Surely this boy had more in him than to make a forester, worthy calling though it might be? 'Would you like your work better if there was more in it to interest you?'

'Oh yes, sir. Do you think the warden...?'

The doctor interrupted. 'No, I'm afraid I'm not able to do much with the warden. As you probably know he is not an easy man, but I might have a task for you that wouldn't interfere with your duties and might make your days more interesting. You see, I'm a bit of a botanist. Nothing special, just an old man seeking after truth and beauty. These woods are rich in plant life and I believe that nature has put her own medicines in the Earth all around us. Many flowers, leaves, roots and seeds can cure ills; it's not old woman talk... there's God's truth in it. The potion I gave you yesterday was made of cowslip flowers... *primula vesis,* a fine remedy for chest complaints like yours.'

'My grandmother used to make such potions, sir.'

'Did she now... and where was that?'

'In Stadt Ilm. Though perhaps I should say she was not really my grandmother... I just called her that.'

'And what did she use?'

'Coltsfoot, sir, and wild irises, and soothing draughts from the berries of the elder. I used to gather them for her.'

'Capital! Then you know these plants?'

'Oh yes, sir! And many more. I used to gather them for her. Many of them grow here too, I have seen them.'

'Now that's just it!' said the doctor. 'I've little time to find all I need. Some of the plants are rare... one can search for hours without finding them; but if I had *your* job, I'd be able to look all day. How would it be if you gathered them for me? I would reward you for it. It would not take much time and it would be an interest for you as well as a service to me!'

Friedrich was fired with enthusiasm. Impatient to be up from his bed and out in the forest again, he recovered quickly from his illness and by the next week was back at work, but this time with a much greater zest. As he went about his duties his eyes were always rivetted on the grass around him. He peered into the brushwood and thickets for the shape of a leaf or the flash of a flower that might lead to the discovery of one of the lesser-seen plants.

As the spring days lengthened and the weather improved he went out again in the evening when the other boys had gone to the village, roaming the glades he had selected during the day as the sources of useful specimens.

Once or twice a week he would go to the village with the others, but not to the beer-garden. He would leave his workmates there and go to the doctor's little house on the outskirts to deliver his herbs... adding to them any new and unknown plant he had found during his explorations.

The doctor was a disciple of the great Swedish botanist Dr. Linnaeus and he taught Friedrich this system of plant identification.

By the light of the lamp Friedrich would use his younger eyes to count stamens and petals, to study the structure of the most minute flowers—some of them mere pin-heads of colour. Until now his knowledge and appreciation of plants and flowers had been superficial, based on their decorative beauty and colour alone. Now he found in each tiny bloom a literal wonderland: the regimental array of myriad stamens in the rose; the hooked hairs on stems and leaves; the symmetrical designs of style and stigma; the endless dainty formation of petals of every shade; the artist's palettes, yellow mauve and white, of the minute milkworts; the tiny trumpets of bugles and ground ivy.

He would peer at them until his eyes ached, but his thirst for knowledge was unquenchable. He found the twisted spikes of Ladies' Tresses hiding palely in the short grass at the forest's edge, the lovely Ladies' Slipper orchid with its butterfly wings of yellow and purple, the ghostly white candles of helleborine and the little pink fairy skirts of the sowbreads hiding under the leaves.

The goblets of the globe flowers could be found in some of the upland meadows; these the doctor used for remedies, as he did many of the saxifrages. Spurges, too, interested him and he showed Friedrich how the juice from the stems of some of them could raise a rash on the hand. It was an endless and absorbing interest which brought as much pleasure to the doctor as his pupil. It only disturbed the old man that one so young should be so dedicated and not give any time to less serious pursuits.

At the end of one of their long evenings together the doctor said to Friedrich: 'Don't you ever get tired of botanising?'

Friedrich showed shocked surprise, even alarm. 'Oh no, sir!

'It's all right,' the doctor laughed 'I'm not sending you away. I just thought that you might like a little recreation sometimes. To go to the play perhaps? Don't you like the play?'

'I have never seen one, sir.'

'Never seen a play! The doctor threw up his hands in mock horror. 'My dear lad! What do they teach you these days? How can you learn about great literature unless you have been to the theatre? Goethe, Schiller... our great poets... and the great Shakespeare... they must be *seen* as well as heard! Did your father not think such things part of your education?

'My father does not approve of the theatre, sir'

'No? Well perhaps not... after all, he's a minister, and ministers can be strict about such things, though why I could never understand. But you are only a minister's son, *you* may see a play surely? We have a good band of players not far from here. Their patron allows them to perform in the grand hall of his home, and all the townsfolk may come for a modest fee. It would be easy for you and I to walk over one evening now that the days are warmer and the light longer.'

So it was that Friedrich and the doctor went to the play. He could scarcely believe that these were the same words that his schoolmaster at Stadt Ilm had delivered to them with so little feeling or enthusiasm. He sat on the edge of his seat tense with excitement. The words suddenly took on a new meaning, the characters were alive!

The doctor lent him a copy of Goethe's works and when he was not walking in the forest in the evenings, or working with the doctor in his study, Friedrich read the plays he had seen, living again their moments of drama, the situations, the characters and the poetic language which delighted him.

Some of the enthusiasm he had to convey in his letters to Uncle Hoffman and his father. Hoffman was delighted; he had always regretted the lack of any theatrical performances in Stadt Ilm, adding a love of good drama to that he had for music. But Pastor Froebel did not share his view. His reply to his son was far from approving: 'I suppose you are old enough to make your own decisions regarding your way of life,' he wrote, 'but I do not recommend you to the theatre. The situations presented are artificial and at most times seldom in keeping with Christian doctrine. There is always the danger that you may be deluded by what you see. Only the strongest character can resist such subtle and insidious temptation, and yours is still young and unformed. I would prefer you to find some other amusement.'

Friedrich read the letter several times but did not tell the doctor about it. Instead he turned his attention even more to study. In addition to his long sessions reading and botanising he had found at the camp a number of books, legacies from previous students and apprentices. Among them were some volumes on mathematics and science, which he had always done well at at school, and some elementary books on geology. The mathematics he found quite easy to understand, and in any case he could always rely on the doctor for help when something proved beyond his comprehension.

Geology was a new venture, but he had always been aware of the contours of the hills and the strata of the rocks. The colour and variety of the stones and boulders which rolled down the scree slopes into the valleys and stream-beds fascinated him with their age and history. His new knowledge lent even greater interest to his daily work on the hillside woodlands, so that the hours sped by and even the long summer days did not give enough time for all he wanted to see and do.

Since his unhappy evening in the beer-cellar two years ago he had avoided the company of girls. He was civil to them but withdrawn, so that his companions dubbed him 'the woman-hater.' He was darkly handsome, thin-featured with high cheek-bones and a slightly aquiline nose which gave his young face maturity, even nobility. He would not have lacked feminine company had he sought it.

Occasionally he had letters from Lotte but they never referred to their childhood relationship. They were all of the present and the future, never the past.

She, too, had been severely reprimanded by her parents when the full story of her affection for the young Friedrich had been disclosed in a letter from Pastor Froebel to her aunt. She was sent to Leipzig with instructions to her relations that she was to be strictly chaperoned and her correspondence scrutinised, for fear that a childish infatuation for a nice but unpromising boy should ruin her prospects of a successful marriage to a young man with more to offer than a forester's career.

Since then her family had moved to Osterode, far away in the Harz Mountains, and many of the old ties had been broken; but there were new links, particularly in the fact that Friedrich's brother, Christian had also settled in Osterode with his young wife, and news of Lotte came to Friedrich from this source as well as her own letters.

Friedrich replied to her letters, but never without a feeling of unrest. The years between had lent enchantment rather than forgetfulness to that summer idyll at Stadt Ilm which even his later experience of remorse and revelation could not eradicate. At these times he would frantically direct his thoughts and energies to a desperate spate of study.

He even set himself physical targets to strengthen his body and subdue the desires which shamed him. He would rise every morning before the other boys to run long distances, he bathed in the cold streams which tumbled down the hillsides from the heights above, he lifted heavy logs until he felt his back would break, and he still kept strictly away from the beer gardens and the village carnivals.

Friedrich had served over two years of his apprenticeship when he was summoned to make the two-day journey back to the pastorate at Oberweissbach. His father, even more deeply absorbed in the rebuilding of his church, had paid little attention to Friedrich's progress as a forester, but the reminder that he had completed two years of his training, and that it was about time that he found a post and began to earn his own living, was brought to his attention by Sofia. The Pastor's second wife already considered that her stepsons' education took too much of the family income; of all the Pastor's sons by his first wife, Friedrich was the one she liked the least.

The warden was not overpleased when he heard the Pastor's decision. Friedrich was beginning to be useful as an assistant and he did not see why he should lose him so soon. The boy had even begun to show himself to be considerably adept at the difficult task of timber-floating, whereby the logs were bound together and slid down the hillsides into the river to drift downstream to the timber-yards in the town.

The warden wrote requesting that Friedrich should continue his apprenticeship another year, but when the reply came that the Pastor considered his son's apprenticeship should be complete, and he would not change his decision, the warden was extremely angry.

Unable to vent his fury on the father, he turned his attention to the son, and in a final letter to the manse at Oberweissbach complained bitterly of Friedrich's conduct and progress.

'I only suggested a further year's apprenticeship,' he wrote, 'because I had the vain hope that I might in that time make something of him, although I doubt if any tuition could have much impression on such a lazy and unco-operative boy. My most patient efforts to instruct him have been thwarted by his lack of attention and stupidity. I wash my hands of him and pity you, his father who must attempt to find him some place in life.'

Friedrich had always gained the impression that the warden, though disinterested in teaching, had been satisfied with his work and he left the forestry camp on his way to Oberweissbach in a reasonably confident and light-hearted frame of mind.

His brother, Christoph, had become minister of a small community which lay between Neuhaus and their home and it had been agreed that Friedrich should break his journey there. After fond greetings, for they had not met for two years or more, Christoph put his arm round his brother's shoulders, amazed to find that they were now almost the same height.

'I am sorry you fared so ill in the forest,' he said.

'Oh, it wasn't so bad,' said Friedrich. I think at least I have learned enough to make a reasonable career for myself.'

I hope our father agrees with you,' said Christoph with a sigh. 'You know, of course, that he has received a bad report of you from the warden?'

'A bad report?' Friedrich was amazed. 'But the warden always spoke well of my work. He was an odd man and not a very good teacher, but I managed to learn something, and towards the end he trusted me with quite responsible jobs, even timber-floating. Why should he report badly of me to father? Are you sure he did?'

'I fear so,' said Christoph sadly. 'I have the letter here. Father sent it to me because he was so concerned and sought my views on its contents... I'll fetch it and show it to you. After all, it is only fair you should know what has been said about you.'

As they walked together in the sunny garden, Christoph read the warden's cruel letter aloud. Friedrich expressing his indignation at every unjust and spiteful sentence.

'It's not true, Christoph!' he cried when it was done. 'Really, it's not true.' For all his nearly eighteen years he was near to tears in his desperation 'It's cruel that a man should write such lies! I tried as best I could... bad teacher though he was. What's more, I have been teaching myself a lot... mathematics, geology. I have my papers with me in my pack... I'll show you!'

Friedrich hurriedly undid the things he had brought with him and showed his brother the pages of neat notes and diagrams on which he had worked during the evenings at Neuhaus. He showed him the folders of pressed flowers and leaves, with their botanical classifications, which the doctor had helped him to compile.

'This is all my work! Is this laziness and stupidity?'

Christoph was immediately convinced and indignant that his young brother should have suffered such injustice.

'You should have complained long ago,' he told Friedrich. 'Why, if it had not been for your own efforts it seems that most of these two years would have been wasted. Why did you not tell father?'

'You know he would never have believed me had I done so. He told me before I left that I was not to come whining to him with complaints, for he would not listen to them.'

Christoph vowed that the injustice should at least be righted now, and he lost no time in writing to his father to tell him that, whatever he had been told to the contrary, Friedrich had far from wasted his two years of study and that he should be given a cordial welcome when he returned to the manse.

This was forthcoming, although Sofia was not so easily convinced that the warden's opinion of Friedrich was not a confirmation of her own belief that he was a useless good-for-nothing. This did not distress Friedrich greatly; he was satisfied at least that his father did not think ill of him. In fact the Pastor seemed quite pleased to see his son again, now that the older boys where all away from home. But Sofia had no intention of allowing Friedrich to stay overlong for fear he might exert his influence, which she considered far from good, over her own Karl.

CHAPTER FOUR

Sofia's relations once again came to her rescue. The same cousin who had secured Friedrich's apprenticeship at the State Forest had contacts in Jena, the University town some forty miles to the North-east, and it was possible that Friedrich, armed with a suitable introduction, might obtain from them a post on one of the estates in the Duchy. This was the most convenient suggestion, as Traugott, the next youngest of the Pastor's sons by his first marriage, had been a medical student at Jena for the past two years and was awaiting his quarterly allowance. It was decided therefore that Friedrich might act as courier for the money and at the same time stay for a short time in Jena while he contacted the official recommended by Sofia's cousin.

The journey from the State Forest at Neuhaus to Oberweissbach, and shortly after on to Jena, gave Friedrich plenty of time for contemplation. His heart lay in the long periods of study he had enjoyed so much with his old friend the doctor, and once when they were together he had been able to express, if inadequately, what he felt in his own words.

'You know, sir,' he said 'until I met you I never learnt how to learn.'

Knowledge at the Stadt Ilm Grammer School had been acquired out of a mixture of pride and duty to please Uncle Hoffman and Grossmutter by his good reports, to be approved by his teachers, wholesome rivalry with his classmates, and the fear of the cane, . . . but never because he *enjoyed* learning. Only with the doctor had he discovered that study could be a deeply satisfying pleasure.

It was this that mostly filled his mind as he travelled to Jena. Would it, he dreamed, even be possible to secure a place at the University? To do so he would be content to perform the most menial tasks, to work long hours, to go hungry if necessary, if it meant that he could share something of the life which had suddenly become all-important to him.

Jena entranced him. The old town, with its narrow streets and red roofs, stood on rising ground, surrounded by steep chalk hills, the highest of which, the Hausberg, crowned one aspect. The steeple of the church, over 300 feet high, pointed a slender finger to the sky in the midst of a cheerful clutter of houses, the market-place and inns. Of the latter, the Black Bear fascinated Friedrich most, for here the great Martin Luther himself had halted in his flight from the Warburg. This true story, more exciting than any fiction, had been told to him long ago by his brother Christoph. To see the actual scene of one of its most thrilling episodes was a tremendous experience.

Jena was Friedrich's first taste of town life, for Stadt Ilm was merely a village by comparison. The University, founded in 1557 by John Friedrich, Elector of Saxony, to take the place of Wittenburg as a seat of learning and evangelical doctrine, attracted students from all parts of Bavaria and Prussia. For some years now it had been the centre of literary inspiration attracted by the residence there of Goethe. Its beer gardens and inns were meeting-places for students of the arts and philosophy, of science and the humanities, and the vigorous life-blood of learning flowed through it with the same impatient vitality as the River Leutra tumbled beneath its bridges towards its meeting-place with the Saale.

Traugott and Friedrich met, as arranged, at Traugott's lodgings, a pleasant attic room above a baker's shop not far from the centre of the town and the university. The brothers greeted each other fondly for it was years since they had met and Traugott saw a great change in Friedrich, who had been a boy when they parted and was now a young man.

'My boots would not fit you now!' he laughed.

Friedrich was already taller than his older brother.

'If they had, father would have had me wearing them!' he smiled. 'As it is, I nearly got Karl's old jacket, but mercifully it was too small for me. Instead I had father's.'

Friedrich had grown philosophic about the sources of his wardrobe, which had always been a series of hand-downs from one member of the family to the other, he being the last of a long line.

'So you are here to get an appointment?' Traugott was standing by the window looking out over the rooftops of the town towards the hills beyond. 'Do you like the forester's life?'

'Not much,' Friedrich replied ruefully 'but what else can I do? It is the only craft I know and our stepmother has provided me with introductions. I suppose there are worse ways of earning one's living.'

'And better...' said Traugott. 'Look, Friedrich, you are here in Jena. This is a wonderful place... I never realised until I came here what we are missing buried there in Oberweissbach. This is life! Don't hurry in your work-seeking. You can live here with me. It's not much but you are welcome to share what I have, and my allowance will easily provide for us both if we are careful. You can even attend a few lectures if you like. There are professors who never pay any attention to the registers and a new face isn't noticed in the crowd.'

'But what'll I tell father?'

'Tell him you are taking your time because you want to be certain of finding the right post. He can't object to that.'

So Friedrich moved into the attic room with Traugott. Every morning they were wakened early by the clatter of the bakery as the baker and his boys prepared the first batches of loaves for the ovens. Soon the warm breath of the new bread floated up the stairs to them, so that hunger overcame their youthful laziness and they too rose to set about the day's business.

Sometimes Friedrich would go with Traugott to a lecture. It was true that a strange face went unnoticed, and Traugott had soon introduced his young brother to his fellow students, so he was accepted as one of the crowd wherever he went. Much of what he heard went straight over his head but there were parts of the lectures which he found surprisingly understandable in the light of his recent instruction by the doctor at Neuhaus and his own studies. He also enjoyed the atmosphere of learning and the happy kamaraderie of his fellow students.

Traugott also introduced him to the University library, where he was able to use books on the botanical sciences which had been his dream during his two years of elementary study.

Their evenings were spent together too in the inns and beer gardens where the students gathered to drink and air their views. Friedrich found these impromptu debates and arguments provided the most agreeable way to spend the long summer evenings.

Austria had joined with Russia, Turkey and Britain in a coalition against Napoleon, anxious to recover provinces west of the Rhine, and the young men were sharply divided in their opinions of the future, political and military, of their homeland.

To these subjects were added others—literature, philosophy, religion... as young, eager minds, exploring their newly-acquired knowledge and inspired by intellectual rivalry, tossed opinions at each other over their beer-mugs late into the night.

Not a subject escaped their attention and women were not left out of the discussions, but unlike the apprentices in the forestry camp the students' approach was one of the mind rather than the body; the latter they kept for their private interludes in the river walks and the sunny hillsides on week-end afternoons. Their discussions therefore were seldom coarse and were much more concerned with the growing belief among intellectuals that women, exceptional women possibly, could contribute to the spheres of learning, at least in literature and the arts.

'Woman is creative by instinct,' said Traugott during one of these discussions. 'She carries the child in her womb, nurtures the seed to fruition, bears it and guides it through the formative years of its life. What artistic achievement can compare with that? She is not creating a mere painting, a book, a work of art, but a human being, the boarding house of the soul! What a challenge! What an opportunity!'

Max, a dark brooding young man studying biology, interrupted him. 'But this is natural to her. Surely a cow, a beast of the field, does all this, not by desire but by destiny? There is no talent in copulation! The lowest of creatures mate and multiply! You forget too that the child the woman bears is the child of its father. He has contributed to that intelligence, that ability, that soul if you like, that you credit to the woman's talent for creation. She is merely the host, the nurse, the comforter.'

'Max, you are a century behind the times!' cried Traugott. 'Who taught you to regard women as a reproductive animal, no more? I tell you, women have minds, *and* souls, as good as any man. It's just that their time is so taken up by child-bearing and domestic duties, caring for old parents, for instance, that they have no leisure for the pursuit of knowledge. I swear that if I could take a girl...'

'You could do *that,* I warrant' interrupted one of the more ribald listeners, but Traugott ignored him, using the pause for breath. 'If I could take a girl away from this domestic treadmill, bring her to the university...' This again was greeted with laughter, but Traugott still ignored interruptions. 'Give her the opportunity we have and she could equal the lot of us, in study, application and the imagination to use her knowledge at the end.' Traugott thumped the table with his beer-mug, out of breath with his oratory.

Friedrich, listening intently, found his brother's theory fascinating. He, too, could see no reason why a woman should not achieve all this. Lotte, he remembered, could talk with him on any subject as well as and better than any of the boys in those long-ago days at Stadt Ilm. In the last years of their companionship they had talked of God, of heaven and hell, of death, of all the subjects that perplex and fascinate young minds on the threshold of adult life, and Lotte had surprised him often by her natural wisdom, which he knew exceeded his own.

When he and Traugott returned to their lodgings that night Friedrich was in a contemplative mood.

'You're dreamy,' said his brother. 'What's on your mind?'

'Nothing, really...just what you were talking of tonight. I think you are quite right...about women, I mean.'

'You're a fine one to be talking of women,' laughed Traugott. 'You never go with a girl.'

Friedrich flushed.

'I'm not jibing you for it.' Traugott put a hand on his brother's shoulder. 'Girls and study don't mix, I've found that. Plenty of time to find a girl when I'm qualified... But you've no studies to confine you... don't you like feminine company sometimes?'

'I feel awkward with women.'

Traugott looked at him quizzically

'I believe you do, too... yet you've got looks enough, you'd not find it hard to please them.'

Friedrich's answer was angry, and Traugott, three-quarters a doctor, diagnosed the reason for his hostility.

He said no more until they had blown out the candle, opened the window and climbed into the large old bed they shared. After they had lain there in the dark a few minutes in silence, Traugott asked: 'What happened, Friedling?'

The use of his old name melted Friedrich's annoyance.

'You knew about Lotte?'

'Yes, I heard from Christoph, but that was a boy's game. You're not still fretting on that?'

'No, its not Lotte... though I still think of her often.'

'What is it, then?'

Secure in the dark as they lay there side by side, uncovered as the night was too warm for blankets, with the stars blinking in the square of dark sky beyond the open window, Friedrich told his brother of the unforgettable memory of his father's lecture when his affection for Lotte had been discovered. He told him of the disturbing and distressing incident in the forestry camp, the coarse stories, the bawdy language.

'I hate it all!' he told Traugott. 'It's horrible, disgusting, degrading! I cannot bear to think of doing such things.'

Traugott in the darkness, frowning with distress at his young brother's bitter revelations, searched for words to comfort him. They must be the right words he knew, for the wrong words now would be as fatal as a slipping scalpel.

'It's not really as you think,' he said slowly after a long silence. 'Oh, I know there is the seamy side... you saw it in the beer gardens, you've heard it. Men can be coarse in their conversation. Much of it is empty boastfulness, trying to prove themselves men when they are boys. But the true love of a man for a woman is not coarse. These things that disgust you might in themselves seem so, but when they express the affection and devotion between a man and a woman, they achieve a tenderness and nobility.'

'But father said...,' Friedrich interrupted.

'I know,' said Traugott patiently, 'I know... he said the same things to me too, though I deserved it more. Our father is a man of sad philosophies but high principles, a man of austerity. He is a good man, and kind, I have found that out since I have grown older; but he is not a man of the world. The God he loves is a jealous God, and I do not believe God to be so. God meant us to love the world and all that is in it as an exercise in our love for Him. And the ways of the world, however strange they may sometimes seem to us, are His ways, and therefore good.'

As Traugott spoke, Friedrich dared again to think of Lotte. There *had* been tenderness, even in his boyish emotion—he recognised that. It was the same feeling of protective concern that he felt for young and helpless animals, the snared rabbit, the barnyard kittens. With the tenderness there was also strength, wonder and humility, all good things in themselves. This he had been prepared to believe until his father's stern reproaches had shattered his belief like brittle glass. Now in the dark of his mind they were beginning to grow together again.

'Shall I ever be as I was with Lotte...?' he asked Traugott.

'No.' His brother would not bolster him falsely with fairy tales. 'Not quite, for this time you will no longer be a boy, you will be a man. It will not be tomorrow, perhaps not even a year from now, ... or even ten years, but when the time *does* come you will know, and when you know you will no longer be afraid.'

As drowsiness overcame him, Friedrich turning on his pillow, allowed himself to live again the afternoon in the woods at Stadt Ilm with Lotte, but this time, for just once in his dreams, he did not run away.

That night of the unburdening of his mind to Traugott left Friedrich refreshed. It was the relief of the confessional, a soothing of spiritual sores which had festered for more than two years. He no longer felt guilty or ashamed; he was no longer afraid to look at the girls in the beer gardens; he could even admire their charms without being either repulsed or unduly disturbed by them. They were like pictures on the walls—a pleasing decorative background to the intellectual stimulation of the discussions around him. Best of all, he was reassured that he was normal. Shy, perhaps, and diffident... but no different to a thousand other young men.

He had already decided that he must stay at the university and had made little effort to follow up the recommendations given to him by Sofia. Of the several he had pursued only one had offered him the prospect of a managerial position on an estate near Oberweissbach. Normally it would have seemed ideal, but now he regarded it as an ominous threat to his hopes to remain in Jena.

At Michaelmas the brothers returned to Oberweissbach for a short vacation.

'I hope you are satisfied now.' Sofia said tartly to Friedrich. 'At least you can say you have been to the university.'

Friedrich had to explain that two or three months did not constitute a university education but Sofia would not listen.

His father, while agreeing, was equally hopeful that the short taste of university life would have satisfied his son's whim. He was not enthusiastic therefore when Friedrich asked him if it would be permissable to persuade his trustees to allow him to have the entire legacy left to him by his mother, so that he could continue his studies at Jena.

After considerable argument and great persuasion from Traugott the Pastor relented and agreed at least that the trustees, two distant cousins of his first wife's family, should be consulted. Traugott again added his reference to the request and the trustees rather reluctantly, agreed. One of them wrote:—'If you have set your heart on this we do not feel that we can refuse you, for your dear mother wished this money to help you in getting a good start in life. I trust your honour that you will use it profitably and not in the wild life of the town, where we understand there are many temptations.'

Jubilantly the brothers returned to Jena in the late autumn of 1799. Friedrich had chosen to enrol for lectures in mathematics, mineralogy and botany, adding to these a course in forestry and practical estate management. He joined the Natural History Society and was inspired by his tutor, Dr. Batsch, one of the university's most progressive professors, in a new natural system of botany. Under the instruction of this scholarly old man he learned for the first time a theory his father would have considered blasphemy, that all creatures were alike in the sight of God.

Another old delight was revived for his leisure hours, for Jena had a flourishing theatre which proved a welcome relaxation from study.

So the old life of study by day and argument by night was happily resumed. They were hard put to make ends meet on their small allowances but managed in the easy going way of all students, by borrowing and sharing among their friends. They never went hungry. The students dining hall provided a reasonable meal at a low price but would not allow the young men to run up accounts. The eating-houses in the town, competing with each other for custom, were not so particular and when funds were low, which they were frequently, they could usually be sure of 'eating on the slate' at one or another.

Towards the end of Friedrich's first year at Jena, Traugott came home one evening from his lectures with exciting news. He had been invited by one of his professors, a surgeon at Jena's hospital, to join his staff as a pupil. This meant invaluable practical experience of both medicine and surgery. However, before Traugott could take this opportunity there was one obstacle to be overcome—the purchase of instruments and apparatus that he would need for hospital work. In his practical work at the university he could usually borrow what he needed, but this would be impossible at the hospital.

The Pastor's reply to his request for assistance was discouraging. 'Much as I regret it, I find I am unable to help you,' he wrote. 'As you know, your small stipend has already been used in university fees. Expenses are great here; the new church building is proving more expensive than we had ever thought and is a constant drain on our resources. In addition, I have Karl's education to consider. Would it not be possible for you to borrow the articles from some other student who does not immediately require them?'

The Pastor did not understand the impecunious state of the majority of the students, many of whom had no coats of their own, let alone the tools of their professions.

When Traugott confessed his predicament to the surgeon professor, who was anxious to know if the young man would accept the post he had offered him, he was offered at least a little encouragement.

'There will be a small stipend for you, you know.' said the older man. 'Not much, but enough perhaps to help you to pay for the things you need.'

Traugott tried to persuade the town's maker of scientific instruments to let him have at least the essentials on an instalment system, but the tradesman had bitter experiences of student's financial circumstances and was not going to risk another bad debt.

'I'm sorry,' he said. 'It's cash or nothing.'

Traugott returned dejected to his lodgings, where Friedrich, unaware of his disappointment, was in a jubilant mood. He had spent the afternoon on the hillside above the town. The day had been warm and sunny, despite the lateness in the year (it was nearing mid-September.) In the short grass on the chalky uplands he had found the rare autumn gentian, a triumphant discovery for a field botanist, as he still was by instinct as well as by instruction.

When Traugott came in, Friedrich immediately sensed his distress: the brothers had grown very close to each other and were quick to catch each other's moods.

'It's no good,' Traugott told him. 'I shall have to give up the idea of working at the hospital. I can't get the post without the instruments and I can't pay for them unless I get the post. It's as simple as that.' He slumped in a chair and dropped his head into his hands.

Always attached to Traugott since their childhood together, Friedrich was distressed to see him so dejected. Impulsively he snatched at the only hope he could think of.

'I've got money, Traug.'

'But Friedling, that's all you have to stay here.'

'I know,' said Friedrich 'but I don't need it all at once. If you buy what you need out of it, you can pay me back with the money you earn. In the meantime, if we are a bit short, old Georg at the eating-house will let us run up a bill on the slate... we won't starve.'

Traugott was reluctant but Friedrich persuaded him. Eventually it was agreed and the amount required drawn out of Friedrich's allowance.

The hospital appointment proved to be all Traugott had expected and more. Distressed and horrified by the sights and sounds of primitive surgery, of the suffering and endurance of the unfortunate men and women who were brought into the hospital's fearful wards and operating rooms, he was determined to overcome his natural reaction to flee from a nightmare by increasing his skill and knowledge so that he might at least relieve a little of their suffering.

He worked long hours at the hospital and Friedrich saw less and less of him, but was happy enough in his own studies, to which he had added physics and chemistry. Traugott faithfully repaid his debt in small instalments with the pathetically inadequate fees he received from assisting the surgeon professor in his work on the more affluent citizens of the town. Nevertheless, money was extremely short, for Friedrich also had to buy books for his studies; both the young men were glad of old Georg's willingness to let their bill for meals at his eating-house run up faster than they were able to pay off their debts.

One evening, after a particularly gruelling day at the hospital, Traugott returned to their attic room looking more tired than usual.

'My head is splitting,' he told Friedrich. 'It's the stench of that place! You'd never believe it, Friedrich! It's ghastly! The reek of decaying flesh, of putrid wounds, of excrement... and of death. Sometimes it seems to seep into me, so that I smell it even when I lie in bed at night.'

Friedrich shuddered. 'It's beyond me how you bear it,' he said. 'I know it has to be borne by someone... but I don't think I could do it. You've got more strength than I have, Traug. I'm too much of a coward.'

'I'm older,' said Traugott. 'You know, as you get older, that some things have to be borne, but it doesn't mean that I like it any better.'

He put a hand to his aching head: the skin was hot and dry.

'I think I'll go to bed, I seem to have a touch of fever. It's probably this unusually warm weather and I've taken a chill. I'll be better after a night's sleep.'

But Traugott was not better. He spent a sleepless night and in the morning his headache was worse and his body burned with fever. Friedrich, alarmed, called the baker's wife to look at him. The good woman peered round the door fearfully, terrified that her young lodger might have the plague. At the sight of the bright fever spots burning on his cheeks and his sunken eyes she hastily withdrew.

'You must call a doctor,' she told Friedrich, 'Your brother is very ill.'

Friedrich hastened to the home of the surgeon under whom Traugott worked at the hospital.

'I'll come immediately,' he said. He knew too well the dangers to which all who worked in the hospital wards exposed themselves, and when he saw Traugott his fears were confirmed.

'He has hospital fever,' he said.

The days that followed were a nightmare for Friedrich. Traugott tossed and turned in his bed, the sheets were drenched with sweat, and the baker's wife, kind though she was, refused to touch them.

'I have children,' she told Friedrich 'I dare not.'

So Friedrich himself struggled to wash the bedlinen in a bucket in the room and dry it by the open window. He sponged his brother's burning limbs with cool cloths, sat up all night, for sleep was denied him in any case in the one bed they usually shared.

The surgeon prescribed blood-letting but Traugott, even in his delirium, refused to allow it. The sights of patients weakened by bleeding were too vivid in his mind.

Time seemed interminable, days and nights rolling into one as Friedrich alternately worked and dozed between care of his patient and snatches of uncomfortable rest in a chair.

On the morning of the fourteenth day, when Friedrich roused himself from a fitful sleep he saw that Traugott was awake too.

'I feel better,' he said.

The fever had abated, but Traugott was a shadow of the strong young man he had been a few weeks before. The surgeon called that morning and congratulated himself, although in fact his attentions had had little to do with the recovery, which was due entirely to the patient's normal natural health and vitality.

'What you need now,' he said 'is building up. You need good food, at least a month's rest and positively no exertion. Any undue effort must have a weakening effect on your heart. I think if possible you should go into the country for a spell.'

What neither Friedrich nor Traugott knew was that the coveted position which Traugott had held at the hospital under the old man had been transferred in his absence to the son of one of the town's rich businessmen, who was also an aspiring doctor and whose father was a patron of the hospital and the surgeon professor. Traugott's departure for the country would not only be good for his health but would also save the old surgeon considerable embarrassment.

'I'll be back in less than a month,' Traugott told Friedrich when he left on the mail-coach to stay with the family of one of his friends, who lived a few miles away in the mountains. 'Will you be able to manage?'

'Of course,' Friedrich reassured him. He could not tell his brother, still pale and weak from his illness, that Georg the eating-house keeper was already pressing him for the money they owed for past meals as well as the nourishing broth which he had provided for the invalid.

After Traugott's departure, Friedrich went to the eating-house.

'I can't pay you,' he said frankly. 'I'll work for you, but I can't pay.'

Georg had heard this story too often. He liked the Froebel boys but most of the students were pleasant young men and nearly all of them owed him money. He had to pay his own bills and a time came when he just could not afford to be sentimental.

'I can get all the help I want,' he said. 'It's money I need. I can't give you much longer.'

In between lectures, which he had been forced to neglect during Traugott's illness, Friedrich made desperate attempts to obtain work. He dared not go near Georg's eating-house, therefore he mostly went hungry; the small amount of money he had left only barely covered the cost of his lodgings. The baker's wife took pity on him, and admiring the way in which he had cared for his brother gave him loaves, which she pretended were stale to placate her husband, and dripping from her cooking. He was hungrily enjoying such a meal when the university proctors came to visit him.

Georg's patience was at an end.

After a short appearance before the court, Friedrich was committed to the Carcer... the university prison where the students who failed to keep the rules of the colleges were detained. He was loath to write to his father of his predicament; to do so would involve Traugott. Better surely to await his brother's return from the country and resumption of work, when at least they might be able to pay off some of the debt, enough at least to secure his release.

In the meantime the Carcer was not so unpleasant as to be really distressing. Friedrich found he was not alone and that one of his companions at least was a friend of his brother's who had often joined them in their evening discussions. Max was renowned for his spendthrift ways and spent long periods in the Carcer before being bailed out by an indulgent father.

Max was a Latin student and, like Friedrich, had been allowed to bring his books with him into detention. Helped by him, Friedrich joined in his studies. Latin had never been a strong subject with him; at Stadt Ilm he had been taught sketchily, and his knowledge, such as it was, was largely confined to his naming of plants in his botanical studies.

In addition to working with Max at Latin he spent the long days writing a thesis on geometry, something which it had long been in his mind to tackle. There were plenty of reference books, mostly left behind by former inmates. Among these Friedrich found a translation of ancient Persian scriptures, which interested him greatly because its truths of life, although unrelated to Christianity, were so similar to those he had been taught to accept.

The weeks wore on. Max was released, his father as usual having acted as bailee, and Friedrich had to continue his studies alone. He sat at the window of the room where he was detained, looking down on the university garden, being greeted cheerfully by his friends as they passed on their way to lectures and looking longingly at the hills beyond the town, where spring was already beginning to cast a mist of green over the trees. He longed to be there on the hilltop, with the short, springy turf under his feet and the first violets growing on short stalks out of the chalky soil.

Traugott's convalescence had been prolonged from a month to over four months by a setback caused by the exhaustion of the journey to the country. Friedrich wrote to him saying nothing of his predicament, for fear that it might delay his recovery further or that he might return too hastily to the town. His friends brought him Traugott's replies, still directed to their old lodgings above the baker's shop.

It was at Easter that Traugott finally returned to Jena, looking thinner but bronzed and fit. When he arrived at their old lodgings to be told sadly by the baker's wife of Friedrich's removal to the Carcer he was horrified, in particular as the debt was in fact his own. He immediately hastened to where Friedrich was detained.

'Why didn't you tell me?' he cried. 'You poor devil, shut up in this place while I was lounging around in the sunshine. I'll never forgive myself.'

'It's not been so bad,' Friedrich reassured him. 'I've even learned some Latin, and look . . .' He showed his brother the neat pages of his geometry thesis. 'You see, I have not been wasting my time!'

'But shut up!' Traugott was still dismayed. 'I never had any idea! You said you were managing well, I thought you had been able to stave off the creditors until I returned. I'll write immediately to father explaining everything. You shall be got out of here without delay.'

It was no use Friedrich protesting. Traugott had made up his mind, and in any case now the added blow was revealed of the cancellation of the hospital appointment and its hope of a little additional money.

'Even if I sell my instruments I'll only get a fraction of what I paid for them,' said Traugott. 'And in any case, I'm sure father will understand.'

The Pastor, however, was not so eager to believe either of his sons. Traugott, he felt, was probably sheltering his younger brother, as he did when they were children. It took several letters before he eventually agreed to advance enough money to free Friedrich from his detention, but he refused to contribute one penny more towards his cost of study, which he already considered excessive.

So at the beginning of the summer session in 1801, Friedrich had to leave Jena. His parting with Traugott was sorrowful.

'I blame myself for all this,' said his older brother. 'I got you into this mess.'

Friedrich clasped Traugott's hand 'If I had more sense I could have extricated myself somehow' he said. 'At least I've added to my experience!'

Although he tried to be cheerful in front of Traugott, who was already cast down enough at the situation, Friedrich was dejected as the mail-coach bore him away from Jena. He dared not look back as the familiar roof-tops faded into the distance and the hopes and dreams of an academic career faded with them.

His arrival at Oberweissbach was no more cheerful. Sofia had lost no opportunity for reminding her husband of her warning that any money spent on Friedrich's further education would be wasted.

The next day he asked his father for permission to use his library. He was told that he could do so provided he kept to certain hours of the day, when he would not disturb the work of the parish. 'But I don't want you dreaming your life away over books,' said his father. 'We must now find some suitable post for you, something where your earlier apprenticeship will be of value.'

So Friedrich was left to carry on with his work, undisturbed for at least a few weeks until news came that a post had been offered him at Hilburghausen, where some of the Pastor's relations had a farm. Friedrich was to be placed as a student of practical farming under a steward who managed the estate.

The farmhouse was large and pleasant, well-built and comfortable, surrounded by neat outbuildings. Friedrich found the lodging and food adequate but the work uninteresting and arduous. Not that he minded hard work; he had grown used to that in his days as a forester, but the farmwork in many cases seemed to be useless drudgery. He was particularly disturbed, too, by the callousness of the farmworkers towards the animals. It distressed him to have to herd helpless lambs away from their mothers and prod them to see if they were ready for the slaughterhouse.

'You're too sentimental,' they told him. 'You'd soon change if your living depended on it. We've got to eat, you know.'

Friedrich knew, but it did not add to his relish of the roasted lamb which turned up with monotonous and sickening regularity on the Sunday dinner table.

As he entered into the routine of the daily milking, work in the fields, seed-time and harvest, rick-building and threshing, Friedrich became more inured to the monotony of the life and even began to enjoy it. It was particularly so with occasions such as ploughing, when he could be alone with his thoughts, the patient steaming horse plodding beside him, its hay-laden breath drifting sweetly into his own nostrils.

In the midst of this gentle, rural existence he began to receive disturbing letters from his brother Christoph, now a frequent visitor to the manse.

'I am concerned about our father,' he wrote. 'He has grown very thin and sleeps badly. We find it difficult to persuade him to take enough nourishment. The doctor has warned him that he must rest or he will not be responsible for the consequences, yet he still spends hours at his desk.'

Friedrich's feelings for his father had always been of awe rather than of affection but these letters still disturbed him. He regretted now more than ever that he had never been able to achieve the closeness which seemed to exist between most of the young men he knew and their fathers. At nineteen he had not reached even a fraction of the intimacy which in maturity often replaces the more formal relationship of father and son in earlier years.

'I wish I could write to him to explain how I feel,' Friedrich wrote to Christoph. 'Do you think he has ever realised how much I wanted to love him, for him to love me?'

As he went about his duties on the farm, in the cowhouse on the cold October mornings when he was up at five for the milking, he sat with his head against the cows warm flanks, his hands monotonously engaged with the teats, his mind preoccupied with the letter he might compose to his father. The letter would explain his efforts to please as a child, his desire for affection and approval, his admiration for his father and, above all, his desperate longing for the paternal friendship and understanding.

The letter was never written, for in November the farm steward summoned him to the estate office. Bad news had come from Oberweissbach: the Pastor was seriously ill and Friedrich must return home immediately.

He found the manse at its gloomiest. Sofia, never a capable woman, had collapsed in the face of the emergency, as distressed over her own future as her husband's illness, and had herself taken to her bed, requiring sedatives and adding to the servants' already heavy nursing duties.

Friedrich was shocked by the sight of his father. He was propped up in his bed against a pile of pillows, his fine face drawn and haggard, his hands on the counterpane thin and pale. His skin had a transparent unhealthiness and his conversation was hindered by a dry cough.

Friedrich appointed himself as the old man's guardian. He read to him from the Bible, but choosing his own passages rather than those of which the Pastor had once been so fond when it came to choosing the texts for his sermons. He read him the Song of Solomon and the Psalms, their poetry lulling the patient into drowsiness. Sometimes he would change to secular works such as Goethe or Schiller, but always something that held light and hope rather than the ominous forebodings of damnation which he felt would only add depression to the already dreary sick-room.

As tenderly as a woman he helped his father with his toilet, lifted him while the servants changed the bedlinen, brought him his food and tried to coax him to eat it.

The old man was greatly cheered by news Friedrich brought him a few days after Christmas. 'You're a grandfather!' he told him, and for the first time in many months the Pastor smiled.

Christian's wife had given birth to a daughter, Albertine, born on December 29th at Osterode, where Christian had a flourishing business as a weaver and dyer of cloth. With the happy tidings he sent a present of new bedcovers to cheer the Pastors sick room and a garland of Christmas roses to hang in the window.

Father and son rejoiced together at the first grandchild in the family. The new year dawned with a burst of false spring, the sun shone as if it were April, and for the first time since Friedrich had returned from the farm his father seemed to improve. He was even strong enough to talk, and when he could not sleep would converse late into the night in a way which Friedrich had never previously known.

'You are a good son' he said one night when they had been talking for some hours and Friedrich was rearranging his pillows. 'I think I misjudged you as a child. If I was a severe father, try to remember that my strictness was born of duty and not of domination.'

Friedrich took his father's hand. 'I think I understand,' he said 'We all understood. We all respected you.'

'But I was harsher with you than the others,' said the Pastor, sighing. 'After your dear mother died I vowed that never again would I allow the love of a fellow human being to deflect my soul's devotion to the whole-hearted service of God. My love for your mother was the ruling passion of my life. When she died I believed she had been taken from me because I had made an idol of her, allowing my passion to overrule my duty to the Lord.'

The old man's eyes filled with tears and Friedrich, standing beside him, felt his own emotion rising. It was cruel to hear such stern beliefs still voiced with conviction, such a harsh creed which could make a man feel that to love was to sin. He could not speak but smoothed the sheets and made the bed more comfortable. The old man now lay silent, the tears rolling uncontrolled down his thin, wrinkled cheeks.

The premature spring quickly faded before intense north winds and the rest of January was bitterly cold, with frequent snow and gales which swept round the manse, crying eerily through the cracks in the doors and blowing the snow flurries into drifts around the windowframes. The Pastor's improvement was equally short-lived and at the end of the month he had a severe relapse. Early in February 1802 he died, as he had lived, with spiritual and physical discipline, a text on his lips, and his hand held by his son Friedrich, whom he had learned to love too late.

Christian had left his young wife and new-born baby to visit his father in the last days of his illness. Finding Friedrich low in health and spirits after his weeks of nursing the old man, he suggested that after the funeral he might like to spend a few days with him and his family in Osterode, a pleasant town in the Harz mountains, some hundred miles away to the north west.

Friedrich readily agreed, not the least because he knew that Osterode was also the home of Lotte. His weeks in the sickroom had given him plenty of time to think and he had become almost obsessed with a mixture of desire and curiosity to see her again.

Christian and Friedrich made the journey together in early March in beautiful spring weather, with the daffodils already carpeting the woods and the first blossom on wild cherry trees in the sheltered valleys.

He had been staying with Christian two days before he met Lotte. Although he knew where she lived, only a few houses away, he could not find the courage to call on her. It was she who came to him, bearing a gift from her mother for Christian's little daughter. Friedrich opened the street door to her knock and found himself face to face with her for the first time since he had kissed her goodbye at their parting in Stadt Ilm nearly seven years ago.

Those years dropped away as their eyes met. She was taller, slimmer, her pale hair drawn into a coil at her neck, but her grey eyes were unchanged, her smiling mouth still with its enchanting tilt at the corners.

He only spoke her name... 'Lotte!'

Their hands met, and as he looked at her long and hard, Friedrich knew that at least *he* had not changed through all the years they had been parted, since the days in the water-garden, the strawberry-picking on the hillside, the night they had buried her dog.

He was unable to speak to her for long and then it was only of generalities. She was full of sympathy for his recent bereavement and enquired anxiously of Uncle Hoffman.

'He is very old, but well,' he told her. His beloved Grossmutter she knew had died while Friedrich was still at Jena.

It was a week before they met again, for despite his delight and emotion at seeing her, Friedrich was still moved by a strange shyness, almost a fear, of trying to resume their friendship. It was as if one wanted to transplant a tender plant and knew that the move could mean its destruction. When they did meet it was by accident, when he was walking in the town, but it was an opportunity he could not allow to pass, for his stay in Osterode was already nearing its end.

'I must see you...speak to you!,' he said. 'When can we meet?'

To his surprise and consternation she seemed distressed and perplexed by his request. Surely she must realise his unchanged devotion to her.

'There is a walk through the woods,' she suggested almost reluctantly. 'I could meet you there this afternoon, but do not tell your family that you are going with me.'

Friedrich felt this strange, as Christian and his wife were very fond of Lotte and knew of his affection for her; but he agreed, if she so wished, to keep their meeting secret.

She was waiting for him, wearing a blue cloak and hood which covered her hair but gave her eyes new exciting depth of colour.

For a while they walked quietly, hardly speaking, she gathering daffodils from the wayside as they went along.

At last he felt he must speak: all his thoughts and dreams of the past days seemed to be bursting inside him.

'You've not changed at all,' he said lamely, hating the stupidity of his own voice and the mundane nature of his remark.

'Oh, but I have!' she laughed. 'And so have you. You've grown up!' She looked up at him. 'Once I was as tall as you, now I only reach to your shoulder.'

He smiled. 'But we are still Lotte and Friedrich...you are still the little girl I wanted to kiss on the hillside, the girl I left with my childhood happiness in Stadt Ilm.' He put his hands on her shoulders. 'I still love you, Lotte.' He had said it now and it gave him courage. 'I know I was only a boy then, but I loved you then...now I know that I still love you.'

He moved towards her and would have kissed her but she turned her face so that his lips only brushed her cheek and he felt her shoulders stiffen under his hands.

'Lotte? What is the matter?' He was alarmed, distressed, puzzled.

'I'm sorry, Friedling.' The old name slipped out, making his heart turn with memories '*You* have not changed, but *I* have.' Her eyes filled with tears. 'I never thought it would be like this, it has been so long and lonely. Why didn't you tell me before? You wrote to me but never, ever, did you say that you still loved me. I thought all that was forgotten.'

'And now it is too late?'

She nodded miserably.

Friedrich dropped his hands from her.

'Forgive me,' he said, 'I should have guessed.'

The daffodils they had gathered were drooping and dead by the time they had walked back together to the town.

*   *   *

By Easter, the affairs at the manse settled, Friedrich left Oberweissbach. He had secured a position as a clerk at the office of the Woods and Forestry Commission in Bamberg.

The Chief Forester was a pleasant friendly man, far removed from his old master at Neuhaus during his apprenticeship. Friedrich was given accommodation in his house with his family. An added attraction was a fine, well-stocked library, to which he was given ready access. The family were Catholics but employed a Protestant tutor for their sons, the young man took an immediate liking to Friedrich and the two soon became firm friends.

His name was Josef Schroeder and together they spent happy evenings in the nearby village, where the young tutor had been received into the families of the doctor, the schoolmaster and the minister and was welcome to bring his new friend with him.

In one company or another they would sit up late discussing Josef's many and sometimes rather revolutionary theories. One of these was that the state should provide all education, even that at university, free to all who had the ability to take advantage of it. He was also a keen supporter of a movement amongst intellectuals to provide higher education for women. In this he had a ready disciple in Friedrich, who found his arguments most convincing, but the minister was adamant in opposition, particularly when Josef insisted that there was no ideological objection to women actually becoming ministers of religion.

This formed the structure of many hard-hitting debates which would end with the friends, flushed with argument and dry with talking, drowning their differences in strong ale (to which even the minister was not averse) and walking home under the stars, still pressing home some point of contention.

Josef was also a traveller. He had already held posts in Holland and in England, and now had his sights set on the New World, where he felt his

progressive theories might have more chance of being put into practice.
All this made Bamberg a pleasant place to be in the full summer of 1802. Even the sad events of the winter, and the unhappy re-union with Lotte, were alleviated by the friendship, and a considerable amount of leisure in which to enjoy the beauty of the countryside and to study.

As the year wore on to autumn and then winter, Friedrich found his responsibilities increasing. The forester, pleased with his work and his personality, gave him new duties which, while interesting, kept him indoors instead of, as previously, spending most of his time in the open air.

It was not so bad during the short, cold daylight of January and February but by March, when the evenings were getting lighter and the countryside began to show signs of spring, Friedrich resented more and more the days when he had to be cooped up in the house poring over accounts and reports.

'I don't think I can endure this everlasting scribbling,' he told Josef.

Political events, in which he normally had little interest, provided an opportunity for his release. In the melting pot of Napoleon's new Europe the Bishopric of Bamberg was to be absorbed into Bavaria. In the course of this transfer a large amount of surveying work had to be carried out and Friedrich addressed himself to the office which was to draw up maps of the district. His application was received favourably and he was given an appointment.

He parted with regret from the Forestry Warden and Josef, explaining his departure as an unrivalled opportunity for advancement without dwelling too much on his delight at the prospect of a life more in the open air.

One of the first tasks in his new post was the survey of a private property owned jointly by a young doctor of philosophy. At their first meeting the young men were astonished to find that they were already acquaintances at Jena. It was a pleasant re-union with much news to exchange and Friedrich found in the professor a happy replacement of the friendship he had enjoyed with Josef Schroeder.

He had been engaged in the survey only a short time when a letter from Christian clouded his happiness, Christian wrote from Osterode in the midst of a warm letter of family news: 'I know you will be glad to know that your little friend Lotte was married at Easter... a nice young man whom we all like, called Levin, a tanner. We hope to see much more of her, for the young couple have moved into a small house opposite us here in Marienvorstadt.'

Freidrich read the letter several times. He had known, he supposed, ever since his last meeting with Lotte that there was no hope for them, but this final breaking of the treasured thread of their relationship hurt pitifully. At first he was angry, not only with the fate that had parted them, but with her, for proving so faithless. Yet had he been any better? His loves had been independence and study. While she had dreamt her girlish dreams, he had been flirting with learning. He had made no effort towards their eventual union, in fact he had never thought of it until the long days of inward reflection during his father's illness. In his heart he knew that of the two of them he was really the most guilty, but if anything this only added to his pique. Worse still, by her distress when he had talked to her again in the woods at Osterode, he was convinced that she still loved him but had pledged herself to this young man Levin and would not go back on her word.

For days he went about moodily, Christian's letter in his pocket, shunning all efforts by his friends to cheer him.

The young professor tried to shake off his gloom by taking him out and about the town, meeting friends, one of whom was an artist who was staging the first exhibition of his works. Friedrich was unmoved by the paintings, although many of them were excellent.

As they left the professor turned to him.

'You think too much,' he said. 'I may have a doctorate of philosophy but I warn you, it can lead to doubt and darkness. Art, on the other hand, gives life, peace and joy.'

'Life, peace and joy?' Friedrich thought later as he ate his supper at home. 'I *have* life. Peace, they say, is within one. But joy?' Joy he felt had died when he left Lotte in Stadt Ilm when they were children, but in their innocence wiser than adults. He spent the rest of the evening writing to her, wishing her happiness, realising that in this way he might keep her friendship, which even marriage to another could not deny him.

Josef Schroeder, tutor to the forester's children, had meanwhile also left his former post and gone to Frankfurt. The news of his departure was unsettling to Friedrich. The surveying work had not proved as interesting as he had at first hoped and he felt that time was slipping by without his having gained much advancement.

It was his friend, the young professor, who drew his attention to an invitation published in a newspaper, inviting surveyors to submit original plans for a country mansion. The imagination involved appealed to Friedrich and for several weeks all his time was spent on the design of such an estate, with out-buildings, a farm plan, and a detailed inventory and map. To his delight his design was accepted and published, with the result that he received several offers of posts. From these he eventually chose, after a great deal of indecision, one at Gross Milchow in Mecklenberg, to be private secretary to President Von Dewitz.

The journey by mail-coach was a frightful one. In a bitterly cold February of 1804, most of the way a blizzard was blowing and the carriage wheels stuck in the snow-drifts and the horses had to be led. Friedrich several times recalled his pleasant surroundings at Bamberg and regretted his decision to move on.

The journey had at least one compensation: the route passed through Stadt Ilm and Friedrich was able to break his travels for a night in order to visit old Uncle Hoffman. He found the old man much aged but still merry, his kindly eyes beaming in his wrinkled face, which had lost much of its ruddy rotundity. He greeted his nephew with joyful emotion. Since the death of Grossmutter, Hoffman had lived alone in the old house by the river, his needs taken care of by a housekeeper, with a gardener to work on the flower-beds which he once so lovingly tended himself.

'We all grow old,' he told Friedrich 'but even old age has its compensations. I find that my tired old body gives my mind more leisure to contemplate. Praise God I can still read, though my eyesight is not what it was.'

They sat up late into the night talking, for although they had corresponded regularly through the years since Friedrich left Stadt Ilm, there was much that could not be expressed in letters.

Friedrich tried now to explain the feelings of unsettlement which he still had, even now that he was bound for a new and apparently promising position. He also told Uncle Hoffman about Lotte's marriage and his own disappointment.

'You cannot expect young women to wait for ever,' said Hoffman.
'You must remember that marriage and children are their life. Men have so much more to consider—their careers, their livelihood.

He questioned Friedrich seriously about his work. Did he enjoy it? Did it fully satisfy him?

'I cannot tell,' Friedrich admitted 'Sometimes, such as when I was preparing my plans for the newspaper article, I am completely absorbed and satisfied. At others, completely the reverse. I find the paperwork dull. I am restless to be out and about, active, doing things.'

'You were the same as a boy,' said the old man. 'Just the same. I used to worry about it sometimes. You never seemed to settle to anything for long and I put it down to your disturbed childhood. Your father was a good man, God rest his soul, but your dear mother's death took the light out of his heart. If only I had taken you to live with me sooner!'

'But when I did come to you and Grossmutter it was the happiest time of my life,' Friedrich told him. 'Anything I am—if I *am* anything, or will be—I owe to you.'

Hoffman put his hand fondly on the young man's shoulders. 'You know you are still so like your dear mother,' he said. '"Liebe Rose", I loved her very dearly. She was my favourite out of all my brothers and sisters. In you I seemed to see her once more, and the love I had for her was yours, and always will be. She was a dear, gentle creature.'

'And yet she died so young,' said Friedrich with sadness. 'No wonder my poor father was embittered. There are such times when it is hard not to question the work of the Almighty.'

'The man who does not do so is a man without spirit, without a mind,' said Uncle Hoffman. 'Of course, we rebel like children when God takes from us the delights of this life, just as the winter takes from us the beauty of the summer. But we do not doubt that summer will return again. It is much harder for us to have faith that we will one day be re-united with those we love, after death.' The old man paused for a moment, his eyes dreaming beyond the present. Then he continued. 'But you will find that even the tragedies have their pattern in life, the sunshine and the shadow. If it had not been for the sad death of your mother, the passing of my own dear Berta and the little one, you would never have come here to Stadt Ilm to live with me, to be my son.'

Friedrich's heart was too full to reply, for although he had succeeded in some measure in reaching an understanding with his father before his death, Uncle Hoffman was much nearer to the father he had always needed.

The few days in Stadt Ilm sent him away refreshed, both physically and mentally.

He arrived at Mecklenberg in sunshine; a thaw had set in and the grass was showing again through the snow. The house was large and handsome and Friedrich's quarters were spacious and attractively furnished, as befitted the considerable importance of his position.

The other members of the staff gave him a genial welcome. His predecessor had apparently been an elderly and rather dreary man who used out-dated methods and who was given to blaming his failures on his colleagues. Therefore the sight of Friedrich, young and vigorous, with a reputation of his success in the newspaper competition having come before him, had been most welcome. The steward and bailiffs eagerly presented to him various ideas and improvements which they had long cherished but had had little opportunity to air.

Her von Dewitz, his employer, was well pleased with his new secretary and allowed him considerable scope. Added to all this busy-ness there was the companionship (similar to that a few years before with Josef Schroeder) of the young tutor of the house, a Doctor of Philosophy from Göttingen University. Through him Friedrich also received various introductions to families in the district and never lacked companionship in his leisure hours, to walk in the hills or to sit by the fire in the evenings.

In July there was an added happiness. Christian wrote to say that his wife had given birth to another daughter, Emilie, a bonny, auburn-haired baby the image of her mother.

In addition to the young children who lived at home, Herr von Dewitz had two older sons at school at Halle. In the summer vacation they came home to Gross Milchow, accompanied by their tutor, a Dr Wollweide, a mathematician and physicist of considerable reputation. Friedrich took an immediate liking to this scholarly man, who reciprocated the feeling. He found his young pupils rather tedious at times and was delighted to engage in more serious conversations with his employer's secretary. He readily advised Friedrich on the books which would further his study of physics and mathematics, and encouraged him to progress further in his already considerable knowledge of architecture.

His life at Gross Milchow might have continued its happy progress undisturbed had it not been for Josef Schroeder's frequent letters, at first from Frankfurt and then from Holland, where he had a post as tutor in a merchant's house. In his replies Friedrich wrote of his increased concentration on architecture and received encouraging response from his friend.

Josef wrote: 'I am delighted that at last you have decided on a truly creative career... and with what scope in these days of change and development! But you are buried there in Mecklenberg! The place for you is in the city, preferably Frankfurt, where, as you know, I have spent considerable time lately. I hope to return there for a short time next summer. Why don't you join me? It would be a happy reunion and I am sure that while you are there you could make successful contacts for your future.'

Friedrich was by now quite decided to leave Mecklenberg as soon as winter had passed and to join Josef in Frankfurt, but how this was to be accomplished he was not nearly so confident.

There was only one person to who he could really turn for advice... and in the long nights of December he spent hours writing a detailed account of his ambitions and desires to Uncle Hoffman. 'I hope you will not dismiss me as a changeable and feckless young man,' he wrote. 'I fear it may seem so as I no sooner settle in one post than I am ready to move on to another. It is not that at all, I am very happy and contented here, with interesting work and congenial companions, but something within me still leaves me discontented. It is as if I must go on towards a goal I cannot even recognise as yet, but there is no peace for me until I attain it. Can you possibly understand?'

He wrote similarly to Christoph, his other dearest friend and counsellor, trying equally to justify his restlessness to himself as well as to his brother and uncle.

Christmas came and went without a reply from either, which was particularly disturbing because both usually greeted him at this season, regardless of the need to answer his queries. Early in January a letter did arrive, from Christoph. When he actually held it in his hand, Friedrich was afraid to open it. The long delay in its arrival had already filled him with the fear that both Uncle Hoffman and Christoph were tired of his vacillations and had decided to ignore him.

He carried the letter around with him all day before he eventually summoned up the courage to open it. The greeting was affectionate, Friedrich noted with relief, more affectionate even than his brother's usual form of address.

'My dearest brother,' Christoph wrote. His hopes rising Friedrich read on, only to have them immediately dashed to distress and despair. For the letter, which he had first thought promised good news, contained the worst he could possibly have received.

'I hardly know how to tell you,' Christoph wrote, 'but our dear Uncle Hoffman died suddenly a few days before Christmas. I was able to reach him before the end and he spoke very fondly of you and begged me to be the father to you that he had always tried to be. He also asked me with particular earnestness to keep the news of his death (he was quite aware that he was dying and entirely unafraid) until after the festivities of Christmas, as he did not want these to be clouded for you. He also spoke at considerable length of your future and was delighted to hear from your letter that you have been drawn towards architecture. (You will recall his own interest in the subject, and particularly in his new church at Stadt Ilm). He said that he could think of no better career for you and that he hoped at least he would be able to do you a small service in that direction. This I understand better now that I have settled his affairs and find that he has left a small legacy to all of us, his nephews, your share of which will be reaching you shortly.'

Friedrich had to read the letter several times before its full implication could penetrate his mind, which was shocked by the sadness of the news of the death of Uncle Hoffman, more a father to him than his natural father had ever been. When he had recovered a little he realised that the die was now cast. Nothing but physical effort lay between him and a career as an architect.

CHAPTER FIVE

At the end of April 1805, having given notice to Herr von Dewitz, who received it with reluctance and not a little annoyance, Friedrich said goodbye to his colleagues on the estate and set off on the journey to Frankfurt.

A week or so before his departure he had received a letter from Traugott, who had qualified as a doctor with considerable distinction and was working at a hospital in Berlin. Traugott had also benefited under the will of Uncle Hoffman and said he was spending a little of his legacy on a holiday in the Uckermark, not far from the city, on the River Ucker, where Max, their old friend from the days at Jena University, had settled on a prosperous farm. 'Why not join us for a while?' Traugott wrote. 'You will have hard work ahead this summer. Enjoy a rest while you can. The weather promises well and it is a delightful place.'

And so it was. That May was the most resplendent spring of many years. The whole of the countryside seemed to be spilling over with blossom, the apple trees were snowy with flowers, the hedgerows were a riot of primroses and dog violets, and the sun shone endlessly from a clear sky, with only puffs of white clouds to accentuate the blue.

It was indeed a spring not to be wasted and Friedrich decided to accept Traugott's suggestion, not the least for the pleasure of seeing him again for the first time since his father's death over three years ago.

The Uckermark district was particularly pretty and the old farmhouse, built on rising ground near the river, was surrounded by carefully landscaped gardens, as Max's wealth had enabled him to improve nature with art.

Traugott welcomed his brother boisterously.

'Friedu! It's wonderful to see you!' He embraced him and Max smilingly looked on, delighted to see both his friends so happily re-united.

They spent the days walking by the river, sometimes fishing, sometimes taking out a boat to lie lazily under the willows, watching the sun through the leaves. Sometimes they swam, naked as fish themselves, then lying on the grass, letting the sun dry their wet bodies.

They talked too, often long after midnight, as they had long ago in the beer gardens of Jena. Only one occupation Friedrich could not happily share with them: when they took their guns and went into the woods for rooks or pigeons.

'They're vermin,' Traugott would explain. 'If Max let them live they'd bankrupt him! The pigeons took all his young cabbages this winter—pecked them to death as they broke through the snow. And the rooks will have the oats if we don't get them first!'

But convincing though their argument appeared to be, Friedrich could not bring himself to accompany them. Even the sound of their guns sickened him as he walked his own way alone by the river, reviving his old delight in botanising.

The water crowfoot had already snowed its blossom over the surface of the backwaters and the yellow flags, late flowering, splashed the banks with gold, only rivalled by the monkey flowers and the purple of the loosestrife. He was particularly delighted to find a few early spider orchids, unexpected purple spikes in the short, tufted grass of the higher pastures, their strange blooms so closely resembling the fat brown spiders which had delighted him so much in the autumn days in the manse garden at Oberweissbach.

He would return from such walks elated, with the specimens he had carefully gathered pressed delicately between the pages of a book, so that when they were dry he could mount and catalogue them and add them to his already considerable collection, started during his first botanising with the doctor at Neuhaus.

Max and Traugott, while not botanists themselves, shared his enthusiasm. Max, who was more familiar with the district, would direct him to places he knew to be favoured by other rare plants, such as the little pink sowbreads, which looked as if they had been blown inside out by the wind, miniature cyclamens growing in the beechwoods near the river.

These early summer days passed delightfully until the time came when Friedrich had arranged to meet Josef in Frankfurt. Traugott and Max tried to persuade him to stay and he would have done so were it not for his promise to Josef and the long journey ahead of him.

Since he had written to Lotte after her marriage, Friedrich had received letters from her regularly: long friendly letters full of news of her own family and his brother's, letters written without embarrassment but always signed with her husband's name as well as her own (although he and Friedrich had never met). Friedrich felt that in this way she convinced her conscience of the propriety of their correspondence.

He found the letters a delight to receive and a relief to answer, using them as a sort of diary, even a confessional, of his experiences, his ambitions, even his fears.

Before leaving Uckermark he wrote to her of its beauties but refraining from the natural instinct to liken it to the old water gardens by the Ilm. 'The more intimately we attach ourselves to nature, the more she glows with beauty and returns our affection,' he wrote, describing his walks which had given him so much pleasure.

Before he left, Max brought him the book he kept on the table in the hall to record visitors. 'You must write something in my album before you go,' he said. 'It is the custom here.'

'Later,' said Friedrich: he could not think of anything that would truly record his feelings about this idyllic visit. He wanted some rarely beautiful quotation but could not recall one, and in any case was rather reluctant to use borrowed phrases on such an occasion. Even when he could put off the task no longer and stood with his pen above the page in the album, he did not know what to write, although he had spent all the time on his last walk by the river desperately searching for words. When he did write it was with a strange, detached compulsion which he himself did not readily understand. The words his pen formed read 'Thou givest man bread... let my aim be to give man himself.'

'I like that!' laughed Max, 'Bread indeed is what I hope to give... if the pigeons spare my wheat and barley. And you are to give man himself. My dear Friedrich, I don't envy you. I think I have the easier task of the two of us!'

*   *   *

Shortly after Midsummer Day, as arranged, Friedrich reached Frankfurt, where Josef met him with joyous enthusiasm.

'Life has begun!' he cried, as they clasped hands. 'I have already made several good contacts for you which I am sure will be successful.'

In the meantime, Josef recommended Friedrich should obtain some temporary situation, perhaps as a tutor, which would provide him with a livelihood and enough leisure to seek interviews with several of the better-known architects in the city.

It all seemed so easy, yet after the elation of his visit to Uckermark, Friedrich began to feel the oppression of the city and once again recognised the old symptoms of doubt and restlessness, even on the threshold of the career in which he had been convinced he would find satisfaction and success.

He confided his feelings to Josef.

'Take no notice,' he said. 'It is the anti-climax to your months of indecision and uncertainty. Do as I say, take a teaching post and you will have plenty of time to settle your thoughts before you proceed any further.'

Josef made even more practical efforts to help his friend to settle down. He came to him a few days later and said that a friend of his, Herr Gruner, the headmaster of the new Model School in Frankfurt, would certainly give Friedrich a post. 'He is always looking for progressive young men whose minds have not been set in old-fashioned methods,' he said. 'Let me introduce you to him.'

The meeting was a happy one. Herr Gruner, himself a pupil of the great Italian educationalist Pestalozzi, saw in Friedrich exactly the type of young man he wanted to teach in his new school. He had the necessary degree of learning, he was vigorous, lively and only twenty-three, eager for new knowledge and with a spark of the revolutionary in him that appealed to Gruner's progressive outlook.

Friedrich told him frankly that he sought a temporary post, but explained his growing doubts regarding architecture as a career.

'Architecture be blowed!' cried Gruner with vehemence. 'Who would build with bricks and stones when they could build with boys? Give up architecture! It's not your vocation at all, I am sure of that. If it were so, you would never have doubts. Become a teacher! We need you here. Say you agree and the position is yours.'

Friedrich liked Gruner, but the whole proposition was so far from his original plans that he hesitated, despite Josef's persuasion that this was indeed his destiny.

He had already had a successful interview with an architect in the city and only needed the arrival of his testimonials from Jena to be accepted as an articled apprentice. The testimonials had been sent to the trustees of his mother's estate after the unfortunate affair which ended his university career, but it seemed a simple enough task to secure them; the news that reached Frankfurt a few weeks after his arrival therefore, came as a bitter shock.

'We deeply regret that at present the papers you want cannot be found,' wrote his cousin, one of the trustees. 'Are you sure they were not returned to you earlier?'

This was a completely unexpected turn of affairs. At first Friedrich was distraught. He considered writing to Jena for fresh copies, but the trouble and delay made him hesitate, added to the fact that he was still uncertain about the course he was going to take.

On the other hand, Josef and Doctor Gruner, convinced that they knew best for their young friend, saw in the apparent disaster nothing but fateful opportunity.

'It's destiny!' Josef cried dramatically when told the news. 'Do not hesitate, my friend. Architecture is definitely not for you . . . the gods obviously decree it! Join Doctor Gruner immediately, while he is still of a mind to have you!'

When he told Gruner of his dilemma the headmaster agreed with Josef, only with less drama.

'But I have never taught before,' said Friedrich. 'Do you think I would be a little instruction and patience you would soon gain experience,' said Gruner. 'I do not want the teachers in my school to have had so much experience in the old ways that they are blind to the new. Here, as you know, we teach by the methods of the great Pestalozzi. Do you know anything of his work?'

'Very little,' said Friedrich, 'but I am willing to learn.' He recalled that long ago in his boyhood, in his father's house, he had read about the Italian peasant who, having taught himself reading, writing and arithmetic unaided, had resolved to make such knowledge available to everyone, however poor.

'Before you begin your appointment I shall send you to Yverden in Switzerland,' said Gruner. 'There you will meet Dr Pestalozzi himself and will gain first-hand experience of his methods and ideals.'

Within three days of their conversation Friedrich was on his way to Yverden, a quiet little town on the far western corner of Lake Neuchatel in the Vaud Canton. Its peaceful setting enchanted him, the still, clear water reflecting the pinewoods and the old castle where Dr Pestalozzi had his institution.

His reception was cordial, but the whole institution was so humming with activity that no one had much time to explain anything to him. He was left very much to his own devices, to look and listen and learn what he could from his own observations. There was also a far more illustrious visitor to claim the attention of those who had any time to spare, namely the Prince Hardenberg, who had been sent to the Institution to investigate its work by the government of Austria.

Pestalozzi himself Friedrich found to be a shaggy lion of a man, gentle of spirit but full of the fire of his own enthusiasm. From their first meeting, despite the difference in their ages, (Pestalozzi was nearly sixty, Friedrich only twenty-three) there seemed to be an inward understanding between them, so that after only three days in the castle by the lake Friedrich felt that he was thoroughly at home, both in the institution and with its founder.

Every morning and evening, Pestalozzi addressed the assembled staff and pupils with touching simplicity, conveying his own gentle faith and setting the whole pattern of life at Yverden, which was reflected, as calmly as the hillsides were reflected in the waters of the lake, in the whole attitude of everyone connected with the institution, down to the humblest servant.

Friedrich also enjoyed the companionship of three of Pestalozzi's young instructors: Tobler (geography), Josias Schmid (mathematics) and Hopf (botany).

These three did their best, in the little time they had to spare, to explain to him the working of the institution, in particular the way in which classes in certain subjects were always held simultaneously, so that there could be an easy interchange of pupils according to their proficiency.

The period of his stay passed so happily that the days flew by. He would sit in on Hopf's botany classes, an incongruous figure among the little children, his long legs sticking out from a tiny desk, but as absorbed as they were as Hopf identified plants by their structure, their leaves, roots and seeds. Equally fascinating he found the geography taught by young Tobler, who would not hesitate to leap from his desk to bring home some point more vividly to his pupils.

Sometimes was he reminded of his own schooldays when for a moment the old parrotwise methods of the past crept in to the German lessons, and occasionally even the active Tobler was reduced to having his class copy out lists of towns or rivers. Emboldened by their friendliness, Friedrich challenged them on this retrograde step.

'We know,' they said. 'It *is* dreary and uninspired, but tell us another way to get facts into young minds and we'll gladly adopt it.' Friedrich could not give them one, although he felt somehow it *must* be possible to free learning from drudgery and monotony.

'One day I may tell you,' he told them... and they laughed good humouredly at him and slapped him on the back.

Once or twice in his stay he was able to snatch a few words with Dr Pestalozzi himself, but when the old man was asked to explain this or that point in his method he would say 'Go and see for yourself... it works perfectly!' with a nod of his leonine head and a benign smile.

Friedrich left Yverden in October 1805, determined to return for a longer stay as soon as possible. On his return to Frankfurt, Josef greeted him excitedly. 'Wonderful news!' he cried. 'I have heard from Dr Gruner that you have a definite appointment from the Education Committee, the Consistorium! You start work immediately;'

After his experience at Yverden, Friedrich was both impatient and nervous. Now he was certain that this was what he wanted to do, but could he do it?

The few days dragged until the Monday morning, when he was due to begin his appointment at the Model School.

He had learned from Dr Gruner that his appointment was part of a plan to establish an entirely new educational course for about 200 boys and girls, with a staff consisting of four permanent and about nine visiting masters.

The class allotted to him for individual attention was to be that of 40 boys aged between nine and eleven, whom he had to instruct in arithmetic, drawing, geography and German.

The Monday morning in late October was crisp and sunny. As he walked through the streets from his lodgings to the school, Friedrich recalled that day long ago when, as a little boy, he had trotted beside his father through the woods to the village school at Oberweissbach. Then it had been warm, but now there was a chill in the air and the leaves had nearly all fallen from the trees. But he had the same feeling of expectant elation as the school bell tolled on the wind and he was passed in the street by young figures hurrying by with books under their arms.

Dr Gruner introduced him to his class. 'This is Herr Froebel,' he said. 'He has just returned from a visit to the great Dr Pestalozzi in Switzerland and he has many exciting new things to tell you!'

'Good morning, Herr Froebel.' The little boys obediently greeted him at Dr Gruner's instruction, and surveying the rows of shining morning faces, Friedrich was vividly reminded of the little girls at Oberweissbach and their chanting recitation: "Seek ye first the kingdom of God."

'Good morning!' he replied and smiled. Forty faces, some round and chubby, some solemn, pale and rosy, straight hair and curly, dark heads and fair, smiled back. His nervousness disappeared. For an hour pupils and master were absorbed in each other so that at the end, when the bell rang for the change in lessons, he was still in the middle of an explanation and could not believe that the time had passed so quickly.

As the children filed out to another class, Friedrich noticed one little boy lingering behind after the others.

'What are you waiting for?' he asked.

The child looked up at him shyly. Without speaking he laid on the desk before him a sticky piece of toffee, blushing as he did so, then turned and rushed out of the room after his playmates.

Later that day Friedrich wrote to Christoph: 'It seems to me that I have found something I have never known before but always longed for, always missed, as if my life had at last discovered its natural element. I feel as happy as a fish in the water, a bird in the air.'

The Model School, though not apparently extensive when seen from the street, was built around a spacious courtyard and garden where the children could play. In many of the games the teachers, including Friedrich, were as happy to participate as the children. In addition it was decided, as part of the new educational course, to which Friedrich had been able to make several contributions, that every week the children and their teachers should go together on an instructional walk.

The subject chosen by Friedrich for his class was the local geography of Frankfurt. Making the town centre his starting place, Friedrich took the boys on long expeditions, making notes and using sandy stretches beside to draw maps on the ground with a stick. On their return to school the children would chart their observations on an old blackboard placed flat on the floor, marking in the hills and rivers, the byways and landmarks. Soon the boys were so familiar with the geographic characteristics of their district that they could reconstruct them alone without any help. In addition, the walks gave plenty of opportunity for pupils and master to enjoy and learn about the plants and wildlife of the surrounding countryside.

Their efforts were shown to parents at a special exhibition of the school's work held a few months after Friedrich had joined the staff.

'You know, I learned the rivers of India before I knew how to travel from Frankfurt to Leipzig,' one father laughed to Friedrich. 'And what good did it do me? *This* is the way physiography *should* be taught! A boy must learn all about the place where he lives before he goes further afield.'

* * *

In addition to his little boys, Friedrich taught drawing, handwriting and elocution to a class of little girls. These classes he particularly enjoyed. He taught the children rhymes he recalled from his own childhood and at term-end they acted a masque, put together from the poems they had learned. The performance also featured pretty programmes which they carefully made themselves to show off their penmanship. As they wrote and spoke their lessons the classroom often rippled with laughter. Dr Gruner, going his rounds of inspection, would smile with satisfaction as he peeped round the door unseen to watch Herr Froebel and his 'mädchen' enjoying their lessons to the full.

'Learning need not have a long face.' He would tell visitors, who expressed surprise that so much hilarity should be allowed in a classroom.

To the young man from the forests and farms of Thuringia, Frankfurt was an enchanted city. Jena had been an exciting experience but even its charms were exceeded by the city on the Maine, with its many crowded streets, its cosmopolitan citizens, many foreigners drawn there as a centre of commerce and culture.

The tree-lined walks by the river were a rendezvous for the students, its side street cafes always full, from morning chocolate-drinkers to late at night, when the beer mugs clinked and the old songs rang out into the darkness under the limes.

In the town centre, the Hauptwache, Friedrich could stand for an hour or more just watching the crowds go by, studying the portly prosperous bankers and merchant sailors from the ships in the docks and the market women with their baskets, priests in black, actors in scarlet, a never-ending motley throng which never failed to excite him.

In addition to his work at the Model School, Friedrich was kept extra busy by having agreed to give some private tuition to three little boys, sons of a friend of Josef's, a Herr von Holzhauser, in German and arithmetic. The lessons took only two hours a day but he also accompanied the boys on their walks and a happy friendship sprang up between them, particularly with the two younger lads, Pieter and Hans. Hans was only six and inclined to tire when the walks were too long; these expeditions usually ended with them riding home on Friedrich's shoulders.

One day, when they had been walking by the river, Pieter asked Friedrich 'Why did you become a teacher? Did you like school when you were a little boy?'

'Sometimes,' said Friedrich, 'but school was different when I was your age, we did not have as much fun as you do. I think I became a schoolteacher to change that... lessons should be fun. Don't you think so?'

'Oh yes!' said Pieter eagerly. 'When I grow up I shall be a schoolteacher, like you, and the children will be allowed to play all day!'

'If they play *all* day they will not learn any lessons,' laughed Friedrich.

'But you make lessons like play!' said Pieter. 'That's the sort of play I mean. I like it better than games, games are silly... let's play botany now!'

Playing botany was one of their favourite occupations on their walks and consisted of challenging each other to name the plants or trees on the wayside; to fail was to lose a point.

*   *   *

Friedrich wrote to Christoph, now the proud father of a son, Julius, a lively boy born shortly after his grandfather's death. 'These little boys are like sons to me. I will never forget the loving care that you and all my brothers bestowed on me when I was a child and often lonely and misunderstood. I do my best to be to them what you were to me.'

'I cannot begin to tell you what a change has come over me since I discovered that teaching was my true vocation. I know now that previously I was just marking time, but I fear that to you and dear uncle Hoffman it may have appeared that I was nothing but a restless wanderer.'

'Now I am quite settled and determined to pursue my career—I think I prefer to describe it as my "calling," in education. I want above all to educate men whose feet shall stand on God's earth, rooted fast in nature, while their heads tower up to heaven and read its secrets with a steady gaze. Whose hearts shall embrace both earth and heaven, shall love life and nature in all its wealth of forms, and at the same time shall recognise the purity and peace that unites the love of God's earth with God's heaven.'

It had been originally agreed that Friedrich should spend at least three years at the Model School, but shortly after the end of his second year he was placed in a dilemma. Up to now Pieter and Hans and their older brother Georg, whom Friedrich had been coaching, already had a regular tutor for their daily lessons. This young man had now given notice that he wished to move to another post and Friedrich was asked by the boys' parents if he could assist in finding a replacement.

Knowing no one himself he wrote to Christoph in the hope that among his parishioners there might be some suitable young man. He received a discouraging reply. 'I don't think you will ever be able to find such a person,' Christoph wrote. 'You set your standards so high. You say you want someone active yet studious, some-one who has experience of life but is not sophisticated. These characteristics could be contradictions.'

Friedrich reported the failure of his efforts to the boys' mother.

'*I* know such a man,' she said.

'But madam! If so, why have you not appointed him immediately?'

'I do not think he is willing to undertake such a task,' she replied.

'I cannot believe that,' said Friedrich 'It is an excellent opportunity ... one I would dearly desire myself if only I had the necessary qualifications.'

'But Herr Froebel, you *are* that man!'

Friedrich blushed with genuine surprise for he had never dreamed of himself in the position, not the least because he doubted his temperament as well as his ability to adapt himself to private tutoring, with all its restrictions and responsibilites.

He discussed the problem with Dr Gruner.

'You are a fool,' said Gruner bluntly. 'Here you are on the threshold of a great career as a teacher and you would throw it all up for a whim! What happens when these boys have outgrown you? Or their parents change their minds about their education and send them away to school? What qualifications and testimonials will you have to show for your efforts other than those that thousands of young men possess all over Germany?'

'I will safeguard myself by a contract.'

'That's all very well,' said Gruner. 'Contracts were made to be broken ... and what about your contract to me? You said you would stay with us for three years at least.'

'But these boys need me,' Friedrich urged. 'I know them so well, they are like sons to me, or young brothers.'

'Good!' said Gruner. 'So you become their tutor and leave your own educational necessities and your own needs out of the question!'

They did not discuss the matter again but when Friedrich declared that his mind was made up, Gruner agreed to release him before the end of his three-year engagement, provided a suitable replacement could be found.

'I know you will never settle now that you have made up your mind to this new venture,' said Gruner 'so you better go and work it out of your system. But believe me, you will not find it at all easy.'

An ideal substitute came, almost heaven-sent, in the form of the young tutor Friedrich had met while working at Gross Milchow. This young man had kept up a regular correspondence since their parting and was actually seeking a new appointment. His degrees from Gottingen University, of which he was a doctor of philosophy, made him more than acceptable to the Model School and the exchange was happily arranged.

Pieter, Hans and Georg were overjoyed that their young tutor Froebel was to become their regular instructor, but Friedrich, delighted as he was at the appointment, remembered Gruner's serious warning. Before finally accepting the appointment he had a serious talk with the boys' parents.

'Firstly,' he told them 'I feel that a city such as Frankfurt is not really suitable for the education of young boys, who need the interests, atmosphere and stimulation of life in the country, somewhere where their high spirits will not be misplaced and where they will not be distracted by the artificial attractions of the town. When you have found such a place I shall require that the boys are handed over entirely into my care without interference, even from you, their parents.'

'Damned headstrong, stubborn and self-willed,' said Herr von Holzhausen later to his wife... 'that's what I consider him. *You* may think him a fine choice, my dear, but I'm not sure... the young man takes too much upon himself for my liking.'

But Frau von Holzhausen was adamant.

'I have watched him with our boys,' she said, 'and I assure you that there could be no better choice.'

*   *   *

Friedrich left the Model School at the end of June 1807 with fond farewells and good wishes, even from Dr Gruner, who still regarded his decision with apprehension, if not dismay. Friedrich accepted an invitation from Christian to visit him and his family at Osterode.

He travelled in two minds: delight at the thought of seeing his brother and his family again, and apprehension that he must surely also see Lotte, herself now the mother of a baby girl.

Osterode itself was at its best in high summer and Friedrich joined in walks and picnics with Christian, his wife and their little girls: Albertine, now nearly six and Emilie, a toddler of three. They made posies and garlands of buttercups and daisies and crowned the little girls 'Queens of July' in the sunny fields by the river. They picked raspberries and gathered bilberries for jelly-making until their backs ached and their necks were burnt sore by the sun. It was a happy time of long days in the open air and warm nights when they sat after dark in the garden watching the moon come up over the pines.

It was a week before he met Lotte and he knew that she had been subconsciously, if not intentionally, avoiding him. His sister-in-law explained her absence with some embarrassment, he sensed. 'She is very busy with the baby,' she said. 'Such a lovely little girl... and the image of her daddy.'

Their meeting, when it came, was unavoidable: on Sunday, when the whole town, it seemed, made its way to church. There she was—unchanged, slender, fair haired, neat and pretty as ever. His heart swung towards her, lost to him but even more beautiful, more desirable because she was unattainable.

They greeted each other with formal affection tinged with shyness.

'So you are a schoolmaster!' she said. 'Who ever would have dreamed it!'

He laughed: 'Least of all myself!'

Their eyes met and he could feel his heart racing with a nervousness he felt she must notice, that her husband standing beside her must be aware of the tension between them, the spiritual union that nothing, not even her marriage to another man, could break.

'Albert,' she said, 'this is my old schoolfriend of long ago... Friedrich Froebel. Albert already feels he knows you from your letters,' she told Friedrich.

The men shook hands.

'I hope you will visit us.' Albert Levin, a gentle-faced, pale young man, smiled friendlily at Friedrich: 'We cannot go out much ourselves because of the baby.'

Friedrich accepted the invitation a few days later. The little girl was lying in the sun in her cradle in the garden, Lotte sitting beside her sewing and her young husband busy with his roses.

'She is a lovely baby,' said Friedrich. He knew little or nothing about babies but this small scrap of humanity lying pink from the sun in her cot was indeed lovely, as all young things are beautiful.

'I hope to have many more like her,' Lotte told him, 'only some of them must be boys!'

'Then I can teach them!' laughed Friedrich.

'Yes, I would like that.'

He talked to Albert Levin about his work—the complicated processes of drying, stretching and tanning leather, the fashions and the markets, and the uncertainty of trade. He was a likeable, friendly young man and he could see how gentle Lotte would have been drawn to him... how she must have felt when he, Friedrich, came blundering back into her life without warning five years ago.

Albert left them in the afternoon to attend to a client.

'I hope you will excuse me,' he told Friedrich. 'This man could not come another time and he has travelled a long way to see me.'

'I must go too,' said Friedrich, knowing he said it because although it was pleasant in the sunny garden he was afraid to be left alone with Lotte.

She walked with him to the gate, keeping the distance between them to a yard or more, as if afraid that, magnet-like, any lesser space would mean their inevitable attraction. She was silent, yet each was conscious of the occasional glance of the other.

It was Friedrich who spoke first.

'You know... don't you?'

'Yes,' she said 'I know.'

He noticed that her small, pale hand, the hand that he would never forget lying in the grass, golden with the sun on the hillside at Stadt Ilm, was fidgetting in her apron pocket. As they reached the gate she held her hand out to him. 'Goodbye, Friedrich... Friedling.'

The use of his childhood nickname turned his heart. As he took her hand in his own it was so small that his own encompassed it.

'I mean goodbye,' she repeated. 'Come to us again... be our friend... but to be our friend, my dear, you must say goodbye to me.'

Now he saw why she had been fidgetting in her pocket, for she was laying in his hand their old keepsake... the little twisted silver nail which was the ring he had given her when she was sixteen.

'I cannot keep it,' she said. 'Keep it for me, in memory of what was ours and can never change.'

His grip tightened in hers until the pressure hurt but the physical pain was almost a relief to them both, although Lotte's grey eyes were brimming with tears.

He left Osterode the next morning for Frankfurt and the three boys who were to be his charge for the next two years.

*   *   *

Despite the excitement of the anticipation of his new position, Friedrich's experience in Osterode sent him back to the city dispirited and unsettled. He had always acknowledged his affection for Lotte but in the busyness of his life it had been until now only a nostalgic background, an accompaniment to the full life of study and dreams and plans for the future. Suddenly at Osterode the realisation of its importance to him had astonished and frightened him by its desperate urgency. He was distressed that he should, even in thought, have allowed himself to violate her loyalty to her husband, yet the loyalty between him and Lotte was so much older in time.

I must not see her again, he vowed. I *must* not... yet his heart turned to stone at the thought. 'I am a child' he said to himself as he tossed on his bed on the hot August night. 'I am still a child! How otherwise could I have been blind so long? While I have been studying life from books, life has passed me by. I know nothing of love, of family life, children... what right have I to think I can educate the young? How could one who knows so little possibly be responsible for the guidance of three young boys? It was audacious presumption! Perhaps further study... another period at the University?'

Deeply perplexed he wrote to Christoph: 'I have decided that I am still totally unequipped for the task of tutoring these young boys and can only think that I should take another course of study, hoping perhaps that I will also gain some practical knowledge of life, for I have come to realise that I am pathetically immature.'

As soon as he had sent the letter he regretted it. Surely Christoph would see in this further evidence of the restlessness of which he had already often warned Friedrich in the past. The restlessness was obviously only another sign of his immaturity and must be subdued.

Almost immediately Friedrich wrote again telling Christoph to take no notice of his momentary confusion.

'I am now much more settled in my mind,' he wrote, 'and looking forward to taking up my new appointment, the three boys are splendid lads and I know I shall enjoy my life with them.'

Hans, Pieter and Georg had no doubts about their feelings for having their beloved young Herr Froebel as their permanent tutor and companion. His stipulation that their education should be undertaken in the country was honoured, and by the early autumn tutor and pupils moved to a farm outside

Frankfurt owned by a distant relation of the family.

Friedrich did not immediately bother the boys with lessons. Making the most of what was left of the warm weather, they spent the days walking and talking or just lying in the sun. The children, by their unending questions born of the inquisitive nature of all young things, turned these happy holiday hours into lessons in the open air.

'What is this?' they would cry, bringing Friedrich a flower or a seed-pod, a snail's shell or some other wayside relic. 'Why?' when he showed them the spiders' webs, the bees on their last flight before the winter, the winged seeds of the sycamore trees.

They would collect bright pebbles and make them into patterns, string nuts on threads for necklaces and make little figures from twigs and pine-cones, sitting happily for hours on the short turf, in the clearings between the pine trees on the hillside.

As the weather grew colder they had to spend more time indoors and Friedrich helped them to make models from card and paper: a little farm, a village, with which they made a pictorial map of the district much the same as that his class had undertaken at the Model School under Herr Gruner. Sometimes they embossed patterns on paper with a knitting needle so that the design showed on the other side. At Christmas he helped them to write and perform a little masque to surprise their parents, who were delighted at the result.

In the spring, at Friedrich's suggestion, Herr Holzhausen arranged for the boys to be given a small strip of land from which to make a garden. Together they roamed the waysides and hillsides collecting plants that might be safely transplanted, heathers and ferns, clumps of primroses or violets, seedling trees, mosses and foxglove roots.

Young Hans was particularly delighted in this venture and would dance in excitedly at breakfast time with the news that some beloved plant had grown new shoots or some cherished seed had just put forth its first leaf. It reminded Friedrich vividly of his own pleasure in the small plot which had once been his in the manse garden at Oberweissbach.

One day Hans proudly brought in a posy of marigolds grown from seeds he had planted himself. The bunch consisted of no more than six or so rather short-stemmed flowers, strong with their bitter-sweet scent and already wilting in his hot little hand. Flushed with pleasure and excitement, he thrust them at Friedrich. 'I growed them for you!' He said. Friedrich took the gift with delight. A long-locked gate in his mind seemed to swing open as he met the little boy's honest gaze...a look of trust which at once elated and frightened him by its tremendous responsibility. He no longer had any doubts about the future.

*   *   *

Frau von Holzhausen was delighted with her sons' progress when she visited them in the summer. She found three lusty, suntanned boys, all grown considerably and eager to show off their work in the garden and play-room as well as their books. Talking later to their father, who was equally unreserved in his pleasure, Friedrich decided to broach a subject which had been in his mind for some weeks.

'What would you say, Sir,' he said, 'If I asked if I could take your sons to Yverden to study in the institution of Dr Pestalozzi? I feel nothing could be of greater benefit to them. As you know, I have some experience in Dr Pestalozzi's methods and I could superintend their work personally.'

Herr von Holzhausen considered the plan excellent. He believed in travel as an education and had heard something of the work at Yverden. By the autumn all plans were complete for Friedrich and the boys to travel to Switzerland.

The long journey from Frankfurt to Yverden was pleasant and full of interest for them all. When they arrived, at sunset, the sky was blood-red, fading to vivid orange, so that the hills surrounding the lake became black silhouettes casting dark reflections into the water, which was itself as molten with fiery colour. The ancient battlements of the castle where Dr Pestalozzi had his school could be seen among the dark trees, outlined against the burning sky.

To their disappointment they found that there was no accommodation for them actually within the institution, already crammed practically to bursting point, but they were able to secure comfortable lodgings in the town and still take their meals at the castle with the other students.

Friedrich became at once master and pupil, sitting in on the classes with the boys and helping them with their private studies. The happiest times of all were those when Dr Pestalozzi himself led masters and pupils on long walks over the mountains, for all his 70 years striding as firmly as the youngest and at the end of a long journey even taking his turn to carry one of the littlest ones, who had tired, on his broad shoulders.

'What? Tired?' he would roar in mock ferocity, puckering his bushy eyebrows and shaking his leonine head at the little one who, momentarily distressed, would then catch the twinkle in his eye as he swept down to perch the little fellow on his back.

When his pupils were occupied in games or other pursuits with their schoolfellows, Friedrich had time to walk alone in the mountains, revelling in the first true solitude he had been able to enjoy for some years, since he had foresaken his work on the land. He wrote to Christoph: 'From the tops of the high mountains nearby I rejoice... in the clear, still sunset, in the pine forests, the glaciers, the mountain meadows. An evening walk here becomes an irresistible necessity to me after each active day. As I wander on the sunlit, far-stretching hills or on the still shore of the lake, clear as crystal, smooth as a mirror, or in the shady groves under the tall forest trees, my spirit grows full of ideas of an almost god-like nature and I feel I can understand at last the priceless value of a man's soul.'

This mood of spiritual elation was due not a little to the inspiration of old Dr Pestalozzi's evening talks with the staff and children. On these occasions Friedrich and the others would sit spellbound while the old man, his face burning with the sincerity of his beliefs, would radiate love and fellowship.

'If only you could hear him!' Friedrich wrote to Christoph. 'I think always of your boys and wish that they too could be given the wonderful opportunity that my young charges are enjoying here at Yverden. I make careful notes of everything which I hope to pass on to you for their benefit.'

These happy occasions were embroidered by the recreations of Yverden, the games and sports which the boys and their young tutor joined in together and, happiest of all, the music—particularly singing, which reminded Friedrich of those long-ago enchanted evenings at Stadt Ilm when he, Lotte, Willi and Gertrud and Grete sat around the fire with Uncle Hoffman and Grossmutter. As they worked in the school gardens, walked the hill-paths in the sunshine, the boys sang, so that the days seemed to be richly filled with music and laughter.

But life at Yverden was not always sunshine: there were times when Friedrich, much as he revered his elderly mentor, would find himself violently in disagreement with him. As they got to know each other better they would sometimes share an evening walk, Pestalozzi, for all his years, keeping the pace of his young companion. High above the little town, looking down on the enchanting view of the lake, they would thrash out their differences, Friedrich pleading for more imagination, for more activity in the instruction.

'The way we teach even our own language is lifeless!' he told the doctor with vehemence.

'For all the boy's brashness I like him' Dr Pestalozzi would say to himself as they walked home. He liked him a great deal better than some of the fawning young disciples who crowded the lecture rooms of Yverden, flattering in their agreement and anxious to further their own ambitions in the Institution.

Hans, Pieter and Georg grew and flourished in the happy atmosphere of Yverden, unaware of any of the shortcomings of the institution of which their young tutor was becoming increasingly aware. Most of all he regretted the lack of attention to natural history, his own theories on education being deeply rooted in nature, from his forest childhood, the botanising at Neuhaus the continuing parallels between the truth of life and the natural order of things in which he based all his own personal philosophy.

Georg was now 19 and ready to go on to the university. He had his heart set on Jena, inspired by the reminiscences with which Friedrich enlivened their walks together. The impending departure of Georg from Yverden seemed to offer the opportunity for a break which was becoming inevitable as Friedrich found himself in conflict more and more with many aspects of the system which he had at first so admired.

Towards the end of 1810 he wrote to the boys' mother: 'Although I am still confident that the teaching at Yverden has splendid qualities, there are shortcomings which are becoming more and more apparent to me. I do not think it fair, either to your sons or to myself, their tutor, to remain here any longer. I hope we may have your permission to return to Frankfurt when Georg makes his journey there in a few weeks' time.'

Frau Holzhausen needed no persuasion, her confidence in Friedrich being complete, and it remained only for Friedrich to break the news to Dr Pestalozzi.

The old man was not surprised. He was already aware of young Friedrich's opinionated views, and although he seldom agreed with them, he respected the mental vigour and independence which inspired them. Frequently he had astonished Friedrich with his humility and diffidence.

'We are all children in the dark,' he would say. 'Just sometimes, God lights the candle, but even then, we in our blindness snuff it out before its light can show us the way.'

'You will do well,' he told Friedrich, as they stood together looking out on the wintery lakeland scene in the late afternoon of the day before he and the boys were to begin their journey back to Frankfurt. 'But make haste slowly. You will be a great teacher, but first you must learn yourself. There is so much to learn and so little time.' He put a fatherly hand on the tall boy's shoulder and Friedrich saw that the old man's eyes were full of tears.

They stood in silence for a few minutes before they turned and walked together down the steps that led to the castle, where the lights were already beginning to shine out into the darkening afternoon. The castle itself was grey against the blacker pines behind, and the lake like steel under the winter sky.

Friedrich was back in Frankfurt for Christmas. It was pleasant to visit the

Model School and his colleagues there. Herr Gruner himself welcomed his former staff member with open arms. 'Come back!' he pleaded, but Friedrich would not be tempted.

'I have much still to learn,' he told him. 'Soon I hope to go to Gottingen, to the Georgia Augusta University.'

Frau von Holzhausen heard this news with dismay.

'But the boys!' she protested. 'You cannot leave them now!'

'There is nothing more I can do for them,' Friedrich told her.

'They have caught up with me. I too must study now if I am to be the person I feel my destiny demands.'

'Stay at least until the summer,' she begged. 'You must know what your companionship and guidance have meant, not only to them but to me and my husband. You have already seen that the little study you made them, with its books and pictures, has been left as it was ever since you went away. I will *never* change it,' she said. 'For the rest of my life and theirs it shall remain to remind me of the way you changed three spoilt little boys into the fine lads who have come home to us from Yverden.'

Friedrich was embarrassed but delighted. He knew that she thought highly of him but this unrestrained enthusiasm was unexpectedly lavish.

'I'll stay,' he promised, 'but only until July.'

Frau von Holzhausen laughed: 'You are always restless in the summer,' she said. 'I will not press you further.'

The rest of the winter, the spring and early summer passed slowly, for having now set his heart on returning to the university, Friedrich found that despite the kindness of the family and the happy companionship of Hans and Pieter, he was impatient to be away.

At the beginning of July he left at last for Gottingen, although it was the middle of the session because he felt that it would take him a few months to settle in his new way of life and get the full benefit from his lectures and study.

Gottingen itself gave him the welcome of its own beauty. He arrived early in a summer evening, when the whole sky above the town, nestling in smiling hilly countryside with wide horizons, seemed to reflect a mellow light which gave the picturesque streets the appearance of an old painting. The narrow byways, with their half-timbered houses leaning towards each other, had a friendly neighbourliness. His first view from the turn of the road as the mail-coach rocked towards the end of the journey was one of re-assuring familiarity, as if he was coming home, although he had never been there before.

He found lodgings near the university in Weenderstrasse, and was soon absorbed in the studious life of the town. He had already decided to concentrate on languages. At Yverden he had devoted much of his spare time to studying Greek and Latin, but now he intended to extend his knowledge to Hebrew and Arabic, hoping perhaps to progress eventually to other Asiatic tongues.

His progress was discouraging. His first elementary text-books baffled him; there seemed no connection with their contents and any living language, and despite his early enthusiasm he found his interest waning. He expressed this concern to one of the younger professors at the university.

'You are a fool,' he said bluntly. 'These are not for you. You are not a man who can bury himself in words. Turn to science ... this is the age of discovery. It's all very well to study the ancients but it is a dead subject. All the discovery has gone before. If I were you I'd leave the Greek and the Hebrew, the Arabic and the Sanscrit, and read natural science.'

Working long hours alone in his lodgings, Friedrich had plenty of time to consider the professor's advice. His journeys abroad were limited—an occasional Sunday he spent walking in the pretty, hilly countryside which surrounded the town. Some evenings he would take a meal in the students' favourite tavern, the Old Finch, where he would enjoy the popular fare with the young men of the university—the 'student's slice,' Gelehrtenschitten ... a piece of toast tastily spread with fried brains, well seasoned. At other times he would prepare some simple meal for himself in his room and go on working uninterrupted late into the night.

The summer of 1811 was long and hot. Even in early September the nights were as warm as July, and the farmers were talking of a record harvest. On these hot evenings Friedrich would work at his open window, finding the gentle sounds of the street below soothing accompaniment to his study. About 10.30 he would leave his books and take a walk in moonlight.

One evening of particularly starry beauty he shut the door of his lodgings and strolled down the street towards the open country, which began almost immediately beyond the ancient medieval fortifications of the town. On the way he met one or two students returning from the beer gardens: handsome young men wearing the colours of their students' guilds. The honour of these guilds was jealously preserved and even blood shed in duels when one guild considered its good name offended by another. Friedrich had little time to spare for these university activities and the noisy Kommers meetings when students in caps of vivid colours settled themselves around tables laden with pitchers of beer and sang long and noisily into the night.

Now he greeted his fellow students good naturedly but left them behind and passed on through the sleeping streets of the town and out through the gates, where a night watchman nodded by his brazier, taking the path towards the hills.

The moon was so bright that he could see not only his way but the view of the town below, the pines on the hillsides as dark as jet and the whole enchanted picture painted in black and silver, the buildings standing out with remarkable clarity.

The sky, glittering with stars, seemed to hang low over the hills and as he walked Friedrich shivered, not with the night air, for it was still warm and scented with the late heather and the resin of the pines, but with the speechless wonder of the scene around him.

The young professor was right. He lifted his head and stared at the velvet sky with its flickering, myriad points of light. The moon, now serried by a few light clouds like black lace across its surface... *this* was life.

What had Greek and Hebrew, even the mysteries of Sanscrit, to offer compared to *this*... the incredible, unfathomable, mystery of the universe?

As he stood on the dark hillside he was suddenly aware that, among the thousand twinklings of the stars, one larger and brighter than all the others was moving with incredible speed across the sky. In an instant he recalled that one of his friends studying astronomy had told him that this was to be the month of a great comet... one that had not been visible from the earth for 300 years.

The flash of its path across the heavens seemed to Friedrich to be linked in some incredible way with his own enlightenment. This surely was a sign, a God-given inspiration? Filled with a surging dedication he fell to his knees on the wet grass. A few wandering sheep, their fleece silvered by the moonlight, moved slowly towards him, gently grazing, the kneeling man seeming to blend into the stillness of the night.

He remained there on his knees for five minutes or more. If he prayed he could not later remember the theme of his prayer, much less any words. But in this timeless moment it was as if he were one with the whole of nature: the moon and stars, the sleeping countryside, the dark trees, the grazing sheep and all the tiny creatures of the night that crept and fluttered, ran warily on tiny legs or flew on soft wings, unaware of the man who had come alone into their realm to discover his destiny...

'Seek ye first the Kingdom of God.' As he walked slowly back to the town, the voices of the little girls in the village school at Oberweissbach long ago in his childhood echoed down the years. Like the sudden sight of the comet, the future seemed to have been made vividly clear to him.

When he reached his lodging it was already long after midnight but he could not sleep. Instead he sat down and wrote to Christoph, feeling he must immediately share with his dearest brother the wonderful experience while it was still fresh in his mind.

'I have no doubts now,' he wrote. 'My vocation in teaching must be built on the corner-stone of the natural laws of the universe. I have decided to conclude my studies of classical languages (still, I fear, very elementary) and pursue instead a course in physics, chemistry and natural history, also perhaps mineralogy.'

Christoph replied with an encouraging letter—his usual reaction to the youthful enthusiasm of his younger brother—but urged him not to overdo his studies. 'A healthy mind must live in a healthy body,' he wrote. 'Don't drive yourself too hard...take a rest now and then.'

The university vacation at Michaelmas gave Friedrich an opportunity to take Christoph's advice. His other brother Christian, now an established tradesman at Osterode, had already invited him to spend the rest time there with him, his wife and family. It was over six years since his last fateful visit to the little town in the Harz Mountains where he remembered all too vividly that Lotte also lived with her husband and children.

Christian and his family welcomed Friedrich with touching affection. The two girls had never forgotten their uncle, who had played with them in the sunny summer of six years ago, and now there were two little boys added to the family, Ferdinand and Wilhelm. Both were sturdy, attractive children but Friedrich was immediately drawn towards the younger boy and spent many happy hours leading him slowly by the hand on gentle walks in the meadows near his home, pointing out the wildflowers or butterflies, helping him to build little houses of sticks and stones, showing him how to cut out fancy patterns from paper.

He was playing with Willi in the garden a few days after his arrival when the rustle of skirts on the grass made him look up suddenly. Almost before he saw her, something told him it was Lotte... turning over inside him, a momentary blurring of his vision which cleared to reveal her, seemingly unchanged by the years, still fair-haired, neat-figured despite her growing family, her grey eyes frank and wide as she held out her hand in greeting,

'Friedrich!'

He took the hand. It was as neat and slim as she was, and cool and relaxed in his.

'I think you have been avoiding me,' she said with mock reproach. 'You have been here several days. My children talk of nothing else but "der Oheim," their new uncle, yet you have not been to greet me.'

Her grey eyes teased him kindly, her mouth was smiling; she was, he realised with a pang, still incredibly beautiful to him. He knew too that he *had* been avoiding her, not consciously perhaps, for the relationship between the two families was so close and informal that it was inevitable that they should meet. He knew this as soon as he agreed to spend his holiday at Osterode, and at a distance had longed for the meeting. Yet as soon as it became a physical possibility he was frightened: that time might have changed her, that the enchantment might have died. That was why he had found excuses for not calling on her, and seeing her now, mocking him gently, he knew that she had felt the same. She was right: her children were constantly in his brother's house, inseparable from his children and he had already grown to love them and to see in them a resemblance to their mother.

'I hear great things of you,' said Lotte. 'That you are very studious and a wonderful teacher. I am so glad.'

'And you, Lotte my dear, are just as beautiful.' He felt no shame, no hesitation or shyness in telling her. What was between them was natural and unashamed.

A flush of colour mounted to her cheeks, but she did not contradict his compliment, nor was she embarrassed or shocked by it. Only the tightening of her hand in his acknowledged their closeness, immediately re-established within seconds of their meeting again after so long a parting.

'Do you like my family? You know already how much they adore you? I am afraid they may trouble you too much if you have come to Osterode for a rest, as I am told you have.'

Her easy manner and frank gaze laid the ghost of his passion for her. He knew it still lay within him, but had been overcome by his love, which was far greater in its intensity than the passion which could wreck her happy life with her husband and her family.

Little Willi had toddled up to Lotte and was holding her skirts. In his fat, grubby hand he clutched a drooping daisy and held it out to her.

'Flower!' he said.

'Yes, darling, pretty flower.' Lotte took the bedraggled object from him with solemn courtesy.

'Daisy,' he said. 'Pretty daisy.'

'I see you are teaching him already,' she laughed.

'Already my children have told me of the games you play with them. It is kind of you to take so much trouble.'

'You know I must love them.' Friedrich did not disguise the feeling for her which showed in his eyes. She in her turn saw how handsome he had become in his maturity. Now nearing thirty he was tall and slim, with an intelligent high-cheek-boned face, deep, dark eyes and a thin, sensitive nose.

Willi had wandered off in search of more daisies and for a moment they were alone.

'I must love them.' said Friedrich, 'because I love you, their mother, and will always love you.'

Again she was not frightened or indignant, not even surprised, for although the blood mounted to her face, she returned his look, gaze for gaze, and answered simply and without embarrasment.

'I know... and I will always love you.'

It was said, and the saying of it had broken the tension between them for ever. He took her hand and she did not draw hers away. Instead she called Willi to her and only broke the clasp of their hands to take his, so that with Friedrich he formed a link between them as they walked together back to the house.

CHAPTER SIX

His return to Gottingen found him more serene than he could ever remember feeling in his life. He settled happily to his studies, adding to them later geology, history and political economy. Furthermore, another small legacy had relieved him of any financial worries, at least for the present, although he knew he might eventually have to augment his income by returning to tutoring.

The following autumn he spent another happy holiday at Osterode. The children had grown, but had not forgotten their beloved 'Oheim' and followed him everywhere, asking questions dancing round each other for the privilege of holding his hand. 'Friedrich and his Kinderbande' Christian laughingly called them.

It was at Christian's recommendation that Friedrich decided not to return to Gottingen in October but to go instead to Berlin, where the famous Professor Weiss was lecturing in natural history and where also it would be easier to earn a little money by tutoring.

The decision was a wise one and Friedrich found the course even exceeding his expectations. He wrote to Christoph, now a minister at Griesheim: 'I cannot begin to tell you my complete satisfaction and delight in this course. The lectures have come up to and passed far beyond my greatest hopes. Suddenly I have become aware of and convinced in the belief that the entire universe is bound together in the same mystical union. There is so much to learn, so much to discover!'

To augment his income he took a part-time post in a small private school run by a Dr Plamann, a pupil of Pestalozzi. It was an uninspired appointment but Friedrich's energies were directed too much towards his own studies for this to disturb him greatly.

Greater events he could not ignore, despite his absorption in his work. Even within the secluded walls of the university the world-shaking political and military events in Europe penetrated into the lecture rooms. In the winter of 1812, Napoleon had been forced to make his disastrous retreat from Moscow. Now the Prussians, long-fretting under the yoke of the French Emperor, began to stir towards new independence and war was declared against the common enemy and oppressor.

A surge of patriotism swept through the university. Bands of students singing songs of the Fatherland marched down the Unter den Linden under the Brandenburg Gate, with its splendid doric columns, erected some 20 years earlier, but still one of the finest new sights of the city.

Friedrich did not join them, he was no hero: the call to uniform and arms did not attract him in any way and he even found some of the sentiments expressed in the fervent songs nauseatingly sentimental and brashly confident. Nevertheless, he was affected by the unity which drew men together as brothers in the defence of an ideal and could not hold himself entirely aloof.

'What can I do?' he wrote to Christoph, as he did in all times of uncertainty. 'The thought of war appalls me and selfishly I do not want to disrupt my studies, yet with my heart set on teaching how can I ignore the fact that the children I shall teach—if God wills—are those who now stand defenceless before this onslaught. What am I to tell them in the years to come if I shirk my duty to take up arms for their future safety and happiness in a united free Germany? I should be rightly dubbed unmanly and altogether unworthy.'

By the end of March 1813, Friedrich had enlisted in the Infantry Division of the famous Lutzowers formed by Baron von Lutzower to encourage the smaller German states to join in the uprising and to harrass the enemy by constant skirmishes. At Eastertide, Friedrich arrived at Dresden on his way to Leipzig. It was a bitterly cold spring and the journey was cheerless. Many of the trees were still bare and only a few daffodils cheered the dank, lustreless grass left after the thawing of the snows. On his way Friedrich many times was sorely tempted to give up and return to the security and comfort of Berlin. The weather improved as he journeyed south and by the time the roof-tops and spires of Dresden were seen in the distance, against a background of wooded hills and vineyards, he was in a more cheerful frame of mind.

His quiet, withdrawn life during the months he spent in Berlin, devoted almost entirely to study, had left him with no friends and only a few aquaintances amongst his fellow students, so it was not surprising that although there were many young men from Berlin among the volunteers he did not know any of them.

The raw band of recruits left Dresden early the following morning for Leipzig. The sergeant in charge was an amiable man, an old soldier but still able to feel sympathy for the young, untrained boys who formed a ragged marching column behind him in an ill assortment of uniforms.

Their way lay beside the Elbe. It was a clear April morning and the sun sparkled on the water as they crossed the bridge towards the open countryside. On the sides of the gentle hills, rising beyond the town, were numerous stately country houses and a few ancient castles more clearly visible for the thin spring foliage of the trees, still a pale golden green in the sunshine.

After several hours' marching the sergeant called a halt and the recruits flung themselves gratefully on to the cool grass by the roadside, pulling eagerly at their water-bottles—for the day was warming—and eating the victuals provided for them by the quartermaster: some black bread and a few slices of sausage. Normally Friedrich would have shrunk from such fare, for he was not a hearty eater, but this tasted wonderful because he was so hungry after the unaccustomed exertion.

As they rested the old sergeant moved among them asking their names and home towns, joking and generally trying to cheer up the few that were feeling the strain of the journey.

'And where do you hail from?' he asked Friedrich.

'Berlin, sergeant... but my birthplace was far from here: in the Thuringen Wald.'

'A Thuringen? Then you have comrades here.' He called across to a group of young men leaning on the fence under a hawthorn tree. 'Langethal! Here is a countryman of yours! A fellow from Thuringia.'

A tall, fair young man left the group and came over to join them. He was obviously younger than Friedrich, scarcely more than a boy, with a boy's eager smile and slightly shy manner. He held out his hand: 'I'm from Erfurt.'

Friedrich took his grasp, it was as warm and firm as his smile.

'And I am from Oberweissbach. My name is Froebel... Friedrich Froebel.'

'I know a Froebel.' Langethal replied eagerly.

'The Pastor at Griesheim.'

'My brother... my eldest brother.' Friedrich could not conceal his pleasure at this acknowledgement, such was his pride in Christoph.

'I heard him preach once,' said Langethal 'he was magnificent.' His boyish enthusiasm was entirely unaffected and he sought only to please. 'I am sorry,' he went on. 'I have not introduced myself. My name is Langethal, Heinrich Langethal. It is indeed good to meet someone from one's own part of the world. These are lonely and disturbing times.'

For all his youth, Langethal had a serious manner which appealed to Friedrich. They exchanged pleasantries and when the bivouac was over and the sergeant called the troop to form up again, Heinrich took his place beside Friedrich in the column and they marched together towards Meissen.

It was a lovely spring day and the road lay between vineyards already busy with labourers tending the vines after the winter and singing as they worked. Some of the young soldiers took up the song as they passed. In the distance the gentle hilly countryside, misty in the early April sunshine, was a landscape in pale blues and greens. Frequently the road wound towards the river, and branches of the weeping willows hung like fine golden hair down to the water. It reminded Friedrich poignantly of the spring days in the water meadows at Stadt Ilm.

There was little opportunity for talking on the rest of the march and Friedrich had time to think... the first time for several days, owing to the change and disturbance of his new life. It seemed incredible to think of himself as a soldier: he who hated the thought of bloodshed to the extent of avoiding the butcher's yard, who never passed a dead animal or bird on the wayside without emotion and distress. Yet he had not been regardless of the political and military disasters of recent years. In 1806, when Napoleon himself had decimated the forces of King Frederick Wilhelm at Jena, Friedrich had been teaching at the Model School at Frankfurt. He had heard the news of the fighting at Jena with particular distress. The beloved sunny hills surrounding the town flowing with the blood of young men—both French and Prussian—filled him with frustration, anger and bewilderment. Several of his own and his brothers' student comrades had died in the bloody massacre of the Heights of Jena... and to what avail? Thousands more young men had perished, in Spain, in Portugal and in Russia, because one man wanted to rule all Europe.

Friedrich and Heinrich Langethal were given a joint billet at Meissen. The lovely spring day had mellowed into a still lovelier evening, warm and scented with the early lilacs which were already beginning to bloom in some of the town's gardens. Having settled themselves in and unloaded their packs, about 20 of the young volunteers, including Friedrich and Langethal, adjourned to a beer-garden near the river. The sun was setting, casting a warm glow on the walls of the ancient castle and cathedral which dominated the whole town in its gothic splendour. Soon the glasses were filled with old Meissen wine and toasts were drunk and friendships pledged in the desperate comradeship of lonely men who find themselves thrown together by the forces of war, united in a common unknown future of hardship or even death. At present all was happiness and light but they all knew that darkness could be just around the corner.

'Remember Jena!' the recruiting sergeant had urged them at Berlin. 'Remember Jena!' The words, hissed as a threat, rang in their ears still, even through the students' songs with which they enlivened the night air of the town.

Among the company Langethal found another friend, a divinity student from the Mark of Brandenburg, Wilhelm Middendorff, the same age or a little younger than himself, who had with him another fellow-student called Bauer. The four of them talked and drank the strong wine until late into the night. It was so warm, there was no inclination to move indoors, and as the moon came up their surroundings became more attractive, the cathedral spires shining silver against the dark sky.

Friedrich found himself in deep conversation with Middendorff. 'How can you, destined for the Ministry, reconcile yourself to the soldier's life?' Friedrich asked him earnestly.

'I'm not sure, even now' replied the young man. 'I hate war but I know that Christ was not a weak man, nor a meek one. He knew righteous anger and He defied tyrants. Our soldiering is against tyranny. We are not fighting to gain any more but our liberty and the right to live in our own country in the way we want to live, to worship freely, to teach our children in the way we consider they should be taught.'

Friedrich nodded in agreement. 'I am a teacher. Like you, I hate war. I admit I am afraid. At this stage particularly I am afraid most of all that I will betray myself, yet I am here because I want the children of our country and all countries to be taught in freedom and happiness not within the fierce and narrow doctrines of a dictatorship.'

The wine in their blood loosened their tongues. What they would have been ashamed or embarrassed to admit even to themselves in the sober light of day was released and in its release came relief and calm. When at last they had talked themselves out the wine-casks were all empty and the innkeeper pointedly yawning; they strolled back to their billets through the moonlit streets in a mood of dedicated elation.

'Let us rise early and visit the cathedral,' suggested Middendorff. 'We may not get the chance again.'

The others agreed. It was a vow rather than a rendezvous, although they made the arrangements lightheartedly.

Soon after seven o'clock the next morning they met on the cathedral steps. Few people were about in the town but the old sexton was sweeping the path and greeted them civilly.

'The doors are open,' he said. 'Go in, young men, and God's blessing go with you.'

They pushed the great doors, creaking on their hinges, and left the early sunshine for the splendid gloom within, the fresh morning air for the bittersweet mustiness of old wood and stone. The cathedral was deserted, the great east window reflecting the rising sun through myriad colours of its stained glass, casting a rainbow of light on the stone steps of the altar before the great cross.

The young men walked through the chancel, their heavy boots ringing on the flagstones, pausing to admire the splendid arch of the roof supported by massive pillars which reminded Friedrich of the great gnarled oaks of the forest. As they reached the altar steps Middendorff simply and unaffectedly knelt, joined by the others, who might have been too self-conscious to do so had it not been for his lead. As they knelt there, the light from the window on four bare heads, two dark and two fair, one of the cathedral deacons, preparing for the morning service, watched them in silence, blessing them in his mind and mourning their youth and the youth of all Prussia and Europe, called to arms.

Middendorff told Friedrich that although his family were living in Brandenburg he originally hailed from Dortmund in Westphalia. 'A proud old city,' he said, 'mourning the recent loss of its independence. Perhaps you will visit us there one day.'

'Not before he comes to Erfurt, eh, Froebel?' laughed Langethal. 'Why even Napoleon honoured us with a visit a few years ago!'

But there were to be no journeys home for any of them for many months to come. The routine of soldiering filled their days monotonously, kit-cleaning, drilling, marching, weapon instruction. Friedrich tried in vain to apply his theories of education to the tuition he was receiving now, even to give a higher meaning to what frequently appeared to be senseless effort. Soon he found that, while the actual military exercises had little meaning to him, their physical performance was satisfying and he even began to enjoy soldiering.

Although splendidly called 'Lutzower's Wild Bold Troop' the main body of the corps in which they were serving had not yet seen any action. In early May they moved up towards Lutzen, south west of Leipzig, where a concentration of Napoleon's troops was reported to be building up, but their arrival, late in the month, was too late. The might of the French had proved too great and the Lutzowers came only in time to hear the news of defeat of the combined Russo-Prussian forces, followed almost immediately in June by an armistice and instructions to the corps to return to Leipzig.

This was splendid news for Friedrich, for Christoph, his brother, had left the gentle pastorate at Griesheim to work in a hospital there. He had written to Friedrich: 'I do not feel that I can take up arms but I will do my part by caring for those who suffer in this bitter campaign. All men are brothers in disease, mutilation and death. I hope I shall not be called upon to differentiate.'

When they met in Leipzig, Friedrich was shocked by Christoph's appearance. He had lost weight and his once dark hair was streaked with grey, although he was not yet 50.

The brothers greeted each other affectionately. Christoph had secured a few hours' leave from the hospital, and his tired face became more strained as he described the terrible conditions of some of the patients brought in after long journeys from the battlefields.

'Their wounds rotting, death already on their throats, yet their eyes burning brightly with the desire to live. Calling out for their wives, their mothers and their sweethearts, falling into delirium and believing themselves back at home in the peace of their own countryside, tilling their land, tending their vines. Can *any* cause be worthy of such suffering?'

*   *   *

The Corps' sojourn in Leipzig, with its advantages to Friedrich of the occasional comfort of the company of Christoph, ended all too soon with a move to Havelburg, a town on the pleasant banks of the Havel some 100 miles to the north.

With Middendorff and Langethal he found a billet on the outskirts of the town where the three of them could spend the evenings sitting lazily in the late sunshine talking after the strenuous physical activity of the days spent marching and taking part in military manouevres. Middendorff, particularly, was a keen listener and critic of educational theories. He and Friedrich would spend hours in absorbed, and sometimes heated, argument. Nevertheless, they became friends—the only close friend, apart from his brothers, that Friedrich had ever made.

The news that Austria and Sweden had joined the Russo-Prussian alliance broke the armistice which had given a sort of uneasy peace to the summer. From Dresden came the news of French victory but this was alleviated by the despatch that the enemy vanguard, despite the dashing leadership of General Murat, had been cut off by a Prussian rally in the mountain passes.

In mid-Autumn the Lutzowers moved south again in answer to an urgent summons from the main allied forces in the area of Leipzig, where it was rumoured a great offensive was to be launched against the enemy. The Corps was divided into smaller commando groups. That in which Friedrich, Middendorff and Langethal were detailed remained some 30 miles north of the city. News was slow but rumours were rife that fighting was already in progress... stories confirmed by the sound of distant gunfire as they marched south.

The evidence of skirmishes on the flanks was left in burned-out farmhouses and cottages, slaughtered horses lying in the roadway, and sometimes a wounded man crying in vain for aid but left unheeded by the marching columns who, now pressing towards action, could not pause even for mercy's sake.

This was Friedrich's first experience of close warfare. Up to now their activities had been confined to firing on distant enemy patrols and some uneventful scouting parties. On the third day of the march they found themselves in a small copse some 25 miles to the west of the city. The firing was heavy now and they were forced to seek the scant cover of the trees. As he lay in the dry bracken, Friedrich knew that he had reached the peak of his fear... the moment of revelation which he had dreaded. The cold sweat broke on his forehead, his limbs felt heavy, hampered further by the weight of his kit, his hands were clumsy as he loaded his musket. All these were symptoms of his undeniable, overwhelming fear; this was not even terror which can give birth to an unreasoning, unthinking boldness and courage. Fear is inactive; you lie there, waiting, knowing that nothing you can do can interfere with what is to be. The scent of the pines in the October sunshine was a mockery: this was the breath of happiness, the air of his boyhood in Thuringia, even the prickly bed of brambles scratched with homely familiarity, even comfort, through his rough clothing.

A thunderous crash brought him closer to the ground and as the smoke of their own musket-fire cleared he saw the bracken had become bloody and a tattered body hung like the devil's washing on a tree-branch, a hand dangling lifeless from a limp sleeve.

His heaving stomach revolted and he was sick, animal-like, without effort, wiping his sweating face with his sleeve so that it stank and added to his shame and discomfort. Middendorff was behind him. Together they went through the disciplined routine in which they had been trained—ram; aim and fire—until their arms ached and their eyes burned with the acrid smoke and staring towards death as if by seeing they might save themselves.

When the sun dropped behind the pines on the further hill they heard, drifting up through the trees towards them, the sound of a bugle, starting as one voice and becoming many... 'Cease Fire.'

They lay over their guns as around them the dead lay, never to rise again, and the wounded groaned and writhed, unmindful that the battle was over... and the enemy in full retreat.

Friedrich opened his eyes as he lay in the bracken and looked up at the sky. It was a deep blue, fading in the west to the palest turquiose. Through the branches of the pines the first points of the stars were shining.

*   *   *

The days after the battle were spent in a sort of stunned routine of re-organisation and rekitting in a mood of fatigue which was more mental than physical. The gaps in their ranks were a constant reminder of the carnage which had taken place only a few hours earlier. Although Friedrich had not lost any of those with whom he was intimate, it was impossible not to miss a familiar face in the mess, or as they went about the camp, and this added to the feeling of depression and anti-climax. They had won, or so they had been told, but there was little atmosphere of victory.

Friedrich got no opportunity to visit Christoph. Leave was not being granted but in any case he realised that the hospital, crowded with the aftermath of battle, would give his brother no time at all for even the briefest meeting, and within a week the Lutzowers had received their orders to march north. The Corps moved off through the Brandenburg marches, a country of lakes and woods divided by vistas of widespread fertile land dotted with little towns, with here and there the turrets of a stately home peering over the tops of the trees, northwards still, through Mecklenberg with its beech forests, and on towards the coast.

Born as he was in an inland village, Friedrich had never seen the sea. As they approached Bremen the fresh north wind, with the tang of salt upon it, roused him a little from the feeling of dull misery he had been unable to shake off.

They marched in to the free Hanseatic town of Bremen early on a November morning, with the sun shining through a sea mist, the twin spires of the ancient Gothic cathedral and the high roof of the Town Hall gleaming copper green. In the front of the Town Hall, in the market place, stood the statue of Roland, of which Friedrich had often heard. Roland was the hero of his boyhood and this statue was a vast figure, six times the height of a man and carrying a sword and eagle-crested shield. As he stood before it, when the assembled force was greeted by the city fathers, he felt a thrill of pride that he should at least be one of the many who had laid aside their personal qualms to fight for freedom and independence, despite the death and destruction, the horror and the seeming waste of young lives.

Their stay in Bremen was short and the column soon moved on in the direction of Hamburg. By this time the campaign was beginning to appear aimless. The route they followed led through heather-clad moors and peat-bogs, ditches and canals threading through the scenery like veins on a flat hand—country very different to that to which he was accustomed. This only served to accentuate his growing homesickness.

Contact with home was sparse, and relied solely on any mail catching up with the marching column, more by luck than judgment. Throughout the campaign Friedrich had received only two letters: one from Christoph when he was leaving the Leipzig area and one from Lotte, like a breath of calm air from the peace of Osterode. She wrote: 'I think of you so much and pray for you every night. The children often ask about you and want to know when you will be coming to see them again. Your brother's little Wilhelm greatly resembles you. He is a lovely little boy and you will be surprised to see how he has grown.' Guiltily he concealed the letter under his tunic, like a talisman next to his heart.

After Jena, Traugott had qualified as a surgeon and now had a flourishing practice in Stadt Ilm which he had left in order to serve in the Army's medical corps. Christoph's last letter had mentioned that the brothers hoped to meet before Traugott also was moved north.

The Lutzowers were billeted in Hamburg for a few days while new orders were awaited and supplies loaded by the quarter-master and his staff. Friedrich enjoyed the unaccustomed leisure, for after the routine tasks had been performed in the morning the men were allowed considerable freedom in the town. He spent most of it exploring the streets and picturesque waterways, lined with old timbered houses and many ancient and historic buildings.

His friendship with Middendorff had been cemented by the shared ordeal of battle; they had become almost inseparable and spent most of their free time in each other's company. On the third day of their stay, Friedrich was cleaning his kit when a message summoned him to the commanding officer's quarters. Such calls, being rare, he obeyed with apprehension, yet holding low rank and little responsibility he could hardly be guilty of any but the most trivial of offences?

When he entered the room in which the officer had established his office, coming smartly to attention in the manner to which he had become accustomed but which was entirely alien to his natural inclination, he saw a familiar figure standing beside the table. It was Traugott, in the smart uniform of a medical officer, his ruddy face more weather-beaten than usual, but still Traugott, his unruly hair sleeked down to meet military requirements.

It was all he could do to maintain military composure. Obeying the leaping pleasure of his heart, Friedrich would have cast convention aside and thrown himself into his brother's arms. Instead he had to remain motionless, only the flush of his colour betraying his emotion until given the order to be at ease. Even then he could only smile his welcome, but Traugott's response was subdued, not that of boisterous enthusiasm to which he was accustomed from this, his most uninhibited, brother.

The commanding officer was a kindly man, a volunteer who was really more at home on his farm than in the field of military operations. He rose. 'I'll leave you,' he said. 'Call me, Herr Kapitan, when you have finished your sad task.'

Alone, the brothers embraced, briefly and with restraint, each now ill at ease, the one with the knowledge, the other with anticipation of ill news.

'What is it?' Friedrich asked anxiously. 'I know now that you come with bad tidings.'

Traugott looked down; he could not meet his brother's eyes. 'It is Christoph,' he said.

The cold fear of battle was joy by comparison to this.

'Christoph?' Friedrich repeated the name unbelievingly, as if he could thus convince himself that he had misheard.

'He died at Leipzig.' Traugott could not spare Friedrich any more than to be swift, as the surgeon is swift with the knife.

'At Leipzig?' Friedrich repeated the words again stupidly. 'But, Traugott, he wasn't in the fighting.'

'He did not die in the battle, he died of hospital fever, of typhus, nursing the French wounded. The disease is raging there.'

The brothers looked at each other in dumb misery, Traugott's own distress heightened by the shocked trembling of his younger brother, already thinner and older by the rigours of long marches and scant rations.

'He said...' Friedrich spoke almost to himself, his voice choked with the struggle to keep back unmanly tears. 'He said he prayed to God that he would never be called upon to discriminate between our own men and our enemies.'

Traugott put his arm round Friedrich's shoulders. 'Then he died as he would have wished, caring for those we have been taught to hate.'

Traugott, the doctor, knew the horrors of typhus, the killer that walked the hospital wards with their stench and filth. Death had certainly been no discriminator: both French and Prussian had succumbed to this common and terrible enemy.

Friedrich returned to his billet alone...Traugott had to leave Hamburg almost immediately. Before he went he had at least been able to assure Friedrich that Christoph's family would be secure, for the time being at any rate, at the manse at Griesheim, where the congregation was determined to do its best by the memory of their well-loved minister.

In the weeks that followed the friendship of Wilhelm Middendorff was the only rock to which Friedrich could cling. Without his kind and sensible philosophy, his patience and understanding, Friedrich felt he might have lost his sanity. The death of Christoph was his first true bereavement, for while feeling a decent regret at the loss of his father, their relationship, even at the end, had never reached any deep emotional warmth. The death of Uncle Hoffman had been a deeper wound, but time had separated them for many years before the parting and the difference in their ages had warned Friedrich, if subconsciously, that it was inevitable. He had never thought of his brothers dying.

Now Friedrich could not forget Christoph. Christoph, who mothered him when he was a sad little boy, opened the doors of nature for him, soothed all his wounds, both mental and physical, and was always ready to give sympathetic and wise counsel. The black void that his death left was an ever-present reality...always there. Every turn of conversation came with relentless inevitability back to some memory of Christoph.

In the night he would wake from the warmth of and blessed forgetfulness of sleep to the swift consciousness of some disaster and break into a cold sweat from a nightmare that was not a dream but an awakening. It brought back the memory of the night terrors at Stadt Ilm when he and Lotte had talked about death.

Now he talked of death with Middendorff.

'There *is* life beyond,' said Wilhelm. 'Not angels in white robes, not golden pavements and marble halls, but *life,* not perhaps as we know it, but just as real.'

'How do you *know*?' Friedrich was despairing.

'I *feel* rather than know. I believe in God because I believe in beauty and love. Where there are these there can be no death.'

Their lodgings looked out on a small garden now white with the December snow.

'This is how you feel now,' he continued. 'The snow is like your sorrow, numbing your heart, but when the spring comes and the sun shines again the ice will melt, new life will spring through the snow. So it will be with you. I know. I have suffered too, although I am younger than you.'

'But my faith, Wilhelm? I think I have lost my faith.'

'We only lose our faith to gain it again, more fully,' said Middendorff. 'Faith is not really something to be picked up on the wayside, it has to be earned, fought for through doubt and questioning. The truly religious man is the one who has come back to his faith through disbelief.'

He put his arm over Friedrich's shoulder. 'Take heart, Kamerade, there is work to be done and work is a great balm for sorrow. Your brother's widow and children, what is to become of them?'

'They continue to live at the manse, at least for the present' Friedrich told him.

'Well, let their welfare be your concern. In that way your grief will turn outward instead of eating into your heart.'

'But how? I have no money. As you know I have hardly enough to pay my fees at the university. What can I do for them?'

'I did not mean financial help,' said Middendorff. 'What about the boys' education?'

'I don't know. I suppose my sister-in-law has made some arrangements.'

Middendorff was still looking into the garden. He did not turn as he spoke, as if thinking aloud.

'Could we not start our own school?'

'Our *own* school?' Friedrich's response was immediate with unconcealed excitement. 'It is the dearest wish of my life! But Wilhelm, it would be very difficult, we have no capital, no property. How could we begin?'

'Not yet, perhaps,' said Middendorff. 'Not yet, but the time will come... and when it comes Friedrich, my dear friend, I will come from wherever I may be, or what ever I may be doing, to devote my life to this great end with you.' He held out his hand and Friedrich took it, like a drowning man clutching at the hand held out to save him. This *was* the saving of his life... the saving of his sanity. The world had a meaning and a purpose again.

The work of the moment was uninspired. The military routine of the last months of the war gave little inspiration but also little time for brooding.

In February the dull days were a little enlivened for Friedrich by good news from Osterode: Christian's wife had given birth to another little girl, to be called Elise and already the darling of her older brothers and sisters.

With the spring Friedrich found, true to Middendorff's prophecy, his spirits rose a little. At the end of May the peace came, before the combined forces could close, as planned, on Paris, and the Lutzowers moved into the Netherlands pending demobilisation.

In July 1814 anyone who did not wish to serve any longer was given permission to return to civilian life immediately. Langethal, Bauer and Middendorff had already been transferred to another section of the Corps and army life without them was becoming increasingly tedious, so Friedrich was glad to take advantage of this opportunity.

Early in the campaign he had met his old professer at Berlin University and this man, in a mood of patriotic enthusiasm, promised him a post in the museum there if victory was secured and they both survived. Now this seemed a reasonably encouraging prospect and Friedrich decided to see whether the promise made in war would be kept in peace. Somewhat to his surprise the professor not only honoured his word but wrote at once and with enthusiasm, saying he badly needed someone to help in the re-organisation of the museum, long neglected during the war years.

Deciding to take the offer up without hesitation, Friedrich determined to make the journey back to Berlin as much a holiday as possible. He chose a roundabout route in order to see as much as he could of the lovely country in the valleys of the Rhine and Maine, and made his first stop by way of Dusseldorf, a lively, artistic town which put him in a holiday mood, and then on to Lunen and thence to Mainz. Between here and Bingen he found one of the loveliest landscapes in the Rhine valley, a land of rich vineyards, low foothills and green water meadows, and so on to Frankfurt, where he enjoyed a happy reunion with the von Holzhausens. Although all three boys were away at Jena University, their parents greeted Friedrich like an elder son and he spent three happy days as an honoured guest in the house where he had once been the tutor.

From Frankfurt he went on to Griesheim, where Christoph's widow was managing as best she could with her three young sons—Julius, Karl and Theodor. He found her calm but still deeply shocked by her bereavement. She greeted him with pathetic relief, and after making him welcome lost no time in unburdening her heart to him.

'Thank God you've come' she cried. 'You have no idea the turmoil I have been in. Friedrich, what *am* I to do with the boys? At present they are so young and I can manage, at least while they allow me to stay here. But what is to become of them later? I cannot afford to educate them as Christoph would have wished.'

He noticed that, as with himself, there was a hesitation in her voice when she used his brother's name . . . as if anonymity took some of the sting out of the reminder of their bereavement.

Moved by his sister-in-law's distress and the memory of his devotion to Christoph, and most of all by the inspiration of his conversation with Middendorff at Hamberg, Friedrich made an emotional and impulsive promise.

'*You* must care for the boys now,' he told her. 'They are still babies and need their mother, but when they are older I will attend to their education. Rest assured, their future is secure.'

Her relief was touching. She wept, and when she had dried her tears she expressed her thanks in the way she best understood—by cooking him a meal, which they ate together in friendly silence.

'I meant what I said,' he told her again when he kissed her and the children farewell.

From Griesheim, Friedrich made the last lap of his journey to Berlin, in a less happy frame of mind than that which had accompanied his earlier travelling. His visit to his sister-in-law had depressed and perplexed him, and the promise made in rash sincerity was now beginning to trouble him. Even the beauty of the countryside brought little comfort, his mind wandered from the past to the present, in a ceaseless, inexplicable state of longing and unrest.

The district abounded in large houses surrounded by beautiful gardens. Passing the gates of a particularly large and lovely estate, Friedrich stopped to look in at the garden beyond. It was a blazing mass of colour, a riot of roses in trailing arbours, banks of delphiniums and hollyhocks and bright pansy borders round beds of heliotrope. As he stood in admiration an elderly man approached the gates from the other side and greeted him kindly.

'I was admiring your lovely garden,' said Friedrich, a little embarrassed that he might be considered rude. 'I hope you will forgive my boldness at staring in through your gates.' 'Forgive? I am delighted! What is a garden if no one admires and enjoys it? Won't you come in and see more of it?' he moved towards the heavy gates and swung one of them open to allow Friedrich to enter.

The larger part of the garden, out of view from the road, was even more beautiful. Carefully landscaped into secluded walks and arbours it constantly presented new delights at every turn: banks of late irises, burning clumps of azaleas reflected in a little stream that flowed gently between mossy stones, and banks of forget-me-nots. The trees were of such beauty and variety that even Friedrich the forester was at a loss to name all of them.

After a while as they walked, talking gently, stopping to admire or to bend towards the scent of the roses, Friedrich noticed that despite the great number and variety of flowers in the garden there were no lilies.

'Lilies do not thrive here, I am afraid,' the owner told him. 'But why do you ask? No one has ever noticed before. Are you particularly fond of lilies?'

Friedrich could not explain, but it seemed to him at that moment that the garden, for all its gaiety and beauty, was incomplete without the pale purity and serenity of lilies.

The old man glanced at him sideways—'a strange, dreamy young man' he thought to himself, 'but I like him' He added out loud: 'I am afraid you must excuse me... I am expecting a caller, but do stay in the garden as long as you please. You can find your way out again to the gate?'

'Oh yes, thank you, sir. Thank you very much.' Friedrich was grateful for the invitation, for much as he liked the old man he was glad of the opportunity to be alone with his thoughts in such a lovely place. He watched his host disappear beyond the trees leading up to the house and then turned his own steps back to the rose-garden. It was late afternoon, the shadows were lengthening, and a light dew on the grass sprayed his boots as he walked. A blackbird was singing and the air was humming with bees busy in the thick borders of lavender. As he stooped to enjoy again the scent of a dark red rose he was startled to hear a sound behind him. He turned and saw a little boy standing in the path. He was fair and chubby and reminded Friedrich of Christian's little son Wilhelm.

'Hallo,' said the child without any shyness.

Friedrich returned the greeting: 'What's your name?'

'Hans,' the little boy replied solemnly.

'I once knew a little boy called Hans,' Friedrich told him, 'but he was a bigger boy than you. How old are you?'

'Three,'

'That's a splendid age to be!'

The little boy smiled now for the first time, showing white teeth like a kittens. He moved nearer to Friedrich and, without saying anything, put his tiny hand into Friedrich's and tugged it. 'Come with me,' he said 'I'll show you the fishes.'

Friedrich bent from his own tallness to accommodate the tiny figure skipping beside him, leading him to the pond, where bright gold-fish played hide-and-seek under the leaves of the water lilies.

'Pretty fishes,' said the little boy.

Friedrich could see his own reflection in the water beside that of the child's. Disturbed by the ripples from the light breeze, the image broke and reformed. It was a moment of peace and tranquility such as he had not known since the news of Christoph's death had shattered his happiness.

*   *   *

He arrived in Berlin in the first days of August 1814. His promised appointment was awaiting him as assistant to Professor Weiss at the Mineralogical Museum of the university. The galleries had been sadly neglected and Friedrich's task was to put them in to some sort of order. The work appealed to him, although it meant days working long hours alone in the musty galleries, with their untidy cases of rock fragments, crystal, quartz and semi-precious stones, all in an unimaginative and untidy jumble. Friedrich found a new fascination in these dumb witnesses of the silent creative energy of nature. Their age fascinated him, their beauty astounded him.

He was laboriously note-taking one afternoon when he was surprised to see that he was not alone in the gallery, which was seldom visited by anyone. It was extremely unusual to see a woman in the university precincts other than the wives or daughters of professors or an occasional laundry-maid, and although the mineralogical galleries were open to the public, visitors to them were extremely rare. This visitor was a woman, tall and dark, probably about his own age, perhaps a little older—36 or 37. Her hair was drawn back from her face, which was fine-drawn and intelligent. She wore a sable hat, which greatly became her, and dark, fitted coat, small-waisted, full-skirted, also trimmed with fur. Her whole appearance was one of quiet serenity, her

colouring, her pose as she bent, absorbed, over one of the exhibition cases.
   Drawn to her by curiosity, heightened by her attraction, Friedrich moved towards her down the gallery. Hearing him approach she looked up and smiled.
   'Good afternoon'
   He returned her greeting, noticing how assured and unaffected she was, with none of the false bashfulness which some of the young women of the day affected. Her dark eyes regarded him with frank interest and friendliness.
   'I was admiring the arrangement of these specimens' she said. 'It really is excellent. I have been here before but I never really understood the formation of these crystals. This arrangement makes it all so clear.' She looked around her. 'The whole gallery is *so* much improved, someone is obviously working on it very well.'
   'Thank you,' said Friedrich 'It is my work. I am glad you like it.'
   'I do indeed! I must congratulate you. But surely you haven't been here very long? I have never seen you before?'
   'I came here last summer, in August to be precise, at the end of the war, to work under Professor Weiss.'
   'You were a soldier then?'
   'I served with the Lutzowers, but you must not imagine that I am a hero for that. The Lutzowers fought bravely and I am proud to name myself among them, but my section only saw action once and then I must admit that I was extremely frightened!'
   She laughed and he noticed that her teeth were white and even and the smile lit up her dark eyes and gave her normally serious face a spark of mischief.
   'How honest of you to admit it!'
   Friedrich laughed too. 'I should be humbug indeed if I did otherwise. And in any case, if I gave myself a heroic reputation someone might expect me to be a hero again one day and then I should be revealed and disgraced indeed!'
   Her merry response echoed in the silent gallery, which seldom heard voices, let alone laughter.
   'And so you came here at the war's end?' she said.
   'That was a change from the soldier's life. Had you been in Berlin before?'
   He told her of his brief period of post-graduate study before his enlistment.
   'And you are studying still?'
   'Greek and Latin'
   '*And* arranging the mineral galleries.' she added. 'Your life is busy indeed!'
   He realised that under her gentle probing, he had already told her a great deal about himself while knowing nothing about her.
   'It is very unusual to see a woman in the university. You cannot be a

student, although personally I would like to see women studying at our universities, and yet I find you in our gallery absorbed in our exhibits. Are you interested in mineralogy?'

'Extremely,' she replied 'In *all* sciences for that matter, but I fear my knowledge is meagre. I try to learn what I can but it is not easy. As you obviously understand, it is not at all the thing in Berlin for a woman to have a zest for learning. In fact it is almost disreputable!'

'If I could help you,' he said impulsively, carried away by his enthusiasm and her attraction. Then, realising that this was a forward suggestion to be made by a stranger, he added: 'If you will forgive me for proposing it... as curator here I am supposed to include guide-lecturing in my duties if visitors so require it.'

'You are the curator!' she cried. 'Then I know who you are! You are Friedrich Froebel! I have heard so much of you from a great friend of my family—your own friend Wilhelm Middendorff! I should have known as soon as you said you had served with the Lutzowers. He told me you were to take on an appointment here!'

'You know Middendorff?' Friedrich cried delightedly. 'This is marvellous news! We were great comrades and it is months since we met. We parted outside Paris and were posted to different battalions. I miss him and my other army friends greatly.'

'Then you will be happy to learn that he is coming to Berlin. We had a letter from him at Christmas. He is coming to continue his divinity studies at the university.'

'This is the best news I have had in months!' Friedrich was overjoyed. 'How glad I am that you came here this afternoon and that we met.'

'And do not forget in your excitement that you promised to be my instructor,' she reminded him.

'Of course, I shall not forget... I am already planning your course of study.'

'I hope you will not find me very stupid'

Friedrich laughed. 'I am sure I shall find you a most apt and intelligent pupil,' he said 'but in case you are *not* I must know your name so that I can scold you!'

She returned his laughter. 'I am sorry... I know *your* name and I have not told you mine. I am Henrietta Hoffmeister, Herr Doktor'—she bobbed a mock curtsy—'and I hope you will not have to scold me too frequently. I will try to be a model pupil.'

The winter sun shone in through the high windows of the gallery, warming their backs as they stood talking. Her company and the news of Middendorff warmed Friedrich even more: the world suddenly seemed a happier place.

CHAPTER SEVEN

Middendorff arrived in Berlin in late February. Friedrich had returned to the lodgings he had occupied before the war and Middendorff joined him there. The comradeship that had been born in war flourished in peace. They worked together, silent in their respective studies. They talked long into the night and at the week-ends. When the weather warmed into spring they travelled to the countryside which surrounded the city, to the lakes or by the river-side, walking all day, eating their lunch in the open air, savouring the peace and leisure which neither had known for many months. As they walked, their favourite topic of conversation was their old dream, born in the last weeks of the war, when they were together at Hamburg: the school which one day they might run together.

Since that time Friedrich has scarcely ever stopped thinking of the school. It had always been his dream since the day he started work with Herr Gruner in the Model School at Frankfurt and realised that teaching was his vocation, but he had never admitted the possibility of its reality until encouraged by Middendorff. Now he could not get it out of his mind.

His reunion with Middendorf fanned his smouldering enthusiasm into flame. Now he could think out loud, his companion eagerly criticising and contributing.

Early in the winter he had had news from Osterode from Lotte. It was her usual cheerful letter, packed with news of her own children and his brother's. 'They are inseparable,' she wrote. 'We are like one family. Your sister-in-law and I scarcely know which children are our own, they are always together!' She added: '... and soon I am to add another little one to our happy family. I hope it will be a girl ... boys are sweet but so boisterous. If all goes well she (?) will be born about Eastertide.'

In late April he heard from her again ... a letter as elated as the sunshine in which he read it and as bright as the daffodils blooming in the park beside the river. 'I have a wonderful little girl! She is tiny and as pink as a rose-bud. We are both very well. Do come soon to Osterode so that you can see her and all of us. I think of you often and pray for your success and safety.'

He read her letter as always, over and over, with a feeling of great tenderness.

Easter brought doubly joyous news in addition to the letter from Lotte: Heinrich Langethal was to join his friends in Berlin. The only tiny cloud on the horizon was the deteriorating political situation. Napoleon's escape from

Elba, the massing of his troops on the Belgian border, had all Berlin talking and it was impossible to ignore even in the delightful days of an enchanted May when the linden blossoms filled the warm air with their heavy perfume and the humming of bees.

'Not again!' groaned Middendorff as they read the latest reports. 'All that senseless slaughter, that waste of life...!'

The thought of war again was even more abhorrent to Friedrich, because he was so happy and life had become so full. To the companionship of Middendorff and Langethal was added that of Henrietta Hoffmeister, a different association to any that he had known before. It was a friendship that had the qualities of comradeship known only between men yet at the same time was softened by a woman's gentleness. He did not feel for her as he had felt for Lotte. Nothing he knew would ever change or replace that; it was part of his life, all that was best of his boyhood, but in Henrietta he found a ready listener, an intelligent but kindly critic. Her quick mind he found a challenge and an inspiration. He was surprised at her knowledge and the readiness with which she responded to his instruction, for he had kept his promise to help her, admitting to himself that it was a happy excuse to spend delightful hours alone with her in the museum gallery. He found she had an aptitude for cataloguing and arrangement and that she was soon able to help in his work as well as increasing her own knowledge, which was not nearly as meagre as she had led him to believe.

Sometimes she would join him and his companions on their week-end walks, adding her quick feminine mind to their more pedantic masculine philosophies.

He had noticed early in their acquaintance that she wore a wedding ring but it was some months before he dared to ask her more. He knew from Middendorff that she was married and separated from her husband, but no more than this. It was she who finally chose the moment. They had been talking of the past. She told him that, unlike most of her generation of women, she had studied under two well-known professors but her studies had been interrupted by marriage at 19. 'How young I was!' she said. 'How much *too* young! He was young too, very handsome, very headstrong. We were warned against hastiness but we would not listen. We had not been married long when I found that he was self-willed and domineering. Perhaps I was to blame too...as you may be aware, I am not the sort of woman who will be happily ordered about. He wanted a clinging creature who would obey him without question: I could not. Then'—she added with a sudden hesitation.— 'then...there were other things that I cannot talk about.' Friedrich noticed that a faint flush had come to her cheeks, something he had never seen before for she was always composed and unembarrassed.

'I left him... It was unforgivable, of course... a man may leave his wife and she will be pitied, but I left *him.*'

'You have no children?'

'Mercifully for them no, that is, not in that sense. I have an adopted daughter, the child of a friend of mine who died tragically soon after she was born. Her father too died when she was still a baby. I had nothing left in my life, neither had she, so I took her for my own. Her name is Ernestine but I call her Tina. She is now nearly 15, a sweet, pretty child and a great joy to me.'

'And your family?'

'My father has never really forgiven me. My husband, you see, was an official in the War Office, junior to my father. My marriage—against my parents' wishes, we eloped—was a scandal. The annulment was an even *greater* scandal. The honour of the *Army* was at stake, you see.' She laughed with a trace of bitterness.

'Why have *you* never married?' she asked Friedrich.

'You were too hasty,' he said. 'I was too slow.'

* * *

The recall to arms came as they feared it must. All three of them, Friedrich, Middendorff and Langethal, re-enlisted within the first few days of the emergency and on account of their previous service were immediately commissioned as officers. The throng of volunteers was so great, however, that orders to join their regiment were almost immediately countermanded and they returned with unashamed relief to their quiet lodgings, assured that their chance of being recalled to active service was remote.

In the late summer, Friedrich made his long-promised visit to Osterode. Lotte's baby was almost four months old, a happy little girl, rather small for her age but contented and uncrying. Lotte, too, was little changed, still beautiful, still young-looking and glad as ever to see him. He told her about Henrietta.

'You should marry her,' said Lotte firmly. 'You are nearly 35, it's time you had a wife and children. You love children so much, what a wonderful father you would be!'

They were alone in the garden under the apple tree where they had sat before the war with little Willi, now grown into a sturdy schoolboy.

'I don't think I will ever marry,' he told her. 'You know why.'

She looked at him frankly.

'I think I do,' she said, 'but it is not a good reason. Perhaps if you did it would be better for us both?' As he looked at her he saw that her lips were trembling, as they always did in moments of emotion, as they had when they were children on the hillside above Stadt Ilm and he had fled from her...

When he returned to Berlin he told Henrietta about Lotte. 'She is married,' he said. 'Her husband is a fine, gentle fellow. I like him and would not hurt him for the world. She loves him truly. I know that what she feels for me is something of the past that lives, as our past must always live in our hearts because upon it is built the present. One cannot cast out old loves because new loves come into our hearts. I will always love Lotte. Do you think it is wicked of me?'

'No,' she said, and he knew that she meant what she said. 'I might if you told me that you would chance wrecking her happiness, and his, by letting the past intrude into the present, or into the future.'

'I would never do that.'

'Then there is no harm. True love has no sin in it. But why are you telling me this?' She looked strangely at him and her eyes were sad. 'Surely this is something between you and Lotte... you should not tell me of it.'

'I would not want you to hear it, or even guess at it, in any other way.' He took her hand and realised how slender and pale it was in his own—large and still tanned and calloused from his soldiering. 'You are a very dear person to me, Henrietta, I cannot tell you what your friendship and company have come to mean to me. Because of this, there can be no secrets between us. I am a man of few secrets. Now you know all there is to know about me, and I hope you will think none the less of me for it.'

'I think much more of you...' She returned the warm clasp of his hand with her own.

* * *

Langethal and Middendorff had both secured tutoring posts to assist their meagre funds, but the friends still had plenty of time together. The dream of a school of their own had never left them and Friedrich in particular. Now Henrietta had been drawn into their plans and discussions. Her views on the part women could play in education were bold and determined.

'It is a woman's vocation,' she said. 'Who should understand a child better than we who bring them into the world and care for them in their most formative years?'

In October 1816 Friedrich had a letter from his sister-in-law at Griesheim.

'I am sorely in need of your assistance and experience regarding the boys' education' she wrote. 'Julius certainly is old enough for serious schooling. Karl and Theodor soon will be. What do you suggest? There is no suitable school here. Should I send them away to Frankfurt or Leipzig? I think I could afford it, but I would miss them greatly, or should I engage a tutor here? If you recommend the latter you may know a young man who would be content with a modest salary in exchange for a comfortable home?'

Suddenly it seemed to Friedrich that this was the moment of decision for which he had been subconsciously waiting. He wrote to Christian at Osterode, asking him for advice.

'I need your help,' he wrote, 'and I need the quietness of your mountain paradise to set my thoughts in order.'

It was a wonderful autumn. The mornings were misty, but when the sun rose higher the days were warm and mellow. The whole earth seemed to be overflowing with bounty. The bramble-bushes were heavy with shiny black fruit, the plums and damsons hung heavily in the orchards where the grass was already bright with the jewels of windfall apples His brother's and Lotte's children played together like boisterous puppies among the hay-ricks. Little Willi was nearly six, with cheeks as round and rosy as the apples. His brother Ferdinand was eight. 'Der Oheim,' as they called him, was their constant companion. They had not forgotten his earlier visits, although they were so young when he last saw them, and welcomed him back to their games with joyous enthusiasm. Their older sisters, Albertine, now nearly 15 and Emilie, 12, were pretty, gentle girls, delighted to mother the latest member of the family, Elise, a chubby toddler of two and a half.

When at last, after a long first day in the autumn sunshine, Friedrich and Christian were alone, Friedrich broke the reason for his visit with some trepidation.

'I'm hoping to start my own school,' he said.

To his relief Christian was astounded but delighted.

'I knew you would come to it!' he cried. 'I would have encouraged you earlier but felt you must reach your own decision in your own time. What has prompted you now?'

Friedrich told him of the letter from Christoph's widow.

'First I planned to take his sons only, as pupils,' he explained. 'But you cannot call three boys of one family a school! Then I thought of your family. Would you entrust me with any one of them? The manse at Griesheim is still available to Marte. I could establish a little school there with perhaps one or two other children. I have friends in Berlin who would be interested, I think. What do you say?'

'I say it is the best thing I have ever heard!' Christian was overflowing with enthusiasm. 'Of course I will help you! The girls, I think, still need their mother, but the boys, I know, would go anywhere with you tomorrow! They never stop talking of their beloved "Oheim" and you have already taught them a great deal, even on short visits, with your marvellous games! Willi spends hours with the wooden ball toy you made him.'

'Then I can take them to Griesheim?'

'By all means! As soon as Marte is ready, if she agrees to your plan, as I am certain she will. I am sure she will welcome you with open arms, poor creature, she has had a sad time since Christoph was taken from her, and she has been very brave.'

Friedrich wrote to Griesheim the next day: 'I would like to bring Christian's boys with me... he has entrusted me with their future, as I hope you will with your own sons. As you know, your husband was the most beloved of all my dear brothers and I can do no better in my devoted memory of him than to be a father to his boys.'

When he returned to Berlin he did not lose any time in breaking the news to Middendorff. 'Wonderful!' cried his friend. 'It's wonderful! When do you begin?'

'Now! ' Friedrich told him. 'I have already handed in my resignation to the university. I leave next week. The only thing that disturbs me is the thought of the loss of your company and Langethal's.'

'It will not be for long, Friedrich. This is only the beginning . I promised you once that when this day came I would make any sacrifice to join you. When you are ready for me I will be here waiting!'

The friends grasped hands. It was a moment of dedication, promise and elation.

Friedrich's parting fom Henrietta was the only other sadness between him and the exciting prospect of his great venture. She was unselfishly delighted for him. 'Of course you must go!' She told him. 'It is a wonderful opportunity to put all your ideas to the test... apart from your duty to your brother's poor little boys!'

'But I shall miss you, Henrietta. I shall miss you sadly. My dear, gentle, wise Henrietta.' They were walking by the slow waters of the Spree, sullen grey as the early November sky. The trees were already bare and a few gulls, driven inland by the approach of winter, screamed above the shore-line.

'I shall miss *you,* Friedrich, the more because I shall not be busy as you will with a new project. You *will* write to me, won't you? Often?'

In the moment of their parting there was an added tenderness he had not seen before. She was a calm woman, not given to displays of emotion, but her voice now was husky with what he might have believed to have been tears had he not expected them from her, as it was he had never seen her weep, nor thought her likely to do so.

'Of course I will write to you.' They had reached the end of their walk and he was standing with her at the entrance to her father's house. She had never invited him to meet her parents but this did not surprise him. As she was composed, so was she independent, an unusual quality in the women of her time.

He took her hand and she looked up at him, for tall as she was he was much taller.

'It will be hard work at the beginning,' he said, 'perhaps always. If I thought you could bear it, and bear me too, I would ask you to share it with me.'

Her look was one of half-belief, half-elation.

'Friedrich! Are you proposing to me?'

'It's not a very romantic proposal, is it? I suppose I should be on my knees and it should be spring, not here in the November fog on a cold street corner. Will you marry me, Henrietta? Share my dream with me... all its probable hardships and disappointments?'

'I'll marry you *and* your dream because I am not sure which I love the most!'

She was in his arms, unashamed, and he kissed her, her face cold and damp with the chill of the fog, its beads of moisture on her dark hair, sparkling in the lamplight.

*   *   *

He left for Griesheim in a mood of such elation that the winter weather seemed like spring. Marte welcomed him with gentle affection.

'I always knew you would come,' she said. 'The boys never stop talking about you.'

Little Wilhelm and Ferdinand his brother settled down happily with their older cousins, and Friedrich set about the first task of converting one of the larger rooms in the old manse into a schoolroom. He decorated it with pictures and garlands of berries and evergreens. It must, he decided, be gay and beautiful; he wanted none of the dreary board-walls of his own childhood. The children themselves collected acorns and chestnuts in the woods and set them growing in glass bottles, eagerly measuring the spiked roots as they grew down into the water.

Marte helped him enthusiastically. He wrote to Christian: 'Sometimes her excitement worries me. Naturally I welcome her help and support, but it seems at times almost too intense, too bright to burn long. It is as if she were waiting for something and I don't know what it is. We have made a pretty schoolroom here, and the children are progressing wonderfully. In addition to their normal studies I have introduced the little ones to simple mat-weaving and making models from card and paper. This they enjoy greatly and learn a lot at the same time about form and pattern and colour. We also have the weather box. This they change daily, using figures I have constructed to show the climate of the day. When the spring comes I hope to start them off with their own little gardens.'

Willi and Ferdinand went home for Christmas to Osterode. Friedrich would dearly have loved to return to Berlin to Henrietta and his friends, or at least to have joined Christian and his family, but felt it unfair to leave Marte and the boys alone, and in any case there was still so much to be done. He thought of asking Henrietta to join them at Griesheim but they were not yet officially engaged and he knew that such an invitation would only cause her embarrassment.

Therefore, Christmas at Griesheim was a very quiet affair shared by him and Marte and the three boys. Between them they decorated the house, the boys making a nativity scene and models for the festive dinner table.

When the meal was over, and he had said grace, the children left the table to play with their new toys and he and Marte were left alone.

'This is the happiest Christmas we have had since Christoph left for the war,' she said. 'You know, Friedrich, you are remarkably like him. As you sit there in the firelight I can hardly believe that it is not he that looks across the table at me.'

'I am sorry, Marte, dear.' Friedrich felt ashamed that his likeness to Christoph might distress her.

'Don't be sorry! It is a comfort to me, just as you are a comfort, Friedrich. I can never thank you enough for what you are doing!'

When Willi and Ferdinand returned in the New Year they were joined by a sixth pupil, a nephew of Langethal's. As the spring approached, lessons moved more out into the open air. The successful experiment long ago at Frankfurt was repeated and the children built a relief map of the district with stones and sand in the manse garden. To their nature table of growing acorns were added the spring branches of ash buds, black as soot, hazel catkins and willow wands and the big sticky buds from the chestnut trees. From the little stream that flowed through the manse garden they collected frog spawn and were delighted to see the specks of life grow into tadpoles and eventually into minute frogs.

In April, Friedrich heard from Middendorff: 'My tutoring appointment has concluded. I have a little capital saved, enough at least to join you for a while. If you can feed me and give me a roof over my head, I ask no more... dreams are not founded on fortunes.'

Middendorff's presence at Griesheim was doubly welcome because Friedrich was beginning to find Marte's devoted attention almost an embarrassment. As the only adults in a community of children, they were unavoidably thrown into each other's company most of the time.

Middendorff's reaction was plain-speaking. 'Have you not told Marte about Henrietta?'

Friedrich admitted that he had not, although he did not really know why. 'We are not officially engaged, you know,' he told his friend. 'I was not sure how she would react to my proposition that I would be shortly bringing a wife to join me here.'

'Very unfortunately, I should say,' said Middendorff bluntly. 'Don't you realise that she is in love with you?'

Friedrich was genuinely shocked.

'Oh no! She's a kind creature and devoted to my work for her children, but not in love with me. Oh no, Wilhelm, you are quite mistaken I swear it!'

'You may swear it,' smiled Middendorff, 'but you don't see it. My dear fellow, anyone with any sense would perceive it a mile away. Oh, I grant you it's three parts sentiment and loneliness and your likeness to Christoph, but when you came here and offered to father her boys she thought you meant much more than you did.'

Friedrich was honestly distressed. It had never occurred to him that his sister-in-law's enthusiasm, even her moments of affection, were inspired by anything other than her gratitude and pleasure in his work for her sons. Now he was at a loss to know what to do about the situation. He obviously could not confront her with it, even now in the face of Middendorff's certainty. He still had to be convinced that it was so. All he could do was to wait nervously for some further development. In the meantime he was even more reluctant to tell her about Henrietta.

A further complication was presented to the Griesheim community, Marte's father, who had been ailing for some time, took a turn for the worse. She had never been greatly attached to him and was more concerned for the future of her elderly mother. In the spring of 1817 he died and after a short journey to her home to settle affairs, she returned to Griesheim with news that was at once reassuring and disconcerting. Far from being poor, her father had left quite a considerable amount of money, enough to keep her mother in comfort, and had even left Marte a small legacy. The disturbing part of this news was that the inheritance disqualified Marte and her sons from further use of the manse, where they had been allowed to live since Christoph's death. However, after the first sense of panic they discovered this was only a momentary setback. A small farm had been up for sale for some time at Keilhau, a nearby village. Marte and Friedrich went to inspect it with Middendorff and all agreed that it would make a comfortable home and also could easily be adapted for school purposes. Marte decided to buy, and in July she moved with Friedrich and Middendorff and their six pupils to the pretty old farmhouse surrounded by a copse of firs on the gentle hillside below the greater heights of the Kirschberg.

The farm itself provided adequate living accommodation but did not have the large rooms of the manse, which were so suitable as classrooms. In September, Langethal arrived from Berlin, bringing with him the boys to whom he was acting as tutor. Confronted with the problem of accommodation he dismissed it with characteristic optimism. 'We have plenty of wood around us,' he said. 'If we want a schoolhouse we must build one!'

Friedrich wrote to Henrietta: 'My household is growing fast and yet I had no house of my own. In a way only comprehensible to Him who knows all things we have managed to build a frame house, although we don't own the ground on which it stands.'

At Christmas, Langethal and Middendorff having arranged to remain at Keilhau, Friedrich joyfully left for Berlin. It was over a year since he had seen Henrietta. When he saw her he could scarcely believe that this delightful, enchanting woman was really his betrothed. She greeted him with tears of happiness in her dark eyes.

'It's been so long, Friedrich!'

He held her closely, her hair smelt of roses and he could feel her heart beating beneath her tight bodice.

'It will not be much longer.' Friedrich told her. 'Very soon now Keilhau will be ready to welcome you. Do you think you will be able to bear our house in the wilds?'

'It will be heaven!' she laughed. 'I was always a wild woman, Friedrich; your house in the wilds will be my soul's paradise.'

It had been arranged that he should spend the festival with Henrietta's family, and much as he looked forward to her company he viewed the prospect with some trepidation. He had met her parents only briefly, on an occasion when he had visited the house with Middendorff, who was already a friend of the family—even, he understood, distantly related. On this occasion they had been friendly and courteous, but the meeting had been of the most formal nature and far different from this at which Henrietta had suggested that he should declare their intention to marry. He had heard enough of General

Hoffmeister to anticipate that the reception he would give to a penniless schoolmaster as a suitor to his daughter would scarcely be enthusiastic. Initially, at any rate, he was made welcome as a Christmas guest, particularly owing to his friendship with Middendorff, of whom they were particularly fond.

On Christmas Eve the family gathered for the traditional exchange of gifts. Friedrich had brought for Henrietta a shawl of fine white lace, which greatly became her dark beauty, and a locket which he had treasured all his life as it contained one of the few portraits he had seen of his mother, set in a simple silver mounting. He had threaded it on a fine silver chain, and as he clasped it at her bidding, he noticed how soft and white her skin was at the nape of her neck above the fastening of her dress, and how the wisps of her dark hair strayed across it, escaping from the ribbon that bound her chignon.

Her mother greatly admired the gift. 'It is a very precious present to give my daughter, Herr Froebel. I hope you will not regret parting with such a memento of your dear mother.' She gave him a quizzical look which made the colour mount to his face.

'Indeed I shall never regret it, ma'am,' he said. 'I am honoured that Henrietta should accept it.' It was a bold speech and he wondered at himself for having the courage to say it.

Later, when her parents had retired, Henrietta and Ernestine were left alone with Friedrich. Ernestine admired the locket. 'Your mother was a very lovely lady,' she told him. 'How sad that you never knew her. I never knew my real mother either,' she added thoughtfully, 'but Mütterchen here'—she kissed Henrietta—'has been all a sweet mother could ever have been to me...'

Henrietta fondled the young girl's hair and returned her kiss.

How lovely they looked together, thought Friedrich: one dark and one fair, one with the mature calm of experience but still beautiful, the other on the threshold of life, eager and expectant.

Now Ernestine turned her bright face towards him in youthful frankness. 'Are you and Mütterchen going to be married?'

'Tina!' Henrietta blushed. 'You must not say such things... it is very rude!'

Friedrich laughed. 'Don't scold her!' he said. 'It's Christmastide. She is young and romantic, it's unfair not to share our happy secret with her. Yes, Tina, I *do* hope to marry your Mütterchen, but first I must ask her father, which I intend to do tomorrow. Until then you must keep our secret. Will you promise? It would be very discourteous if he were to hear it from you before I have spoken to him.'

'Oh, I promise, I promise!' Ernestine's eyes were sparkling and she jumped up and clapped her hands... then suddenly stopped, as if remembering

something. 'But if you marry, will she have to leave Berlin? To leave me?'
'No, no liebling!' cried Henrietta. 'You will come with me, won't you? To live with us at Keilhau, where Uncle Friedrich has his new school. You will love it there, it is in the country and very pretty.'
'Oh, I know I will love it!' Ernestine was sparkling again. 'And I love you too!' she added impulsively and threw her arms round Friedrich and kissed him. He lifted her up although she was a tall girl for her age, laughing up at her merry face and her fair curls bobbing in the candlelight. 'You shall be the first girl in my boys' school!' he said. 'How shall you like *that*, little Tina? Do you think they will bully you?'
'Indeed they shall not! I can hold my own with any boys... you ask Uncle Middendorff, he knows! I can run fast and climb trees and do a thousand things as well as any boy!'
'So she can!' laughed Henrietta. 'And often I have had to scold her for it. She is a tomboy, I fear, one day I shall have to try and turn her into a young lady.'
'There's time enough for that,' said Friedrich, suddenly serious. 'Time enough and too little time. Stay as young as you can for as long as you can, dear Tina, for all our sakes.' Tina was irrepressible for the rest of the evening, so much so that had it not been near to bedtime, Henrietta and Friedrich feared that their secret would be discovered.
'That child is over-excited,' said Henrietta's mother. 'All this gift-giving and rich food has been too much for her.'
On Christmas Day, after they had attended morning service, Friedrich took the opportunity of the time before the mid-day meal to approach the general, who was sitting alone in his library. He was a handsome old man, tall, though slightly bent now with his years, with a proud head and a mane of white hair.
'What do you want of an old war-horse like me?' he asked. 'Help for your new-fangled school no doubt! Well, I warn you, I've no patience with these modern educational ideas. The old way was good enough for us. All this playing about never did children any good, they need discipline.'
'Discipline, yes, Sir, all young things need discipline, I don't dispute it— young plants, young animals— but it must be *natural* discipline... training them in the way nature intended, not in the way we may want to force them.'
'I don't know what you are talking about,' said the old man tersely. 'But it all sounds a lot of nonsense to me... and I've already told you... you're a nice young fellow, but you can't talk me round. You'll get no help for your school from me, for all young Middendorff may do to try and persuade me. I hear you've involved him in all these mad schemes of yours.'
'I did not involve him, sir, he *is* involved, but it is his own decision. In fact it

was he who inspired me to start my own school . . . if you can call six little boys in a farmhouse by such a grand name. In any case, it is not for help with my scheme that I have come to see you.'

'Then what *do* you want?'

Friedrich felt it was no use bandying words with this abrupt old man.

'I want to marry your daughter, Henrietta.'

'Henrietta! Marry her?' The proud old face flushed, the eyebrows bristled, he half rose in his chair and choked on his words.

'God Almighty! And Christmas-tide too! How dare you come into my home as a guest at this season and have the effrontery to ask my permission to carry off my daughter to your god-forsaken, hare-brained school in the wilds of the country, without a penny to bless yourself with, no prospects, no sensible plans for the future! Dammit man, are you out of your mind? Go on with your wild schemes if you want to but don't involve poor Henrietta in them! Hasn't she had enough trouble in her life already? I suppose you know about that?'

'I know all I need to know,' said Friedrich calmly, 'and I was very sorry to hear it. I had hoped in a small way to make up to her for any unhappiness she may have had in the past.'

'Make it up to her! You'll make it up to her!' the old man stormed, 'At least she might have chosen a *man,* not an eccentric dreamer! Whatever her husband may have been, at least he was a practical fellow with good prospects. Perhaps you think she has money to invest in your scatterbrained schemes. If you do, you are wrong. She hasn't a penny, except for the small allowance I make her, and she shan't have that if she chooses to go gallivanting off with you!'

Her father's shouting had brought Henrietta and her mother from where' they had been quietly arranging the table. Now they stood outside the library door unashamedly and fearfully eavesdropping.

There was little more to hear.

'No! . . . that's my final word. No! And again No!' The general emphasised his refusal by stamping his foot. 'I cannot stop Henrietta doing what she wants to do, she is no longer a child, but whatever she does with you it will not be with my blessing. Now go! You've ruined my Christmas.'

Friedrich left the room, almost knocking over Henrietta and her mother, the latter flushed and twittering with distress while Henrietta herself was pale and calm. 'If you are leaving I am leaving too,' she said.

Friedrich put his arm round her. 'Don't do that,' he begged her. 'You will make them all unhappy and really spoil the feast that I have already put in jeopardy. I will go, but not far, don't worry, and later when things are calmer I will return. You will have had time to think.' He kissed her on the cheek and went upstairs to his room.

Once there he sat down on the bed trying to collect his own thoughts. He had not expected the general to be over-whelmingly in favour of his proposal but this vehement rejection had shaken him. Say Henrietta decided to abide by her father's advice? The thought of losing her made him cold with distress, he could not believe that there had ever been a time when he had not wanted her to be his wife. All the time, at Griesheim and Keilhau every plan, every achievement, had been incomplete until he had been able to write to her with news of it.

Downstairs the sounds of Christmas festivity were already invading the house. Ernestine was playing a little carol that she had been practising for weeks; he was to have sung it with her and he imagined her disappointment when she heard that he was not to be there. She alone of all of them would know why. Delicious smells of food also crept up into the top floors of the house. All this only served to accentuate his own unhappy position, to which was added a new fear, something which had always lurked in the back of his mind since he had revealed his feelings to Traugott long ago in Jena: a painful uncertainty which had made him shy away from the thought of marriage, the fear that physical intimacy might revolt him.

He knew he did not lack spiritual passion: his feelings for Lotte and, lately, for Henrietta made this plain, but more than this he had never known. He was embarrassed in his soldiering days when his companions, moved by wine and homesickness, had recalled their conquests, afraid that they might discover that for all his mature years he was uninitiated in those arts of love that they found so commonplace, if delightful. Henrietta's father had even accused him of unmanliness. Perhaps it showed in his manner? Horrible doubts beset him, far worse than his immediate disappointment.

He was still sitting miserably on his bed when the early darkness of December dimmed the room. Earlier Henrietta had crept upstairs and left a tray of food for him but he had not had the heart to touch it. The party was still progressing downstairs when he put on his cloak and slipped quietly down into the hall. He was just opening the front door to let himself out when he heard a light step behind him. It was Henrietta. She too was cloaked. She put her finger to her lips and indicated to him to continue, following him into the street.

It was cold... a light powdering of snow making dizzy patterns in the light of the street lamps. She slipped her hand into his own and he saw that she was still wearing his locket.

'You shouldn't have come, it's very cold,' he said.

'It was colder inside without you. Don't worry about father... his bark is worse than his bite, and in any case it makes no difference. You were going to marry a poor enough wife anyway, now I am afraid she will just be poorer!' She laughed and looking down at her he caught the laughter in her eyes and laughed too. His doubts and fears seemed groundless now as they walked together through the silvered streets, the light snow crunching under their feet and the church bells chiming for Evensong.

*   *   *

Friedrich returned to Keilhau in early January. He had spent the rest of his Christmas holiday at his old lodging and had not returned to Henrietta's home, although they had met daily... precious hours in odd meeting-places: in their old museum gallery, in the university library, in cafés, even in churches, anywhere where they could be alone and whisper their plans for the future.

His departure from his house had not lessened her father's fury. 'He's hardly spoken to me since,' Henrietta told Friedrich. 'Mother is not so bad about it, but she's completely dominated by father. Oh, it makes me furious to hear her! "Yes, dear," "No, dear," as if she had no right to have a mind of her own.'

'By the end of the summer all will be ready,' Friedrich told her. 'Our schoolhouse will be finished and I will have a home for you and Tina to come to... Oh, Henrietta! You will love it there, I know you will. The farmhouse is on the hillside and in the autumn the woods are burning with colour, flaming and glowing! You'll love the children too! Little Wilhelm is such a merry little fellow, full of energy and fun. Ferdinand, his brother, is a dreamer... they say he takes after me, so be warned! The other boys, Marte's sons, are charming lads. Julius is the adventurous one—he goes off for long walks alone in the hills, searching for new plants for his collection. Karl is the leader of them all, although he is only a middleman in years; it's always Karl who decides what game they shall play. And finally there is Theodor... he's the artist of the family. Do you know, he actually helped me in the drawing-up of the plans for the schoolhouse and garden, although he is only ten?'

Henrietta listened with glowing attention to his plans and his dreams, adding her own to them. In the cold of December their hearts were warmed by the thought of September to come.

Their parting was alleviated by the anticipation of the work ahead. Back at Keilhau the boys welcomed Friedrich with tremendous excitement, during the time he had been away they had carried on working on small jobs in the schoolhouse, even the littlest of them doing something. Julius had put up shelves, Karl and Theodor had polished the wood walls until they shone like satin, and between them Willi and Ferdinand had gone out into the winter woods gathering enough tinder to keep the school-room fire burning for many weeks.

Marte, too, was delighted to see him. On his part the meeting with her again embarrassed him. He was still very conscious of the thoughts sown in his mind by Middendorff, thoughts heightened now by the warmth of her greeting. 'I've missed you so!' she said. 'It's so lovely now that we are all together again.'

He knew he could not now delay telling her the news that he had already broken to Middendorff. As he expected, his friend was delighted. 'My dear fellow!' he cried. 'We knew you would! Heinrich and I had bets on it, if you must know! And I've won! He said next Christmas, I said the autumn... but we both agreed it must be' then he added soberly 'Have you told Marte?'

'No. Do you think you could tell her?'

'Oh no!' Middendorff was adamant. 'That's not fair, Friedrich, I know it will be difficult but it would hurt her much more if she were to hear it from anyone but you.'

So he told her, one evening when they were alone together in the schoolhouse sorting out the children's playthings. He told her quickly, perhaps brutally, because he had to get it over before he lost the courage to do it at all.

'I'm engaged to be married, Marte.'

He heard the quick intake of her breath, but it was the only break in her composure.

'Oh Friedrich, how lovely! I'm so glad! Is it Henrietta? Wilhelm and Heinrich have told me about her. I am sure she is a very sweet person.'

Friedrich looked at her. Dear, gentle Marte, unselfish and brave. Was Wilhelm right when he said that she loved him? Looking at her now he saw that her eyes were soft with tears.

'Marte! Don't be sad! This is happy news. You have told me I should marry, and it will make no difference to your part here. You are an essential member of our community.'

'No, Friedrich,' she said sadly. 'I cannot stay. A home can only have one housewife. It would not be fair to your bride for her to come into a house where another woman held the reins, and I could not play second fiddle. I am not big enough. You see.' she looked frankly up at him—'once I thought that I might be that housewife when you were so kind to me and to my boys.'

So Middendorff was right. Friedrich was hot with embarrassment.

'Marte...I did not...could not...you know I love you as a beloved sister... for his sake, for Christoph's... and I love your sons as if they were my own. Forgive me, Marte, if I have in anyway misled or distressed you, for I never intended to do so.'

'No.' Marte replied. 'It was no fault of yours. It was my own foolishness. You see, you are so like Christoph. I see, in my longing for him, his face in yours every time I look at you. But it is memory I love, Friedrich, only memory. Thank God for us both that you have not let me try to make that dream a reality. A man cannot live as the shadow of another, even if that other is his brother. It would have brought unhappiness to us both.'

'But what will you do?' Friedrich was anxious for her. She looked so small and frail and alone, kneeling there among a disarray of toys on the schoolroom floor. 'Must you go? Henrietta will love you I know, for all your fears. Why not stay and go on with us as now, together?'

'No.' She was adamant. 'It is better this way. I will not leave immediately, but later, in the summer, before Henrietta comes here, I will go. I have friends at Volkstadt who will welcome me I know, and you shall care for my boys as you care for them now.'

After that evening she never referred to the subject again. She was cheerful and normal in her manner, working busily about the house, helping in the school, preparing meals and generally sharing in the happy life of the community.

Towards the time of her intended departure she came to Friedrich one afternoon as he was busy fixing tiles on the roof of an extension to the schoolhouse. She watched him silently for a while, and when he stopped working and looked down at her she smiled up at him.

'Your Schoolhouse is growing,' she said.

'Not mine,' he told her. 'Yours... it's your farm, Marte. We are only here by your graciousness... I never forget that.'

'That is why I have come to you here,' she said. 'I have just heard from my lawyers, Friedrich. Keilhau is yours.'

'Mine!' Friedrich nearly fell from his place astride the roof. 'Marte! What are you saying?'

'Simply that I have arranged for Keilhau to be made over to you, the land and the buildings, for the school which you founded for my sons.'

It was a strange situation in which to receive such momentous news; she on the ground below him in her kitchen apron, her sleeves rolled up from baking, he on his roof, hammer in hand, the hot sun burning the back of his neck. Descending the ladder, dropping his tools on the grass beside her, he took Marte in his arms and kissed her.

'Dear, gentle Marte! How can I ever thank you? Are you sure? Are you really sure?'

'Quite sure,' she said calmly and smiling. 'I know that Christoph would want it to be this way. I have never felt closer to him than I do now.'

He could not wait to tell Middendorff and Langethal and when they heard they too hugged Marte and kissed her.

'We spent the evening rejoicing,' Friedrich wrote to Henrietta. 'For the first time after so many tribulations and problems I felt that fortune was beginning to smile upon our venture. From now on we can look forward to even greater things. We are working very hard on the buildings and you should be greatly surprised by our progress when you arrive here.'

In late August, Friedrich left Keilhau again for Berlin. This time Middendorff travelled with him, Langethal staying behind to attend to matters during their absence. Marte's sons had gone to join their mother at Volkstadt for the summer holidays and Wilhelm and Ferdinand had returned to their family at Osterode. In fact, news from Osterode was the only cloud on the horizon when Friedrich set out on what was to be his wedding journey. Christian's wife had just written to him in concern about Lotte: 'She does not look well,' she wrote. 'She has grown so thin and pale and is troubled by a cough which she has been unable to shake off since last winter. I have begged her to go away for a rest but she says she cannot leave the children.'

Friedrich added his concern to that of his sister-in-law and had written to Lotte urging her to take this advice. She knew of his forthcoming marriage and had written to him long and lovingly of her thoughts and good wishes for his happiness. Of her health she added only a postscript: 'Do not worry about me... I am as strong as an ox.'

*   *   *

In Berlin, Friedrich's reunion with Henrietta was all he had dreamed of and more. She greeted him with tenderness, her dark eyes sparkling and his heart quickened at the sight of her, the warmth of her smile and the eager way in which she listened to and questioned all his news of Keilhau and the home that awaited her there.

Middendorff was delighted in his friend's happiness.

The wedding was to be very quiet as Henrietta's father was still unreconciled to her marriage and it seemed as if there would be no one there except bride and bridegroom and their two witnesses, Middendorff and Ernestine. Friedrich was sorry that none of his brothers could be present, but Christian was much occupied with his work at Osterode and Traugott, still at

Stadt Ilm (where he had recently been appointed burgomaster), was a busy doctor. Neither could be expected to make the long journey to Berlin.

The days before the wedding were busy. Friedrich and Middendorff had many purchases to make for the school. Their visits to the city were few and they needed books and other supplies difficult to obtain in the nearer towns.

Henrietta was equally occupied in her final packing for a new and entirely different life. Consequently, meetings between her and Friedrich were brief for a betrothed couple on the eve of marriage. These times were all the more precious and consisted of walks by the river in the warm September evenings, short meetings in one of the little coffee-houses, or quiet moments in the garden of her father's house, when he was away during the day at the War Office, where he still worked although in semi-retirement. Henrietta's mother believing that such meetings did not strictly defy her husband's decree that 'the schoolmaster shall not enter my house again.'

The ease of their relationship seemed unaffected by the length of their parting since Christmas.

'I can hardly wait for you to see all we have done at Keilhau!' Friedrich told her. 'I know you will love it. It will be quiet after your life here in Berlin... no parties, no friends except for Middendorff and Heinrich Langethal and the children. You won't be lonely, liebchen?'

'Lonely!' she laughed. 'Friedrich! With all those children! How could anyone be lonely among the merry throng that you have assembled there. I am only afraid that we will never have a moment alone with each other!' She took his hand, 'And you, Friedrich. Are you sure? Am I *really* the one to share this great adventure with you?'

'There could be no other...'

'Not even Lotte...?' She had said it—what she had never before dared to say, the question always in her heart.

The name lay like a ghost between them. He drew a deep breath and looked at her honestly.

'Not even Lotte.' It was not enough, he knew. He went on bravely, praying for the right words that would not betray his memories or his loyalty, yet would reassure her whom he now loved with all his soul.

'Lotte was the sweet companion of my childhood... the lost dream of my youth. Now she is my dear friend. I hope she will be your friend too, Henrietta, but you... you are to be my wife.'

Now she looked fully and frankly into his eyes, deep-set eyes in a dark, intelligent face, thin-nosed, high cheek-boned. He heard the catch in her breath, almost a sob, and saw that her eyes were filled with tears.

'Oh Henrietta...' He held her to him. 'My dear, sensible, wise Henrietta!

Have you really been jealous of little Lotte?'

She nodded dumbly, her head buried on his shoulder as he held her close to him, kissing her hair which always smelt so sweet. He was 38, almost middle-aged, and to be married tomorrow. As he stood with her in her father's garden, hidden from the house by the shrubberies, the fact of it hit him with sudden awareness, as if he was detached from the scene and looking down on it. He who had said with conviction that he would never marry. Holding her still close and looking over her dark head up into the dark branches of the trees, he prayed: 'Let me be worthy, God. Let me be worthy!'

They were married next day, quietly, according to the Lutheran form of service, with only Middendorff and Ernestine to see the minister bless their union. Friedrich had arranged to stay a few nights at his former lodging before they all journeyed back to Berlin together.

Henrietta had chosen for her wedding dress a travelling coat of deep blue which would be useful in the cold months to come. With it she wore a bonnet in matching velvet, tied with a wide ribbon bow under her chin. Her hands were concealed in a little beaver muff and a tippet of beaver-fur finished the neck of her coat. Seeing her, Friedrich could not believe that this pretty creature who was also so wise, could have chosen to cast her lot with him in the dream of his heart.

They celebrated together with a meal at one of the cafés where they used to meet, with Middendorff and Tina. The latter bubbling with excitement at the romantic occasion and keeping her companions busy with questions about Keilhau and the life that awaited her.

Middendorff took Tina back to her grandparents' house before returning to his own lodging, leaving Friedrich and Henrietta alone in the room where he had spent his student days in Berlin before the war and later when he was working at the museum. It was a small, sparsely furnished room but clean and tidy and blessed with a tall window which presented a roof-top view of the city, now silvered by the light of a full harvest moon.

Friedrich lit the lamp and Henrietta took off her bonnet and tossed it on to the bed with its clean white counterpane. It lay there, its blue ribbons looking strangely out of place in the austere masculine surroundings. She unbuttoned her coat and he saw that beneath it she was wearing a dress of warm chestnut brown with buttons from neck to waist, closely fitting her slim figure. How lovely she was! The incredibility of the situation still amazed him ... frightened him. The dress revealed the curves of her still youthful high bust, and his eyes, drawn to the beauty of its little flaring points, brought a flush to his face which embarrassed him. She seemed to sense his feeling, for it was she who moved towards him, who raised her hand and gently touched his cheek.

'Have you nothing to say to your wife, Friedrich?' her voice was gently mocking, the humour which had always delighted him.

'Only that I love you... that I love you so much that I am afraid.'—he had admitted it to her—'afraid that I have been so busy planning other men's lives that I have not learned the lessons of my own. It all seemed so easy, and now, now that we are truly together, man and wife, I am afraid that my ignorance will displease you, that I will fail you.'

'Fail me?' Henrietta puckered her brows. 'Friedrich, you could never do that.'

He turned his back on her and gazed out at the familiar roof-top scene that had so many times earlier been his consolation and pleasure, but now served to hide his embarrassment.

'I told you long ago,' he reminded her, recalling the time when in a mood of nostalgic revelation he had unburdened some of the distress and confusion he had suffered in his boyhood.

'But Friedrich, those things are long ago. You were only a child!'

'I know I was a child. But am I yet a *man*? Oh Henrietta!' He buried his face in his hands; the thought of what he was trying to say appalled him. She was standing behind him. Her hands on his shoulders, and he felt her breath softly warm on the back of his neck as she answered him.

'I think I know what you are trying to say.'

Did she? He still could not face her. How had he dared marry her? How had he dared not to say what he was saying now before they had reached the point of no return? But she went on talking, her face pressed against the rough stuff of his coat, her body so close to his that she could feel the beating of his heart against her own ribs.

'I understand,' she said. 'You forget my years with Fritz.' The memory of them still horrified her. 'It was worse for me, Friedrich. I am no longer a child, but I was a child *then,* when I married him...'

He turned now, warmed by her confidence, by her tenderness. She continued: 'It was I who was afraid then, Friedrich.' She was looking up at him, and her eyes had tears in them. It was only the second time in their long knowledge of each other that he had seen her so moved... and that twice in two days.

He kissed her with tenderness... it was a kiss of understanding, of promise, which warmed to passion as her lips parted softly against his own.

He lifted her up into his arms as he had carried little Lotte across the brook long years ago. The feeling came surging back, timeless, as his body, still strong and youthful. bore the weight of Henrietta. Then it had been the feeling of a boy; now it was that of a man. It was a feeling of protection, of strength of rising passion. Later, her soft body close to his in the dark, his hands exploring the secret sweetness of her, he knew the time had come at last, the time that Traugott had told him *would* come, that night in Jena when he was a young boy, puzzled and ashamed... and he was no longer afraid.

*   *   *

They left Berlin on a warm late September day, accompanied by Ernestine and Middendorff, loaded with luggage, books and bundles—all the paraphernalia of a happy journey—and arrived at Keilhau in equally lovely weather. The farm was smiling to greet them among the autumn woods, the stubble cornfields on the hillside golden in the sunshine and late poppies still glowing in the hedgerows.

The children had already returned and had spent days preparing their welcome. Sheaves of corn and poppies decorated the house and schoolroom, branches bright with berries garlanded the doorway, and as Friedrich led Henrietta through the front porch, little Wilhelm, his merry face flushed with excitement and embarrassment, thrust a posy of late roses into her hand.

Langethal welcomed them back with delight: there was so much news to exchange, so many plans to make, that they all sat up very late, long after the children had gone to bed.

The first evening of their return set the pattern for the days to come: days filled with the busy adventures of the school, and nights talking, planning, adding accounts—always adding accounts and seldom making them balance. Their impecunious situation did not worry them greatly. Henrietta proved a clever housekeeper, and there was always plenty of produce from the surrounding farms and their own garden. The children regarded gardening as a game, and if anything preferred growing vegetables and fruit, with the sense of actually producing something which could be used, to flowers, which already grew all around them naturally on the hillside meadows.

They also entered with a will into the work on the schoolhouse, and soon the measuring of timber, the drawing of plans, the calculating of the amount of bricks or mortar they would need, became a practical part of their arithmetic lessons. The little ones made models, the older ones drew up professional-looking bills of quantities, kept accounts, made reports, wandering around the outbuildings with books and papers like a band of businessmen.

Less serious were their expeditions into the hills when, led by Friedrich or one of the other grown-ups, they would spend a whole day walking, collecting wild flowers, listing the plants and trees, exploring the water-life in ponds and streams, coming home at dusk, hot and tired but full of the interest and excitement of the day.

The days, the months, sped by. Christmas came and went, the spring gave way to summer, long, hot days, a lot of work on the school buildings, lessons in the open air and the old delights of blackberrying and apple-picking, children and adults working side by side in the orchard with the wasps buzzing drunkenly, soused with apple juice, and the September sky deep blue between the branches above.

It was an idyllic existence which should have been marred by their constant lack of money. However, all went well otherwise, so this could not instil a sense of real anxiety in any of them, least of all Friedrich, who saw in the thriving children, growing in stature both mentally and physically, the happiness of his friends and best of all the happiness of Henrietta, his life's dream coming true before his eyes. From its first day his marriage had proved to be a union of mind and body which he never dreamed was possible and still had him humble and amazed.

Tina had an added delight to her life, the companionship of Heinrich Langethal. Almost from the moment of her arrival she had attached herself to the young professor, a handsome 26 and some years her senior, but who accepted her devotion with reciprocal admiration and affection. Being older than the other children she needed a certain amount of individual instruction, and Langethal appointed himself her personal tutor, much to her delight.

Willi was now nearly ten and Ferdinand twelve; both had grown almost beyond belief and brought back to their parents at Osterode the living proof of the success of Friedrich's methods. Christian was particularly delighted that his faith in his brother had been so well-founded. He had always secretly fretted over his own lack of further education, the small manse fortune having been expended on Christoph and Traugott at Jena University while he had been apprenticed to a trade. Now he saw his sons working towards the goal he himself had never achieved he was overjoyed. His wife shared his enthusiasm, even when he suggested that the two younger girls might share their brothers' life at Keilhau. Albertine, the eldest daughter, was now 19, Emilie not yet 16 and little Elise not quite six.

'The only thing is that I shall miss them terribly,' said his wife. 'The house won't be the same without the children and Keilhau is a long journey from here. Elise is still a baby... perhaps Emilie should go alone—after all, she will have the boys there to keep her company.'

Friedrich made no secret to Christian of the fact that the financial position of Keilhau left much to be desired. He wrote with good humour: 'If only the money grew on the trees like the apples we should have little to worry about. Unfortunately my creditors all have full orchards of their own... so I cannot pay my bills in kind!'

Doubtful as to her reaction, Christian broached his wife with an idea that they might in some way assist the struggling school at Keilhau. 'We have a little saved,' he said, and the boys are progressing so wonderfully there. What do you say? Can we spare them a little to get them out of their immediate difficulties?'

The answer she gave surprised him. 'I have a better idea,' she said. 'It will solve both problems, for then little Elise can join her brothers and sister: let us *all* go to Keilhau. Let us throw our fortune, such as it is, in with that of Friedrich and Henrietta! I am sure we will never regret it. You have always hated your life at the mill: you could be happy at Keilhau and I would be happy with you!'

Christian was overjoyed: for months this had been a secret desire he had hardly dared to admit even to himself. Now it seemed that his wife had read into his thoughts and grown to share the desire with him. He embraced her fondly. 'Of course we shall go!' he cried. 'Of course we shall! It is the turning point in our lives!'

Within months they had wound up their affairs at Osterode. Their only sorrow in leaving was the inevitable parting from their friends and neighbours, the Levins. Elise particularly grieved at the prospect of losing her friend Luise, a year her junior and an inseparable companion. Even the promise that she should have all the toys discarded in the move would not console Luise, who regarded the older little girl as a sister. The other children were equally upset at the thought of leaving their friends behind and promises were exchanged that visits should be made at least once a year.

Christian was deeply anxious over Lotte. Her health had not improved, she tired easily, and her once glowing complexion was pale and transparent. He urged her to see a doctor. 'Friedrich would grieve if he were to see you now,' he said. But she, as usual, rejected his concern. 'We all grow older,' she said. 'Some grow fat... some thin. I am one of the thin ones!'

Christian and his family arrived at Keilhau in the early summer of 1820. It was a joyous arrival. Albertine immediately took to the pretty Tina and they became bosom companions. Middendorff, now 27, was equally delighted by Albertine's arrival, and as Langethal had devoted himself to Tina, he took charge of her pretty companion, the four of them spending their leisure hours picnicking together in the woods or taking a boat on the river which flowed through the farm fields at the bottom of the hill.

Christian not only added his small fortune to the project but the labour of his hands, and worked throughout the long light midsummer days until late in the evening, building additions to the schoolhouse and outbuildings, always with a band of young assistants, sometimes getting in the way but insisting on trying to be helpful.

Life at Keilhau was very happy that summer.

CHAPTER EIGHT

It was two years before the main school house building was completed—simple and unpretentious, but light and airy and big enough for more pupils than it was required to house. The time had gone so quickly, the days so full of activity, the happiness of the household so satisfying, that none of them could believe that so many months had actually passed by.

One of the first visitors to Keilhau after its completion was Middendorff's nephew, his sister's son, a young divinity student, Johannes Barop. He was nearly 21 and in his first year at Halle University. He was deeply impressed with what he saw and, after he had returned to his parent's home at Dortmund, wrote to say that he would be overjoyed to join the Keilhau community at the earliest opportunity.

When he was not teaching or building, Friedrich was writing. Keilhau lacked only pupils. The way to get pupils was to spread the knowledge of the existence of Keilhau abroad: soon its founder pupils, Marte's sons, Willi and Ferdinand, would be grown up and beyond the limits of Keilhau. Without fresh blood Friedrich realised his dream of the education of men must die. He worked late into the night, sometimes all night, much to Henrietta's concern.

'You'll make yourself ill,' she warned. 'A man cannot work *all* hours.'

But he would not listen. Already his *Letter to the German People,* published several years earlier, had received some publicity, not all of it favourable.

Again Henrietta counselled him. 'Don't make it too obtuse! Others do not think as you do, Friedrich. If you cannot take them into the depths of your mind, at least enable them to skim over the surface and learn a little that way.'

He tried to explain some of his work to her.

'No one thinks of interfering with young plants or little animals,' he said. They are left in peace, yet young human beings are looked upon as pieces of wax that can be moulded into a set pattern, regardless of its natural inclinations.'

One day, when they were in the garden together, they came upon Elise, now ten, collecting stones from the stream which flowed between the orchard and the out-buildings.

'What are you doing?' Friedrich asked her.

'I am making a fairy grotto.' She took his hand and led him to a corner where she had arranged the stones with fern fronds and tiny wildflowers into a little garden barely a foot square. 'They don't look so pretty now though,' she said, disappointed. 'When I took them out of the stream they were all coloured and shiny. Now they are all dry and dull. Why is it, Uncle Friedrich? Why don't they stay pretty?'

'Because they are meant to be in the water and you have moved them,' he said. 'All things are best where they are meant to be... but never mind. It is still a pretty garden and you have made it very well.'

Later he described the incident to Christian.

'As I watched her,' he said, 'I realised that to her these pebbles in the water were the material with which she was building her dream-world. A child must know all about all things... their innermost nature. That's why the baby takes an object in his little hand, holds its, strokes it, looks at it, even puts it in his mouth and sucks it, sometimes breaks it. I well remember as a little boy breaking an egg to get out the chicken that Christoph told me lived inside and weeping bitterly to find nothing but a mess of yoke!'

Christian and his family had frequent letters from Osterode but seldom from Lotte, who occasionally wrote to Friedrich letters full of news about her growing family but little about herself.

In June 1823 Friedrich had a letter from Osterode in a strange hand. When he saw it something about it disturbed him: who would write to him but Lotte? It must be bad news... she must be ill. He slit the letter urgently in his alarm, startling Henrietta as they sat at the breakfast table. There was silence as he read—cold silence which held his heart and brought a chill sweat to his brow and made the neat, small writing of Lotte's husband merge into an unintelligible blur. Lotte, his beloved Lotte, was dead, at the age of 41 from the lingering illness which had disturbed and distressed them all but which she, in her concern for her young family, had chosen to ignore until it was too late.

Friedrich wept openly as he told Henrietta. She took him in her arms, stroking his back as if he was a child in need of comfort and pressing her lips against his hair.

'Friedrich... Friedrich!' she comforted, 'Lotte will never die in your heart and I would not have it so! Dreams never die and to you Lotte will always be alive and beautiful, always 15, as she was when you were children together. Only you and I will grow old.' She looked sadly beyond him, beyond the bowed head, stroking the nape of his neck with a gentle hand. She was a remarkable woman, Henrietta, without envy or jealousy, possessing an infinite tenderness.

*   *   *

That summer, Lotte's sons came to stay at Keilhau for a happy holiday with Willi and Ferdinand, their old friends from Osterode. With Karl, Julius and

Theodor they set off on long walks over the mountains, camping out under the stars, cooking their own food, growing sun-tanned and strong-legged with open-air and exercise. When the weather was not so good they would sit for hours making a model farm for little Luise, left behind at home as she was too young to go on a holiday by herself.

Stunned by the death of Lotte, Friedrich tried to bury his sorrow by working even harder on his pamphlets and his book. All the pamphlets he published privately, although Middendorff, in particular, warned him that it was a mistake. 'It's too expensive,' he said. 'Let the publishers bear the cost.'

'And take the profit,' said Friedrich.

'My dear friend, you'll be lucky if you make a penny profit... the public does not buy such books for fun. A good publisher would know his market, however, and get your works to the right people.'

'I shall still publish them privately,' said Friedrich stubbornly.

The following Christmas he prepared as a surprise gift for his pupils and their parents, also his friends, a little book called *Christmas at Keilhau*. It was his fifth small work, but *The Education of Man* was still unfinished.

Less serious events still had their place in the life of Keilhau. The happy associations between Tina and Langethal, Middendorff and Albertine, had blossomed from friendship into romance. On her twenty-fourth birthday, three days after Christmas 1825, Albertine announced her engagement. Ernestine and Langethal had already become betrothed in the autumn of the same year and the girls planned a joint wedding in the coming May.

A new member had also joined the Keilhau community that year—a young man from Hildeurghausen, Wilhelm Carl, who came to teach music and singing. With him, and the regular visits of Johannes Barop, the school household was made happier than ever, particularly by the approaching marriage of four of its members.

The wedding was fixed for Ascension Day, 1826, and the ceremony had the added solemnity and promise of a dedication as well as a physical and spiritual union of four delightful young people.

The growing boys formed a choir for the simple service, Christian's younger daughters, Emilie and Elise, acted as bridesmaids, and the brides were dressed alike in simple white muslin dresses tied with blue ribbons, and carried posies of wild daisies and buttercups. The little church was decorated with flowers and garlands picked and arranged by the children.

Christian gave his daughter away and Ernestine was given to Langethal by Friedrich, for whom the marriage was the culmination of a friendship of many years with the young man he had first met on the march to Dresden nearly 13 years earlier.

He returned that evening to the farmhouse with Henrietta after the young couples had left on a brief honeymoon and wrote uninterrupted and inspired for the rest of the night, long after Henrietta had gone to bed and the pale crescent moon had faded into the light of the dawn sky. When he finally put down his pen *The Education of Man* was finished.

*   *   *

If all was harmony within at Keilhau, outside influences were not so favourable. The long turmoil of the Napoleonic wars had ended, but the youth of Prussia, intoxicated with the wine of liberty, and inspired by earlier events in France, were seething with rebellion. Students associations, mostly of a revolutionary kind, flourished at all the universities and the government became increasingly critical and alarmed. Any hope of financial assistance for any sort of educational movement from official sources was out of the question. The attitude of Henrietta's father towards the 'scatter-brained schoolmaster' was by no means unique.

The Education of Man, on which Friedrich had worked so long and with such dedication, received either the most unfavourable notices or, worse still, no notices at all. Friedrich, bitterly disappointed, wrote to Traugott at Stadt Ilm: 'I thought at least that scientific, learned men, the universities, would recognise my efforts and try to help me by word and deed. I was mistaken. The universities have paid no heed to the simple schoolmaster, and as for the able editors, they think very differently from me... in fact their notices seem mainly concerned with degrading me and my work. They are not even *constructive* in their criticism.'

Henrietta did her best to console him, but it was a bitter disillusionment. 'I'd have done better to have called my book *The Education of Footmen* or *Housemaids, Shoemakers or Tailors!*' he told her. 'Then I should have gained fame and glory for the great usefulness and practical nature of our institution, and everyone would have rushed to acclaim it as something worthy of support by the state. I should have been held as the right man in the right place by the state and the world, and much more so because as a state machine I should have been engaged in cutting out and modelling other state machines. But I only wanted to train up free-thinking, independent *men*... so no one is interested... and everyone is afraid.'

'Too damned independent,' said Henrietta's father when he read the book which his daughter had sent him, hoping it might change his opinion of her husband. 'If I had *my* way the authorities would put an end to the whole business! If you ask me he is training a band of young revolutionaries in that hill fortress of his at Keilhau.'

'The young revolutionaries' spent a happy summer, working and playing in the idyllic surroundings which even poverty could not affect... the hot sun on the water meadows, the cool shade of the woods, the nature walks, the singing in the evenings, and just the happiness of living at Keilhau, which seemed removed and remote from the turmoil of the outside world.

Johannes Barop was serving his year with the Army as a volunteer in Berlin, but spent any leaves he had at Keilhau, where he was obviously attracted not only by his interest in the educational experiment but by Christian's second daughter, Emilie, now 23 and a sweetly pretty girl with gentle ways. A practical man, he was delighted with life at Keilhau but rather horrified at its haphazard financial position.

'Your money is disappearing like drops of water on a hot stone!' he told Middendorff in alarm. 'Don't any of you realise that you are heading for disaster?'

From Yverden the news of the death of Dr Pestalozzi depressed Friedrich even further. It seemed that the lamp he had hoped to light was dying out; all he had was the love and loyalty of those few around him and the happiness of the children, now rapidly growing into young adults. Whether there would ever be any other children to follow in their pioneer footsteps at Keilhau seemed terribly uncertain.

The bills piled up. 'At times it seems as if the devil himself must be let loose against us,' Middendorff wrote to Barop, who had returned to Berlin. 'The number of our pupils has sunk and as the small receipts dwindle more and more, so the burden of our debts rises higher and higher till it has now reached a giddy height indeed.'

He was right. Creditors stormed from every side, urged on and accompanied by their lawyers. Only Middendorff seemed able to quieten them.

'You see them, Wilhelm!' Friedrich would beg him.

'You can *talk*, I cannot. I am either tongue-tied or, I lose my temper; either way they write me off as a madman.'

So Middendorff would plead, excuse, postpone, anything but pay the money which they had not got.

The worst creditor was an irritable builder from whom they had purchased a large quantity of timber and bricks on a year's credit, hoping that by then they would have been paying their way, but the debt was long overdue.

'We will take your children as pupils, free,' Middendorff offered but this only inflamed the man's temper.

'I'll be damned if you will!,' he stormed. 'Do you think I want my innocent offspring brought up as revolutionaries in this ridiculous establishment, run by that mad schoolmaster? Look at him!'—He pointed up at the hill behind the house 'There he goes as usual, afraid to look an honest man in the face.'

In the direction where the builder pointed, Middendorff could see a rangy figure walking among the trees. As usual, his friend had left the house by the back door as his creditor came in by the front. Most of them were too old, and certainly too fat, to follow him and they could only shout. Even then their words were soon lost on the wind.

Up on the hillside, however, Friedrich was by no means remote from the troubles below. The turmoil in his mind was not even soothed by the beauty around him. He tried to pray and failed; his mind was rivetted on practical problems, so that attempts at spiritual communion seemed almost blasphemous. When he was alone on the hillside he often thought of Lotte. Strangely her death had allowed him to think of her more often, without the guilt that he was being disloyal to Henrietta, in thought, if not in deed. Now, high above the neat little schoolhouse, surrounded by its garden, he thought how small it looked—how insignificant down there, just a speck in the rural landscape, his great dream which seemed to be coming to nothing.

Down below, Middendorff was dealing with another creditor, but a very different fellow from the earlier visitor. This was the village locksmith, a kindly man who had known Friedrich's brother Christoph and mourned his untimely death, and had affectionately watched his young sons growing up.

'I don't want my money,' he told Middendorff. 'I've not come for that. I've come to tell you not to worry. I know you'll pay me when you can, and don't take any notice of my lawyer! "Bring action against the scamps," he told me. I told *him*.' he said indignantly. '*Scamps* indeed! And me a member of the late young Pastor Froebel's flock at Griesheim! I told him I'd rather lose my hard-earned money than doubt your honour, and nothing was further from my thoughts than to add to your troubles in any way!'

The locksmith was only one of many kindly workmen and traders who forebore to press for their debts to be paid. Those who had children were invited to send them to the school and most of them accepted gladly.

So Keilhau continued, if precariously. In the following year, Barop concluded his Army service and came to live with his friends at the schoolhouse, much to the displeasure of his father, who refused him any assistance whatsoever.

But the fame, or infamy, of Keilhau was spreading further afield. Some six years earlier Friedrich had contributed some articles on his institution to a scientific journal in Rudolstadt called *Isis* founded and edited by the famous naturalist, Lorenz Oken. The articles were immediately criticised by the most eminent philosopher of the day, Karl Krause, who had been a professor at Jena but not in Friedrich's time there. Krause criticised, among other things, the aims of Keilhau as an educational centre for all Germany. The criticism had stung at the time but Friedrich, wrapped up in the practical affairs of teaching, building and writing, had no time for arguments. It was not until now, six years later, faced with the overwhelming problems of continuing at Keilhau in any form, that he gave thought again to Professor Krause's criticism of his schemes. Was the Professor right, then? Was he no more than the hair-brained dreamer that most people considered him? Friedrich's spirit was low and he was beginning to doubt himself. Searching, thinking, desperate for an answer, he set himself to reply to the Professor's theories.

Middendorff found him writing late at night, as he often did when Henrietta, worn out with the physical and mental exertion of the day, had gone wearily to bed.

'What good can it do?' Middendorff, battered by his eternal bargaining with creditors, was also beginning to despair. 'It's all so long ago, this man Krause will have forgotten us! And even if he has not, what can he do to help us? All he can give us is words. Words! Words! Words! There have been too many *words!* We want practical aid if we are to live.'

'And who can give us that?' Friedrich retorted irritably. Tempers lately had often become frayed in the tension of their situation.

They had not heard Henrietta come downstairs. She stood in the doorway, wrapped in her blue dressing-gown. Even in his misery Friedrich was intensely moved by her beauty as she stood there, her dark hair loose about her shoulders.

'Are you two arguing?' she scolded sadly. 'I heard you, you were shouting.'

'I'm sorry,' said Friedrich. 'It was selfish of us, we forgot you were trying to sleep.'

She smiled. 'Don't worry, I wasn't asleep. It's too hot tonight.' She looked out at the sullen dark clouds outside the window. 'And I, too, was shouting—to myself! I am as worried as you are, you know. It's my dream too.'

'Who do we know?' she went on, running her hand through her hair. 'Who will help us? Don't we know *anyone?*'

'There is the Duke, I suppose.' Middendorff was speaking in a doubtful, half joking way.

'The Duke? Do we know such a person? Which Duke?' Friedrich's surprise would not have been much greater had his friend suggested the Devil himself.

'The Duke of Meiningen.'

'Do you know him?'
'No, but Henrietta does.'
'Do you?' Friedrich was incredulous. 'Do you know the Duke of Meiningen? You have never mentioned him to me.'
Henrietta laughed. 'Wilhelm exaggerates,' she said. 'The Duke visited us once; he was concerned with some business with my father. I hardly spoke to him except briefly at dinner.'
'But could you claim any acquaintance? Enough to get us a hearing?'
She looked doubtful, then her face cleared 'We can try!' she said. 'Yes, we can try. I will write to him. Certainly he was a progressive man then—he had plenty of arguments with my father. They used to shout at each other, like you do!'
The tension broke between them just as outside the dark clouds rumbled with thunder and the first heavy rain began to fall. 'I'll write tomorrow,' said Henrietta, 'Before we lose our courage. After all, he cannot shoot us.'
'Can't he?' laughed Middendorff. 'With all the things that are being said of us I shouldn't be too sure of that!'
But they shared the joke with him and the future seemed at least a little brighter.
The Duke responded quickly. Of course he remembered Henrietta and he had heard of her husband's work. It interested him and he would like to hear more about it. 'As you know,' he wrote, 'I have long been interested in progressive education and am particularly concerned about the future tuition of my own son. I would be grateful if your husband could advise me in this direction also.'
The whole community at Keilhau threw itself with enthusiasm into the task of preparing a report for the Duke. Friedrich wrote immediately advising him on his son's future.
'Whatever form of education on which you eventually decide, he *must* be brought up with other boys. Children, just like young animals, do not thrive in solitude and often learn more from each other than we, who think ourselves so wise, can hope to teach them.'
The advice pleased the Duke for it co-incided with his own opinions. 'Come and see me,' he replied, 'and bring your plans with you.'
Friedrich travelled alone to the Werra Valley between the mountains of the Thüringen Wald and the Rhone. It was his first parting from Henrietta since they had been married.
He took with him an elaborate plan to which every member of the Keilhau community had contributed. The plan outlined an educational establishment in which not only academic subjects would be taught but crafts such as

carpentry, weaving and bookbinding. Half the school hours would be devoted to studies, the rest of the time to handicrafts.

The Duke, a lively, practical man, heard the scheme with interest. He liked the enthusiasm of the dark, intense schoolmaster, his frankness about his financial difficulties.

Friedrich brought with him some of the constructional toys he had already introduced to his younger pupils, fitting brick blocks, wooden balls, and other building materials.

'Children must do things to learn them!' he said. 'This way their minds become inquisitive and it is the searching mind that acquires knowledge, just as the dry soil soaks up rain. At Keilhau we lack technical teachers, but worst of all we now lack pupils. Is no one willing to believe in our ideas?'

The Duke listened patiently and at the conclusion of the interview he was brief and to the point.

'I have made up my mind,' he said. 'I like your plan and the complete and open way you have laid it before me. I shall make available to you my estate at Helba with 30 acres of land and a yearly subsidy of 1,000 florins. All I ask from you now in the form of a guarantee is that you should let me have some account of your past career, your academic qualifications and so on, so that I can satisfy my advisers and the parents of your future pupils whom I hope to find among my friends and acquaintances.'

When Friedrich returned to Keilhau the whole community was overjoyed. Ernestine, the most emotional of the young women, wept. Henrietta merely took his hand, but all her heart was in the warmth of her grasp.

For weeks Friedrich was occupied with his future plans. The letter to the Duke of Meiningen was long and detailed. In brief breaks from it he again took up his idea to reply to his old adversary, Professor Krause. The one letter was in some ways complementary to the other. Both were extremely lengthy, both gave the very fullest details of his early life and in some way gave him a feeling of relief, as if by expressing on paper some of his early sadness and disappointment he had purged his memory of its unhappiness.

Recalling his own schooling he wrote to Professor Krause: 'I want the exact opposite of what now serves as an educational method and teaching system ... the method which involves learning by rote dulls the edge of all real mental insight.'

Krause was impressed with this belated and lengthy reply to his earlier criticism. He replied in a friendly and enquiring letter in which he invited Friedrich to visit him at any time when his travels brought him near Gottingen.

Plans were practically completed for the move to Helba when Friedrich received a further letter from the Duke. Even its opening salutation chilled him, for instead of his now customary 'My dear Froebel.' the Duke began 'Dear Doctor.' The letter continued in most formal vein and explained that the Duke was having difficulty with his advisers, one of whom had warned him that the central government might not look favourably on his patronage of this educational movement, which some even regarded as revolutionary. Would it not be better perhaps to start in a more modest way? With 20 pupils only, as an experiment?

As Friedrich read the letter disappointment quickly boiled into fury. He tore the paper in two.

'I've finished!' he cried. 'I'll have no more. We are not paupers that we must take orders like this.'

In vain Middendorff and Langethal, Barop and even Henrietta, whose advice he usually took, argued with him in an attempt to persuade him to swallow his pride and grasp at least the straw which the Duke still offered him, but Friedrich was adamant.

When Barop, who had long been attached to Emilie, finally asked her parents to approve their marriage, Christian's wife asked him if they intended to stay at Keilhau.

'Yes,' he told her, 'I shall remain. I am sure that in the end men will come to believe in us.'

Christian had never doubted either and he grasped his future son-in-law's hand with affection. His wife was less confident: she and the other women at Keilhau were growing increasingly alarmed by the privations of life in the little upland community. Her older daughter, Albertine, and her husband had already had a baby girl and now Ernestine was expecting her first child. Every new member of the household was an extra burden, for though they never went actually hungry, there were sheets and blankets to be provided, and warm clothes, for the winter months in the hills could be very cold.

It truly seemed, as Middendorff had written bitterly some years before, 'that the devil himself must be let lose against them,' a belief strengthened by a tragedy which clouded the lovely summer of 1829. On a beautiful August evening, young Wilhelm Karl, whose music had done so much to cheer their dark days, was bathing in the nearby Saale when he was seized with cramp and drowned before any of his companions could reach him. He was buried after a simple service in the little church at the foot of the hill where he had so often led the children in their Sunday hymn-singing. The darkness had truly blotted out the sun for the Keilhau community.

* * *

Christmas was a poor pretence at merriment, kept only for the sake of the children. Early in the New Year, Friedrich received a final letter from the Duke, who had received further warnings of the possible dangers of the Helba project.

'I will not be *mistrusted!*' Friedrich stormed when he read the letter. 'Even Krause, who criticised me so bitterly, never doubted our honour.' When he and Middendorff had visited the old man at Gottingen some months previously he had received them with courtesy and honoured them with introductions to all his learned acquaintances at the university.

'I am going to Frankfurt.' he told Henrietta.

It was a sentimental journey. It brought back the memories of those days over 25 years ago when he had first decided that teaching was to be his vocation, at the Model School of Herr Gruner. Then he had been a boy, just 23. Now he was nearing 50. As he walked down the familiar streets he was overcome with nostalgia and sadness. His life was almost two thirds through its allotted span and he still was no nearer the fulfilment of his dream.

The most cheering aspect of his return to Frankfurt was the opportunity to visit Frau von Holzhausen, with whom he had kept up a regular correspondence throughout the years since he had been tutor to her sons, Hans, Georg and Pieter. They were now in their thirties, all married and living away from Frankfurt.

She received him with sentimental delight.

'We have never forgotten you,' she told him. 'Never! Come and see the room where you taught the boys. It's quite unchanged. I keep it that way always, although my husband laughs at me!' She led him upstairs to the little study which they had used as a schoolroom. It was exactly as he remembered it: the table, chairs and draperies looking strangely old-fashioned and on the walls the pictures the boys had painted, an illustrated map which Pieter had made after one of their many walks and excursions in the city. There, too, was the model of the farmhouse made by Hans, and some of the mats which Georg had woven with coloured straws. It should have all been sentimental and delightful but instead it served to heighten his nostalgia and depression.

'You look ill,' Frau von Holzhausen said anxiously. 'You have been overworking!'

'I am not ill,' Friedrich told her, 'Only worried and discouraged.'

'Discouraged?' she cried '*You* discouraged? You who were always filled with hopes and plans?'

'That was the young Froebel,' he said ruefully. 'The middle-aged Froebel— and I am middle-aged, you know—has run out of plans and hopes.'

'Oh no!' She was amazed at his despair. 'I have never known you like this!'

He told her of his latest disappointment. 'One cannot blame him,' he concluded, after describing the Duke's apparent change of heart. 'After all, our financial state at Keilhau is not exactly the best of references. We could paper the wall with our bills! Why, I have no longer much faith in myself. Why should he have faith in me?'

'I will not hear you talk like this!' Frau von Holzhausen was distressed and disturbed; she had never known him to have reached such depths of despair. 'We have only to think! Frankfurt is full of progressive intelligent people who will see the truth in your ideals and be eager to help you.'

Her optimism was not entirely justified. She invited several of her more influential friends to a soiree to meet the 'Professor from Keilhau.' They were politely interested but offered no practical assistance. One or two were even a little alarmed for fear of being associated with one who already had been labelled too progressive for safe conservative society. But one at least of Frau von Holzhausen's society friends remained behind after the others had left. His name was Schnyder, a Swiss musician, who had already gained some renown in Frankfurt for his compositions. He was on a visit from his home in Wartensee in the canton of Lucerne.

'Do you include music in your curriculum?' he asked Friedrich.

'Indeed yes... and particularly singing, which has a very important place in our system.'

'I am glad—I feel that to be very important.' Dr Schnyder spoke with difficulty in heavily accented Swiss-German but Friedrich found him intelligent and a congenial conversationalist. Their hostess had joined them, for the other guests, well satisfied with the food and the wine, had gone their several ways. She was frank in her appeal.

'I asked you tonight because I thought you at least of all of them might help Herr Froebel,' she told Schnyder.

'But, Madame, you know I am a poor man! I'd gladly help if I had any means, for I see a great deal of sense and truth in what I have heard from Herr Froebel tonight.'

'You may not have much money,' she said, 'but you have your castle at Wartensee. You know it's much too grand for you with your simple tastes. If Herr Froebel could leave Prussia, where he is being persecuted for his advanced ideas, I am sure he would progress better. The air of learning in Switzerland is freer than here. You are an independent people. He could breath more freely in your beautiful Lucerne.'

'Would you come to Lucerne?' Schnyder looked enquiringly at Friedrich.

'Gladly! Some of the happiest years of my life were spent in Switzerland—at Yverden with Dr Pestalozzi, when I was tutor to Madame's sons.'

'Then you are doubly welcome!' The kindly man held out his hand. 'Switzerland eagerly awaits your arrival! My humble home is at your disposal. The only thing I must insist is that you make no structural alterations. I am sure you will understand this reservation. The castle is my family home and I only hold it in trust.'

'Indeed, sir,' Friedrich told him. 'It is more than generous of you to offer us a home. I can assure you we would not abuse your kindness in any way.'

He returned to Keilhau jubilant. Perhaps after all the institution might survive. Henrietta shared his delight, as did all the others, but it was evident at least for the present that only a few of them could make the long and expensive journey, and in any case Keilhau, with all its effort, sacrifice and achievement, could not be abandoned lightly.

'Take Ferdinand,' said Henrietta. 'He is young and enthusiastic. He will work hard and be of great assistance to you.'

'But what about you?' Friedrich was concerned. He knew that the help of his young nephew, now 22, would be invaluable but his heart cried out that Henrietta herself should be his companion.

'I will join you later,' she told him. 'As soon as you are established you shall send for me and I will come flying. But in the meantime you need someone vigorous and active like Ferdi... and I am needed here.'

He embraced her tenderly—his faithful, adoring, wise Henrietta. At that moment the thought of parting from her, even for a short while, seemed almost unbearable.

Nevertheless, the opportunity could not be neglected or delayed. Ferdinand was delighted to be the one chosen to accompany his uncle on the long journey and to share with him the excitement of this new and vital project. They were given a festive send-off by the other members of the little community that was not without tears. Emilie was particularly sad that her beloved Oheim could not be there for her wedding to Johannes Barop, which had been fixed for Midsummer Day 1831.

Friedrich's happy memories of Switzerland were revived and intensified by the beauty of the Wartensee. The lake was smaller than that of Lucerne itself, but still beautiful. The mountains dropped into its calm depths with their feet in the water, their majestic outlines reflected in its mirror-like surface. The castle itself was elegant and beautifully appointed, and Herr Schnyder's welcome warm and generous.

'My home is yours,' he told Friedrich. 'The furniture, the plate, my library, which is quite extensive, you must use them all as if they were yours.'

Friedrich wrote to Henrietta: 'His generosity can never be too greatly admired or praised but I fear, for all their beauty, the rooms here do not lend themselves easily to our system and this can only be regarded as passing assistance of the most temporary nature. Also, I am much disturbed by the ill-will of some of the clergy. We had hoped to find complete freedom of thought here in Switzerland but I fear that here, too, bigotry and prejudice are rife.'

Friedrich and Ferdinand had by now been away from Keilhau for some months and this letter, and others in similar vein, alarmed Henrietta and Ferdinand's sisters, Albertine and Emilie. It was Emilie whose concern finally broke down the objections which the men of the community had made so far to any suggestion of interference with Friedrich's plans.

'You *must* go to him,' she urged her husband, Barop. 'Ferdinand is only a boy! What can he do to help Oheim? He needs someone like you...someone practical.'

It was brave of Emilie to suggest it. She knew that Henrietta was pining with anxiety but she too had her problems and fears, and she was carrying the child of the man she was urging to make a long and possibly hazardous journey.

Nevertheless, Barop agreed to leave Keilhau and go and see for himself exactly how they were getting on in Switzerland. With only ten thalers in his pocket, wearing his old summer coat and carrying a threadbare frock-coat over his arm, he started off to make the journey of many hundreds of miles, on foot, relying only on the kindness of passing travellers for the assistance of an occasional lift in a carriage or mail-coach.

It was an arduous journey, as he knew it would be, but eventually he arrived at Lucerne and from there made the final stage of his travels to Wartensee. He asked as he travelled if the people of the district had any news of Herr Froebel and his nephew. 'The heretics?' said one of the men he questioned, a storekeeper in a neighbouring village. 'They are well enough. We've nothing against them, but the priests warn us to have naught to do with them. They seem a harmless enough pair, for all their funny ways...always playing games they are with the children, though they be grown men, and one of them quite an old 'un, too.'

Barop found Friedrich and Ferdinand depressed. Surrounded by the splendid appointments of Schnyder's home, the beautiful furnishing, tapestries and pictures which if anything only served to emphasise their own poverty, they had made little or no progress.

'Our only pupils are the village children,' said Friedrich with a sigh. 'Dear little creatures they are...so merry and eager to learn. But where are the pupils that will *pay* for our school? We cannot run as a charity...much as we might like to. No children come from any distance because their parents are afraid to send them. I have told you of the hostility of the priests.'

Barop told him how he himself had heard them described as the 'heretics.'

'Heretics!' That is nothing!' Friedrich replied. 'Some have accused us of devilry and witchcraft—just because they saw me in a circle with the children playing a singing game!'

The weather did not reflect their unhappiness. The summer was glorious. The pines on the hillsides filled the air with their aromatic resinous scent and the sun shone from a clear sky from dawn to sunset. Barop, Friedrich and Ferdinand would walk together after the day's work, trying to be hopeful because all around them seemed so full of beauty and promise.

'All life has a serene pattern but ours.' Ferdinand, the youngest of the trio and still in his early twenties, was the quickest to let his discouragement get the better of him. His hopes had been so high when he and Friedrich had left Keilhau and so few of them had been realised.

They continued with their walk, down through the pines across the lower water meadows to the village where a friendly tavern welcomed even heretics if they could afford to pay for their drinks. They sat outside with their beer-mugs, watching the moon rise, a pale crescent in the darkening sky.

They had been there about half an hour or so when they were joined by three strangers. They were cheerful businessmen on a visit from the neighbouring town of Willisau. Having had a successful day among the lakeside farmers of the Wartensee, they were celebrating before retiring to bed. Their success and merriment was in sharp contrast to the depression which had sunk upon Friedrich and his companions, a depression obviously evident for it was commented upon by one of the strangers, a white-haired, rosy-faced man who slapped his beer-mug down on the table and wanted to know why they were spoiling the evening with such long faces?

The enquiry was made with mock severity and his manner so friendly that none of them could fail to respond to his cheerful, well-meant attempt to stir them out of their misery.

'Our business is obviously not so successful as yours,' Barop told him. 'We gather from your smiles that you have had good fortune in Wartensee. We, I regret, have not.'

'Then what is your trade, sirs, that you fare so badly? Perhaps your goods are not to the villagers' liking?'

'We sell education,' said Friedrich 'and it is not I fear, a very marketable commodity.'

'Education!' The man's laughter was joined by his friends. He slapped Friedrich on the back. 'No wonder you are not doing well! People do not expect to *buy* education. They hope to stumble upon it in the street, like finding a lost thaler and claiming it for their own by putting their toe on it. When it is not there they blame their ill fortune, not their laziness! How do you sell this 'Education' then?'

Warmed by their companionship, the excellence of the beer and the glorious summer evening, Friedrich and Barop tried to explain as briefly as possible their plans and their failure to put them into practice.

'Everywhere we go we seem dogged with ill-fortune,' said Friedrich. 'You would be ostracised here if you were to be seen talking to us. Do you not know we have been branded as devil-worshippers by the priests?'

'The priests! A pox on them!' said another of the men. 'They tyrannise these country simpletons. It's not the same in the town, you know. People there have minds of their own.'

'I tell you what,' said another of the strangers. 'Return with us to Willisau. I am sure that you will get a fair hearing there, away from the bigotry of these damned priests. We all have children... maybe you'd take *them* in your school? They seem to learn precious little where they are at present.'

'It's a wonderful idea!' Ferdinand, the least cautious, the quickest to depress, was also the first to respond to encouragement 'We'll go, won't we, Oheim? Johannes? Should we not go?'

'It seems a reasonable idea,' said Barop. 'If these gentlemen really consider that we should be welcome. I do not fancy a whole town rising against us!'

The citizens from Willisau assured them that as they were all held in considerable esteem in their town they could vouch for their safety. Friedrich, Ferdinand and Barop returned to Schnyder's lakeside castle in a much improved frame of mind to that in which they had set out earlier in the evening.

'Shall we go?' Ferdinand was the most impatient to be away: the atmosphere of the castle, although beautiful, depressed him.

'I am willing,' said Friedrich. 'What do you say, Johannes?'

'We have nothing to lose,' Barop agreed. 'Here we are, failures, we can only be bigger failures in a bigger place!' He laughed as he spoke: it was the first laughter the three had shared for many days.

CHAPTER NINE

At least twenty of the wealthiest best known families in Willisau welcomed them when they travelled there from the Wartensee a few weeks later. Under the leadership of their friends at the inn the families had already formed themselves into an association and had secured permission from the authorities of the Canton of Lucerne to use a small castle-like building as a school, and about 40 pupils were immediately enrolled.

'At last we seem to have found what we have been seeking so long.' Friedrich wrote to Henrietta. 'But the priests are still furiously against us, and with a really devilish force, which seems strange in men who should be holy. We are often warned by kindly people to turn back when we are walking towards secluded spots, or along the outlying mountain paths. They really feel that some physical violence might be used against us. But do not worry, we are quite able to look after ourselves, and in any case I am sure that all their threats are merely words and that they would not dare to lift a finger against us in violence.'

This letter was no comfort to Henrietta, Friedrich had already been away nearly a year and she was desperately lonely and worried. He missed her, too, particularly the comfort that her companionship would have given him in the dark days at Wartensee. 'But it is too uncertain for you to travel so far,' he had written to her. 'It would be better to be miserable together than parted like this, but how can we afford for you to make this long and expensive journey when we can scarcely pay for our own food here, although we eat it off Herr Schnyder's splendid plate.'

The move to Willisau eased this situation at least and in answer to her desperate pleas Friedrich was at last able to send Henrietta her fare to make the journey, for which she had waited so many lonely months. Keilhau gave her a gala farewell. Christian and his wife still remained as the oldest members of the community, with Langethal and Ernestine, Middendorff and Albertine, all now with children of their own.

An equally joyous welcome greeted her at Willisau. Friedrich himself wept openly with happiness when he embraced her, unembarrassed in the delight of their reunion. He was amazed in the rediscovery of her beauty. Although she was now 52, her dark hair was only touched here and there with grey, her figure had kept its slenderness, her dark eyes sparkled, and the lines on her face were only those made by her smile.

'You are lovely!' he told her. 'My beautiful, beloved Henrietta!'

It seemed at last that the dark days were over and the sun was shining upon them again.

The school was flourishing, Herr Amrhyn, one of the businessmen who had been mainly responsible for their move to Willisau, was delighted, for some of their popularity reflected on him and his already important status in the town had been considerably enhanced. It was he who persuaded Friedrich that it would be both diplomatic and a symbol of their place in the community if the new school took an active part in the annual church festival at Willisau, to which visitors came from all parts of the canton. At this festival the highlight of the religious ceremonial was the showing of a communion wafer miraculously spotted with blood. The drops of blood were all part of a miracle story cherished by the population. This told that two criminals who had gone into the church for refuge and to share their spoils had fallen out with each other. In their rage one of them struck the effigy of Christ on the Cross with his sword, and drops of blood from the holy figure fell on the communion wafers that lay below it on the altar. Every year these holy relics were honoured with a service of much pomp and ceremony, and people came from all over the canton to attend and join in the big procession which was the climax of the festival.

Friedrich was not over-enthusiastic at the invitation to join in a religious ceremonial that appeared so alien to his Lutheran upbringing, but he was so delighted with the present success of his and his companions' efforts that it seemed rash to offend their new friends. At the same time, he did not want to take risks which might once more bring the disapproval of the priests upon them.

'Are you sure?' he asked Amrhyn anxiously. 'After all, we are strangers. Perhaps the people will consider we should not take part yet in something that belongs especially to your town. Say there is a protest or outburst of some sort? It would undo everything that we have so far achieved, and do us and you irreparable harm.'

But Herr Amrhyn was adamant. 'To the contrary,' he said. 'If you do *not* take part, it might be construed that you disapprove in some way of our religious customs.'

So it was decided that the pupils of the school should lead the singing, a prospect which greatly delighted and excited them and vastly pleased their proud parents.

Friedrich, still apprehensive, cautioned Barop and Ferdinand who with him were to accompany the children to the church.

'Keep quiet under any circumstances. Whatever happens we must not get excited. I am sure no harm at least will befall the children.'

The children themselves unaware of any tension, took great pride in their new clothes: the girls in white dresses, their hair tied with blue ribbons, the boys in white shirts with embroidered waistcoats and velvet breeches. As they walked to the church in a tidy row, two by two, the little girls carrying posies of wild flowers, the townspeople applauded them: they made such a pretty sight.

The service opened with singing and the children's voices rising sweet and clear in descant above those of the congregation. The sun shone down through the coloured glass of the church windows, casting shafts of light through the blue smoke of the incense from the swinging censers of the acolytes at the altar. The ornate ceremonial was strange to Friedrich, used to the simple forms of service of his own church, but he enjoyed its spectacle and particularly the joyous part played in it by his own schoolchildren.

The singing was finished and the time had come for the sermon when suddenly, instead of the expected preacher—a mild old friar who had never shown any hostility to Friedrich or the school—there was a scurry at the altar steps and from the assembled clergy a Capuchin monk broke away from the rest and mounted the steps to the pulpit.

He stood there for a moment, his eyes blazing fanatically as he glared at the congregation.

'God forsaken!, he declared 'God-forsaken, unhappy people of Willisau! What good can you do yourselves on your knees praying when your hearts are sick with sin? When your spirits are black and bedevilled? Only hell-fire awaits you! Only the searing white agony of the flames of hell, the torment of burning, the everlasting damnation which will blacken and destroy your writhing wicked souls!'

By now his voice had risen to a scream. The children sitting neatly in their pews were looking pale and frightened and some of the younger ones were crying; many of the adults looked scarcely less disturbed. Now the Capuchin, having exhausted his denunciation of the wicked townspeople, turned his attention to the heretics whom the now alarmed Willisauers were harbouring in their midst. Fiercer and fiercer grew his threats, coarser his insults, more horrible his descriptions of the tortures of hell.

Fortunately the monk was so taken up with his own tirade that he did not notice that many of the people, including the children and their parents, had quietly faded from the congregation and the church was rapidly emptying. Friedrich and his companions in their pew at the front of the church were directly in front of the preacher. To Friedrich, whose eyes seemed to be in a direct line with those of the fanatical priest, it seemed as if the burning glare of that venomous gaze was boring into him. His heart was racing, he was frightened yet elated. It was not the cold fear of the battle that he had known long ago at Leipzig, but something fiercer—a mixture of fright and anger which left him almost numb, yet ready for action if need be. Ferdinand and Barop seemed equally affected. They looked directly ahead of them, giving the monk look for look, but their faces showing nothing of their emotions.

'Win then for yourselves everlasting treasure in heaven!' the Capuchin screamed at the conclusion of his tirade. 'Bring this misery to an end and suffer these wretched men to remain no longer among you! Hunt these wolves from the land, to the glory of God and the rage of the devil. Then will peace and blessings return and there will be great joy in heaven and for those who serve God and his saints.'

Hardly had he uttered his 'Amen' than he swung down from the pulpit with a rush of his sweeping robes and disappeared through a side door and was away.

Friedrich, Ferdinand and Barop got up together and walked quietly through the remaining congregation, most of whom stood staring and bemused, too shocked and frightened to react in any way. One or two of the bolder members, those most affected by the priest's encitement, mumbled threats and shook a fist as the three passed, but no hand was actually raised against them.

Friedrich wrote to Christian: 'Danger lies about us on every side and it is no pleasure to recognise that the sword of Damocles always hangs above our heads. Mercifully the parents of our pupils all seem quite unaffected by this outburst and in fact are all the more enthusiastic to maintain our school and its principles. They are however equally anxious for our safety and we have agreed that Barop and I shall travel to Lucerne to see the Abbe Girard, of whom you will surely have heard as a Swiss educational writer of great power (and charm!) and to the Mayor, Eduard Pfyffer, to beg that they should provide for our security with all the means in their power.'

Friedrich and Barop made the journey without delay. On their way they stopped at an inn hoping to find lodging there for the night . Among those drinking in the crowded bar-room as they entered was a priest of the same order as the fanatical monk. Friedrich hesitated when he caught sight of him; after all, it was stupid to court danger.

'Let's go,' he whispered to Barop. 'If we stay here there will only be trouble.'

But Barop was firm. 'If we go now we will be branded cowards as well as heretics,' he said. 'Come on, walk in as if you had noticed nothing.'

The men in the bar turned their heads casually towards the strangers but one or two had been in the church at Willisau on the day of the Festival and recognised Friedrich in particular for his height, gait and thin features, which had become more angular with the years.

'It's them!' said one man in a whisper that could be heard across the room. Mugs were put down and conversation died as Friedrich and Barop walked across to the bar.
Barop addressed the landlord, a jovial-looking man wiping beer-mugs on the other side of the counter.
'Good evening, innkeeper... my friend and I seek lodging for the night. Have you rooms for us?'
The innkeeper looked awkward. He was a kindly man and the strangers looked tired.
'Well, I'll not be rightly knowing,' he said, embarrassed. My wife sees to the rooms. I know she's pretty full up at this time of the year, but I'll ask her.'
He put down the mug he was drying and moved to the foot of the stairs and called up. While he did so one of the men, now openly listening, addressed Friedrich and Barop.
'Aren't you the schoolmasters from Willisau?'
'We are.' Barop told him.
'Why do you come here?'
'We are travelling to Lucerne on business and seek lodging for the night, as you just heard me ask the landlord.'
The priest, who had been sitting quietly in the corner, a dark figure in his black robes, spoke for the first time.
'There will be damnation on any house that gives you shelter' he said, his fiery tones contradicting the stillness of his posture, for he had not stirred nor moved a muscle of his impassive face; only his eyes burned brightly with hatred. 'You are heretics.' he hissed at Friedrich and Barop.
'And as heretics you will be destroyed and with you all those who harbour and encourage you.'
The men in the bar began to mutter among themselves and to cast anxious glances at Friedrich and Barop and at the priest.
As he had in the church, Friedrich felt almost elated with the tension of the situation.
'If it is heresy to desire the happiness of little children, then we are heretics,' he said simply. 'For that is all my friend here and I desire in life: to see your children and the children of the whole world taught to live full happy, useful and Christian lives.'
'Christian!' The priest almost screamed in his fury. 'Blasphemers! How dare you use the name of Christ!'
Barop, calmly and unemotionally, crossed the room to where the priest still sat, his face contorted with fanatical rage.
'Do you know, sir, who Jesus Christ was... and do you hold him in any

particular esteem?'

The men looking on, stared unbelievingly as the priest, quite nonplussed by this firm and quiet approach, stammered: 'Certainly I do... He is the Son of God, and we must all honour Him and believe in Him if we are to escape everlasting damnation.'

'Then perhaps you can tell me.' Barop continued, in the quiet manner of one asking a direction, 'whether Christ was a Catholic or a Protestant?'

There was deathly silence, broken only by the clock ticking on the wall and the shuffle of an embarrassed foot in the sawdust.

The priest did not reply. He rose without a word. gathered his cloak about him and left. As he moved to the door the tension broke, the men began to laugh and applaud. They gathered round Barop and Friedrich, slapping their shoulders, offering them drinks.

'Tell us about your work!' they cried. 'Who are you to see in Lucerne? Can we help you?'

The innkeeper joined them. 'My wife has a room for you' he told them, 'and she says that there is a fine pork roast in the oven if you are hungry after your journey.'

The evening sun shone warmly through the window of the bar parlour. For that night at least they were secure.

*   *   *

In Lucerne they met the Mayor, Eduard Pfyffer, and as soon as they saw him they liked him. He was a large, rather clumsy man with an ugly but agreeable face, big hands and feet and a smile as broad as his massive shoulders.

'You've got a hard task ahead of you,' he told them. 'The people here are bogged down with superstition—religious superstition too, the hardest to combat. The only way you can do it is to start at the beginning with the children. That is why the priests fear you. You may break the hold that they have had on the people for centuries.'

'But we do not *want* to undermine their religious faith.' Friedrich assured him. 'As you know, we are not Catholics, but I would not deny any man the right to worship as he pleased.'

'This is not worship of God,' cried Herr Pfyffer. 'This is tyranny, even idolatry, and the people are to blame because they are too slothful, too lazy-minded to think for themselves. They would suffer any tyranny of thought rather than make the effort of using their own brains. That is why I welcome

you in our midst. In you and your new school I see hope for our children.'
'We cannot tell you what this means to us.' Barop told him. 'For years we have worked, striven, sweated even, building our own schools, and all we have got is abuse and penury. Here in Lucerne we have met the first true encouragement and kindness we have yet known, yet this is marred by the actual physical danger in which we are finding ourselves through the fanatical opposition of some of the clergy.'

'There is only one way to ensure your safety,' said Herr Pfyffer. 'You must win over the people. Work on a little longer and then invite everyone, all who like to come, to an open day, a festival, I have heard something of your methods. Let them see the children at work and at play. Then they will see for themselves that you mean nothing but good. If this wins the crowd to your side, then, and only then, will you be out of harm's reach. It will need courage and boldness but it is the only way. If I was to make a decree for your protection it would be playing into the hands of your enemies. You would be branded government spies.'

It was wise counsel. Friedrich and Barop recognised it as such, though it was not what they had expected. Nevertheless, they returned to Willisau already eager with plans for the open day which Pfyffer had suggested.

No one was happier, nor worked harder for the new project, than Henrietta. To be together again after their long separation and at last to see some hope ahead for their dream: the summer days were not long enough to contain all their happiness.

The open day was planned for the last days of September and the chosen date dawned fair and warm. The lake gleamed in the sunshine and the trees on the hillside below the fir line were turning red and gold. Bright late poppies still glowed in the hedgerows and the Michaelmass daisies, which grew in the school gardens, were banks of rich mauves and purples.

The event opened soon after dawn and by seven o'clock people were beginning to arrive from Willisau. Within an hour or two the school and gardens were crowded. The opposition of the priests to the strange German schoolmasters of Willisau had attracted the attention that Herr Pfyffer had been sure it would. It had gained them notices in many Swiss journals, which might otherwise have dismissed them as cranks. The visitors therefore included quite a few journalists as well as teachers from many parts of Switzerland, who had made considerable journeys to see what all the fuss was about.

In the classrooms, people from the neighbouring towns and villages examined the children's books, collections of simple compositions and pictures, but all their own work and full of lively, creative imagination. They saw, too, the models made to illustrate various lessons, such as the panorama of an ancient lake village, made from natural materials, sticks and stones, shells, mud and reeds from the lakeside. The children were eager to explain their work and answered the questions put to them quickly, intelligently and courteously. In the garden, groups were engaged in exercises and singing games, all dressed alike in matching pinafores and much enjoying the unaccustomed attention they were receiving.

The day concluded with an assembly, just as the sun was setting. The children, teachers and the crowd of visitors, which also included delegates from the neighbouring cantons of Berne and Zurich, joined in a simple hymn and a prayer.

When the last of the visitors had left and the children had gone home, tired and happy with their proud parents, Friedrich and Henrietta, Barop and Ferdinand and their few willing helpers, were left behind to tidy up. They, too, were tired, tired to the point of exhaustion, but jubilant.

Their jubilation was well-founded. Herr Pfyffer, already an enthusiastic supporter of their cause, gave a glowing account of the open day to the Great Council of the Canton of Lucerne. Others joined in, in support of his views, and it was decided that the castle in which the school was housed and its outbuildings should be dedicated to this use for an indefinite period at the lowest possible rate. Furthermore, the Capuchin priest who had led the attack upon Friedrich and his companions was to be expelled from the canton with the promise of like treatment for anyone who acted in the same way.

Willisau became a mecca for educationalists. Scarcely a day went by without someone coming to see the school, to talk to Friedrich or one of the others, to question, criticise or admire. Among these visitors was a deputation from Berne. They stayed all day until both Friedrich and Henrietta, who had accompanied them on their tour and entertained them at mealtimes, were quite exhausted.

As they finished their evening meal the senior member of the deputation, an elderly councillor, turned to Friedrich. 'It has been a wonderful day, Herr Froebel,' he said. 'All and more than we had dared to hope. I am most impressed, and I know that I speak for my colleagues.' His companions nodded their agreement. 'Now I feel the time has come to tell you that our visit is more than curiosity or even intelligent interest. We hope very shortly to establish an orphanage at Burgdorf. We wondered if you would agree to undertake its organisation?'

Friedrich was amazed. It had never occurred to him that the visitors from Berne were there out of anything but purely academic interest in his methods, and the offer of a post from them was entirely unexpected.

'I will have to think about it,' he told them, after thanking them for the honour they did him. Later in the evening, as soon as they had left for their lodging in the town, he asked Henrietta what she thought about the proposition.

'It's exciting,' she said, 'but I do not think this institution should be devoted to teaching orphans only. For one thing, it's bad for the poor motherless little ones to feel that they are something apart. They will benefit from the company of children who have happy homes, and the children from these homes will appreciate them the more for knowing that not all children are as fortunate as themselves.'

Friedrich told the elders from Berne of his decision, for he agreed wholeheartedly with Henrietta, but like her was excited by this new challenge. The Berne deputation, much to his surprise, agreed gladly and without reservation. 'Anything you suggest, Herr Froebel!,' said their leader. 'We are entirely in your hands. The institution shall be of a mixed nature, with children from families as well as those who are parentless, and from all walks of life.'

It was settled that as soon as arrangements could be made for someone to succeed him at Willisau, Friedrich and Henrietta would travel to Burgdorf.

'First of all we need a holiday,' sighed Henrietta, and Friedrich noticed suddenly that she looked tired. She had lost weight and the approach of the winter had brought on a troublesome cough.

Where else for a holiday but home to Keilhau—their first home of happiness and dreams, where the old faithful community still lived and worked? Barop asked to go with them. His son was now a year old and he had not yet even seen him. When asked, Middendorff, who had been struggling to keep things going at Keilhau, readily agreed to travel to Willisau to join Ferdinand, who was now a responsible and valued member of the staff.

The return to Keilhau was an occasion of great rejoicing.

Henrietta wept as she embraced Ernestine. For her the homecoming had lost its savour owing to the fact that she was mourning the death of her little daughter, taken by one of the dread diseases of childhood, diphtheria. Her husband, Heinrich Langethal, also looked tired and thin with this sorrow added to the burdens of his responsibilities. Nevertheless, the return of Der Oheim and Henrietta acted like a charm.

Elise, Christian's youngest daughter, had grown from a gawky girl into a lovely young woman of nearly 21 and there was exciting news of Julius, Christoph's eldest son. After studying at Munich, Jena and Berlin he had just been appointed Professor at the Polytechnic in Zurich. He had also had several learned books and treatises published and was already held in high regard in university circles. His younger brother, Karl, had a tutorship in

England, after graduating from Jena and had recently published a pamphlet on Euclid. Only Theodor was left at Keilhau, where he had transformed the rough and ready garden into landscaped rockeries and terraces.

Their success in itself was a tonic to Friedrich, in addition to the happier situation at Willisau and the anticipation of his own new post at Burgdorf.

The day after their return to Keilhau, Friedrich went out alone into the garden. The sun was just setting behind the distant hills, the pines were black against the sky and the evening air was warm and scented with lavender from the hedges that Theodor had planted along the narrow paths. Over the years the scent of the lavender had always carried him back to the days of the manse garden at Oberweissbach, to Stadt Ilm and his happy life with Uncle Hoffman and Grossmutter. To Lotte, too. Lotte! He saw her now, not as a ghost but in her shining sunlit girlhood, the hot sun on her brown arms as he carried her across the stream. Henrietta had been right when she said that Lotte would never die in his heart... never grow old.

Old! He supposed he was old. His dark hair was greying, he looked down at his hands. In the orange light of the evening they looked dark and lined. They were a working man's hands rather than those of a scholar, for his building had been with wood and stone as well as with pens and paper, but he was not ashamed of that. 'My heart, too, is scarred,' he thought as he saw in his hands the marks of his labours, the place where he had driven a nail as he laid the shingles on the roof of the Keilhau schoolhouse, the jagged scar of a slip with the axe edge when he was working in the Thüringen Wald nearly 40 years ago.

'And where am I now?' He spoke out loud to the silent garden, to the rooks circling above the elms, croaking their evensong. 'Where am I? Where am I going?' There was no answer but the mocking of the owls in the darkening woods beyond and the echoing silence of the hills.

There was little more time to brood. Their short stay at Keilhau, packed with preparations, passed quickly and soon it was time to return to Switzerland, to Burgdorf, where an overwhelming task awaited him. From Keilhau, Langethal journeyed with them, Friedrich feeling that the sheer physical effort of the foundation of a new school might be too much for Henrietta to share with him alone.

They found the canton officials of Berne friendly and helpful, the premises in which the new institution was to be housed, pleasant and spacious.

Apart from the school work, which progressed easily and happily, Friedrich found that in his position as director he was responsible for the refresher course for teachers. The regulations of the canton laid down that all teachers must take three months' leave every two years for post-graduate study. During this leave they assembled at Burgdorf to exchange experiences and ideas and to attend lectures and debates. Friedrich had to preside over these meetings and assist and guide their studies as well as lecture. This he found as enjoyable and inspiring as his work with the children.

Most of the sessions were informal and would often take place in the school gardens, or even on walks beside the lake or in the mountains. But even as he was absorbed by their conversation he was distressed by their common conviction that nothing they could contribute by means of education could compete with the influence of a bad or indifferent home life.

'How can I tell a pupil it is wrong for him to copy from his friend's exercise book when his father openly boasts of his thefts of ideas from a business rival?' said one young teacher. 'My children use bad language,' said another 'but so do their parents.'

'It is the parents we should have in our classes... not the children!' laughed another 'And I'd love to give the cane to some of them!' The others joined in the laughter at the thought of a row of portly citizens under instruction, but Friedrich cut short their merriment.

'You are right!' he cried 'You are so right! It is the parents we should be teaching! The mother first, the fathers too, but the mothers first of all. It is the mother that teaches the child to feed itself, to walk its first steps, to speak... the mother's opportunity is so great and yet so seldom taken!'

'Here at Burgdorf we have such young children, poor little mites who are motherless and fatherless, their only family this institution, but we can teach them and make them happy, responsible citizens. Look at them!' They were standing on a hill-side looking down on the garden of the institution, where, through the trees, they could see a group of children playing singing games, snatches of their voices coming and going on the wind.

'Mothers all over Switzerland could be playing such games with their children, teaching them movement and rhythm, teaching them to know and love words, to appreciate nature, to marvel at a daisy, to watch the busy worms, the snails, the bees, all the living playthings of the world around us... let them touch, feel, explore, question!' Friedrich's eyes were bright as he spoke, to the little gathering of students, listening to him spellbound. It seemed as if the burden of his years of disappointment had suddenly dropped from him.

Only one shadow clouded the horizon. Henrietta, whose energy was always so unflagging, who in her early fifties had still retained so much of her girlish beauty, was tired and ailing in the brisk, boisterous mountain air. Whereas she once could outwalk him on their hillside rambles she would now beg to rest awhile and sit pale and breathless while he watched her anxiously. 'You must not walk any more,' he told her.

'But I love the mountains!' she protested 'It is the only time we can be alone together.'

But by the end of 1836 it became apparent that Henrietta could no longer stay at Burgdorf. The physician they had consulted told Friedrich bluntly 'If you want your wife to live you will leave Switzerland. She cannot, in her condition, stand the altitude, nor the cold of another winter.'

From Willisau, too, came bad news: the temporary peace had been shattered by a change of government which was now in favour of the Jesuits and once again the opposition of the priests was becoming an embarrassment, if not an actual danger. Decisions had to be made quickly. Friedrich, normally an indecisive person, was spurred by the increasingly alarming condition of Henrietta. He wrote to his nephew Ferdinand at Willisau:

'I need you here and you can do far more good than any you hope to achieve now in Lucerne under your present difficulties. But first and foremost I must get Henrietta to a better climate for I fear greatly for her.'

Langethal stayed at Burgdorf with Ferdinand, who came as soon as it was feasibly possible in answer to Friedrich's appeal. Friedrich and Henrietta left for Berlin, where she had relatives and they could stay at least for some time while she received specialist treatment. He was alarmed at her great weakness, when he helped her from the carriage she leaned heavily on him, and would have fallen if he had not taken her weight. She protested, nevertheless, that she was alright and only needed rest and a change of air.

In some respect it seemed that she might be right; and in this and other ways their visit to Berlin was a happy one. To start with, it revived memories of their first meeting and early associations. Henrietta's health *did* improve and as she grew stronger they were able to visit their old walks by the lakes, the little cafes they once knew, and even the old museum gallery where Friedrich had lectured the pretty young woman on mineralogy and found the blue of her eyes more fascinating than the stones they were studying.

Friedrich used this time of enforced leisure to explore further an idea which had long lain in the back of his mind—the construction of a set of educational toys for young children, which would direct their play along constructive lines and teach them as they amused themselves, fitting together building-blocks, placing wooden balls in set places, making patterns. 'My gifts' he told Henrietta as they sat in the evenings with him whittling away at wood, stringing coloured balls on thread.

As Henrietta's health improved they planned to return to Keilhau. 'I am sure that's all I need now,' she said. 'At Keilhau I will be really strong again.'

Friedrich also longed for Keilhau, for its quiet hills, its peaceful garden and the friends he knew would surround him there and with whom he wanted to share his newest idea—that of a school for really young children, babies of three to five, ages at which no one had so far thought of beginning to teach children, but which to Friedrich now seemed so important.

Middendorff and Barop had both returned to Keilhau and Friedrich valued their opinions above all except Henrietta's.

'But it is no use here!' said Middendorff when at last Friedrich was able to tell him of his new scheme. 'Why, in Keilhau there is only a handful of little children and you cannot expect parents to send such young children away from their homes. Your new school must be in a town, somewhere where mothers can bring their babies for a few hours each day.'

'Why not Rudelstadt, then?' Barop suggested.

'Too far,' Middendorff argued, 'And too big. It would take too long for our existence to become known.'

'Blankenburg, then?' It was Friedrich who thought of the little town between Rudelstadt and Schwarzburg, about ten miles away.

'You'd only need a room to start with!' Middendorff, as usual, was the most enthusiastic. 'Let's start immediately... tomorrow! We can go to Blankenburg and see what can be found there. We have nothing to lose, and everything to gain! Say we shall go tomorrow!'

'It will take money... and we have precious little.' Barop, the businessman, was the cautious one, as always.

'Not much, Johannes! I have a little, the Burgdorf Institution paid me well, you know, and Henrietta and I were very modest during our stay in Berlin. I will take the room and furnish it, then we have little else to spend except for some simple equipment, and our own labours.'

So the Babies School opened in Blankenburg in 1837. It was a very modest affair indeed—no more than, as they envisaged, a room simply but brightly furnished, with little tables and chairs, and window that looked out on the garden where the children would be allowed to play in fine weather.

Henrietta was well enough to make the journey by carriage from Keilhau and was there to greet the young mothers when they brought their babies to their lessons.

'My youngest-born!' Friedrich called it, teaching not only the children but their mothers who stayed to play with them the lesson-games which they so much enjoyed.

It was a success. There was no doubt about it. Pupils soon crowded the room and there was no space for movement, so extra accommodation had to be found.

At Keilhau, too, extra pupils had enrolled, drawn by the considerable publicity which had followed Friedrich from Willisau to Burgdorf, and home again. From the community itself Middendorff's little daughter and Barops' son had become pupils, so a second generation of children was growing up in the Froebel tradition.

'I feel at last as if I am beginning to see my dreams come true!' Friedrich told Henrietta, as they walked together one evening in late October. She was still weak and their walks were limited to the garden and the nearer, gentler slopes of the hills beyond which the great shadow of the Kirschberg towered dimly in the early autumn twilight.

'It may be the end of my dream.'

Henrietta beside him turned her gaze to his. 'Friedrich, do not be frightened or sad by what I am going to say to you. I must say it because we have never had secrets from each other. I have a strange feeling that I shall never see another autumn here at our beautiful Keilhau.'

Friedrich, alarmed, drew her to him.

'You are ill! You are worse! My darling, what is it? I thought you were so much better!'

'Liebchen! Now you are frightened! I am *not* worse! ... Only very tired.' Her voice was quiet and calm, soothing him as a mother soothes a fearful child. 'All I am trying to tell you is that if my time has come I am ready. Once I was so afraid to die—when I was first ill I was so frightened! You see I had never been really ill before, and I was very afraid.' She shivered now as he held her in his arms. 'But all that is changed. They say animals know when the end is near and I think that is the feeling that I have. I am tired, Friedrich, so tired, with a tiredness that sleep never seems to ease, and I am no longer afraid of death. I used to lie in the night, awake and cold with terror, imagining darkness and nothingness.'

To Friedrich his memory of Stadt Ilm the night he and Lotte had buried the dog was as vivid as if it were yesterday. He, too, had lain awake shivering in the dark. The terror sometimes took him still and now it made him clasp Henrietta closer to him, as if this might shield her from that inevitable terror too.

'But that has passed,' she continued, drawing away from him slightly, to see him better. 'Believe me, darling, I am *not* afraid. In one of those dark terrible nights I suddenly felt a great peace come upon me, an indescribable sense of peace and security and happiness. I knew then I would never be afraid again ... only sad at the thought of parting from you, if only for a little time, before eternity.'

But Friedrich was afraid. Afraid for her, but most of all afraid for himself, because he dared not try to imagine life without her.

As was his nature to do so, he buried his anxiety in work and within weeks had published the first of a new periodical, *The Sunday Journal*.

In March 1839, after two months of bitter snowy weather in which it had been impossible for anyone to travel from Keilhau to Blankenburg, Henrietta was taken ill again. At first it seemed that it might only be a chill, but as the days wore on and there was no sign of her fever abating, the old village doctor who was attending her could not conceal his anxiety from Friedrich. 'She is already too weak from her earlier illness to stand this strain,' he said, 'and she seems to have no will to recover.'

There was no let-up in the weather. Snow swirled in drifts against the house walls, bowed the branches of the trees in the garden to the ground, lay thick in wedges on the window sills and doorsteps. Henrietta, who had always loved the snow, did not see it. Exhausted by her illness she had sunk into a coma. Friedrich sat with her through the dark days in which the sun never shone and the short hours of daylight blurred into the long, fear-ridden nights. He held her hand, but it was limp in grasp, her breathing was short and rapid, her face flushed. He recalled in those long hours of vigil the nights he had spent sitting beside Traugott at Jena, his father's last illness, and the times his imagination had worked on the death of Lotte when he had not even known to pray for her.

Now he could not pray for Henrietta. In his desperation the words would not come. It was only a desperate longing to have her restored to him, a bargaining with God in which he offered all he possessed in exchange for her life. This he knew was not prayer as he had been taught, but it was all his torn heart could achieve, and even then it brought on a kind of superstitious uneasiness that the very out-reaching of his mind to God might turn His attention to Henrietta and He would take her away from him.

Towards midnight on the third night of his watch by her, she suddenly flickered her eyelids, their first movement in days. Eagerly Friedrich leant over her.

'Henrietta!'

She opened her eyes, and he saw with poignant pain that they were still beautiful, even in the extremity of her illness. A faint smile flickered across her lips and her limp hand took a faint pressure of life within his.

'The sun is shining!' she whispered. 'It must be Spring at last.' Outside it was dark as pitch and the snow was blowing in little flurries against the window-panes. 'Draw the blinds, liebchen,' she said more softly, so that he could scarcely hear. 'The sunlight is so bright!' She closed her eyes again, but the faint smile still played on her lips as her hand fell from his, and with it her life slipped away into the night.

Middendorff found him an hour later when he came to take his turn watching in the sick-room. He was still sitting beside the bed, holding Henrietta's lifeless hand in his and staring unseeing before him. The light of his own life had gone out and it seemed that it would never be lit again.

*   *   *

For weeks Friedrich was stunned, unable to work or concentrate. Middendorff carried on as best he could, feeling that only time could heal this most terrible wound that fate had dealt his friend just at the time when it seemed that the tide of his fortune might be turning.

'Nothing can save him now but work,' he told Barop as they watched Friedrich set off on one of his morose, lonely walks in the hills. 'How can we inspire him to work again?'

'Another Babies School' said Barop. 'Another school somewhere way from this place and its memories, somewhere, anywhere, but it must be a city, a place that will be a challenge. We have a little capital and he has Henrietta's small estate.'

'Do you think he would do it?' Middendorff was doubtful. 'He seems to have lost his spirit. He is like a man whose mind has moved into the shadows.'

'Dresden?' Friedrich repeated the name dully when they suggested to him that he might open a Babies School there. Dresden he recalled dimly from his soldiering days; it did not inspire him greatly but Middendorff, having broached the subject, pursued it relentlessly.

'Yes, Dresden. Why not? It's a big city; the people there will be progressive, ready to accept new ideas. It's just the place. Say you will do it!'

Friedrich looked at them: Middendorff, his dear friend of so many years, and Barop, faithful, business-like Barop, both regarding him with anxious eyes. He had not the heart for their plans but he could not find it in himself to disappoint them. He put his hands on their shoulders.

'Alright! I will do it! When do we start?'

Friedrich and Middendorff left Keilhau in the early summer for Dresden. They found the journey tedious but their arrival rewarding. The beautiful old town at its best in the June sunshine, the wooded hillsides lush and green, the vineyards blooming and the Elbe flowing calmly beneath the old bridges, giving an air of peaceful timelessness.

Middendorff had an introduction to one of the town's schoolmasters, a young man called Adolf Frankenburg who received them enthusiastically. He had read of their work in Switzerland and more recently at Blankenburg and was eager to join their enterprise.

'A Babies School in every city, in every town... that must be our aim!' he said. He was young and an impractical idealist, but his eagerness encouraged them.

'Next year it will be Frankfurt,' Middendorff told him, although no such plan had yet been discussed between them.

The gamble had come off. When they returned to Keilhau, Middendorff told Barop 'We have snatched him back from despair. He is sad... but he is alive again.'

*   *   *

They were right. Friedrich had emerged from the dark valley of his despair, but he was still a long way from happiness or even hope. The bright spark that burned within him seemed to have gone out. Even when he was told the good news that the Babies School at Blankenburg continued to flourish, he was apathetic.

'We must expand,' Barop told him, for it was he who had nursed the Blankenburg venture while his friends had been in Dresden. 'The opportunity there is too great to miss and interest is growing. You must see for yourself, as soon as possible. Tomorrow, even, if you feel strong enough.'

'But Johannes, I have nothing more to give! *You* go with Middendorff, find new accommodation if you think fit. I will stay here at Keilhau, I trust you both, there is no need for me to be there.'

'There is *every* need!' Barop turned on him fiercely, 'Friedrich, this is *your* dream. Yours and Henrietta's. Are you going to desert us and her memory now, when we need you most? The school at Blankenburg is asking for 'Der Oheim.' The young mothers who bring their babies ask anxiously for a word with 'Herr Doktor' about their little ones. It was inevitable that you should stand in the shadows in the time of your great sorrow, but you cannot *stay* there. You *shall* not. Wilhelm and I will not let you!'

'I will come tomorrow.' Friedrich did not turn in anger on his friend. As a soldier takes an order he acquiesed, and in his humility Barop saw the full depth of the man's cutting sorrow, for Friedrich never took orders from any of them. He was self-willed, stubborn even, convinced that his way was right. This man who meekly took a reproach without retaliation was a man whose heart was broken, and Barop grieved for him, but wisely did not let his sympathy turn him from his purpose.

The three friends set off early the following morning. It was a wonderful day with a light mist shrouding the early sun, giving the promise of clear skies to come.

Their way lay through the Steiger Pass, the mountains closing in on either side of the road until they seemed to squeeze it almost into nothingness. At this early hour the sun could not reach down to touch it but eventually they came out into the wider country and the full warmth of the sun struck their backs, making them sweat. After a while the road turned round the shoulder of the hill and down below they could see Blankenburg, its red roofs sparkling in the sun after a sharp shower of the kind which can fall from apparently clear skies where there are mountains.

Friedrich looked down at the little town.

'Is it there, then? Is this our destiny? It looks so small down there, like a toy town! Is it here that we are building our new dream... our...' He paused, all the way over the hills he had nagged in his mind for a name for his newest dream but nothing would come to him. 'Our *school,* Wilhelm?' He discarded the term as he spoke it. 'A school is too big, too solemn a name for such tiny children... it could frighten them.'

As they stood on the hillside in the sun looking down on Blankenburg he tried to recall again his first vision of the Babies School... children playing to learn, learning to play, growing in the sunshine naturally, just as the flowers grew around their feet here on the hillside... the buttercups and daisies, the bright blue of the gentians and the scarlet poppies. Suddenly, as he stood, he saw his dream as a garden—a garden which grew children as its flowers. He shouted to the hills with such force and suddenness that his companions were startled. 'I have it! I have it! *Kindergarten!*' The garden of children! That shall be the name of our new venture. Kindergartens!' He laughed aloud as the name rolled from his lips and echoed in the surrounding hills. It was the first time he had laughed since Henrietta died.

CHAPTER TEN

In 1840 the 400th anniversary of the invention of printing was celebrated with exhibitions all over Germany. In June the little Babies School at Blankenburg, now greatly enlarged and improved, was officially opened as the first kindergarten, with Barop's business-like backing of a joint stock company. In December, another kindergarten opened in Rudolstadt. Events were moving with encouraging but almost alarming swiftness. Friedrich was also engaged in the collecting together of his songs and singing-games for children, which he was hoping to publish, either separately or as part of his *Sunday Journal,* which still occupied a great deal of his time.

Time... it seemed only yesterday that he had come to Keilhau, to the newly-widowed Marte and her children. Friedrich, standing at the window looking at the snow on the New Year Eve of 1841, let memory carry him back to Stadt Ilm, to his forestry days, his botany with the old doctor at Neuhaus, long since dead, to Jena, the war, and finally to this burning destiny which drove him against his natural slowness and diffidence, with ever-increasing and relentless force to build a dream of which he would never have believed himself capable. Soon he would be off again. Middendorff was already planning the next journey, this time to Gera, where a Madame Schmidt, a distant cousin of his family, had already agreed to undertake the preliminary work.

At Keilhau the round of work and domesticity went on with its usual happy regularity. From Elise, Friedrich learned snatches of news from Osterode, where Lotte's family still lived. Her husband had only survived her by a few years, and her children were now all grown-up and married with the exception of the youngest girl, Luise, Elise's correspondent since they were children. Then, Luise, two years younger, had needed help to write her little messages to her friend, whom she missed sadly when Christian and his family had left the Harz mountains to move to Keilhau.

The little girls had exchanged seeds for their gardens, had sent news of each other's pets and dolls and laid the foundations of a lasting friendship that had endured despite distance. Both had to bear sorrows beyond their years. Elise, now 29, had spent a few years at Willisau with her brother Ferdinand before returning to Keilhau, where she hoped to be married. Her betrothed was a young man who had long been a faithful friend of the community there. Within a few weeks of their marriage he had taken a slight chill which worsened into a fever and pneumonia, and despite Elise's devoted nursing had died a few days before his thirtieth birthday.

   Luise, motherless at seven, had seen her father die of consumption when she was 13. Other deaths followed in tragic succession in the family, darkening her young life. Her two brothers, one a bookseller at Elbing, the other a lawyer at Osterode, were both left widowers after only a few years of marriage, and her eldest sister also lost her husband in the prime of life. Luise became a sort of travelling aunt, journeying from family to family, soothing sorrow with physical comfort, cooking, cleaning, caring for motherless babies. It was a hard life but not unsatisfying and she was a happy-natured girl with the same solemn beauty which had been her mother's great charm. She also had her mother's grey eyes and fair hair, and men would have found her attractive had she ever stayed long enough in any one place for them to notice her. As for her own feelings, she was too busy to dream, though occasionally, when moved by poetry or music—of which she was particularly fond—she would wonder sadly if there would ever be an intimate personal relationship of her own which was not related to her family duties.

   'But don't pity me,' she wrote to Elise. 'For all the hard work, I am happy. I love the babies as if they were my own and I only wish I had more knowledge! I confess I find my own education sadly lacking. Why do they not teach us more when we are children?'

   Elise read the letter to Friedrich. 'It's true,' he said. 'Here in Germany, where we teach the humblest chambermaid to make a bed, we expect young women to train their children by instinct. It's nonsense! Training a child is the most difficult task in the world and yet there is no pattern of preparation for it.'

   Friedrich himself was still busy with his collection of singing-games which he had now decided to publish as a book, separate from the *Sunday Journal,* although Barop warned him that the project would probably prove costly and lose him money. The book was completed by the spring of 1843, in time for the opening of his fourth kindergarten, at Darmstadt.

   'You must travel now,' Barop told him. 'Stop this writing and day-dreaming. It's a nice little book but it will not make our fortune or secure our cause!' He threw *Songs for Mothers* on the table. 'It's *you* the people want to see. You must travel to other parts of Germany. I'll arrange it.'

   Friedrich agreed. He had learned that to do otherwise with his friend Johannes Barop was only asking for trouble and in any case he was usually right.

   Despite his reluctance to go he was happy once the journey had begun. Barop had decided that his best route lay through the valleys of the Neckar and Main rivers, delightful countryside dotted with mellow old towns, dreaming over their own reflections in the rivers, the sun deepening the red of their roof-tops. In August he was in Markgröningen in time for the Shepherds' Festival on St Bartholomew's Eve, when shepherds from the whole district performed a 600-years-old tradition by marching through the town in a colourful procession, in red-lined coats and scarlet waistcoats trimmed with silver bells and ribbons flying from their crooks. It was a brilliant sight, with fifes, violins, bagpipes and clarinets echoing through the narrow streets, as the shepherds danced for their prizes, a crown and a fat sheep into the bargain!

He wrote to Middendorff at Keilhau: 'I would like to see our children perform such a masque, perhaps at Christmas. The colour and life of it made my soul sing again, and such old beautiful customs should be kept alive in Germany.'

Indeed his soul *did* sing as he travelled back to Bamberg, where nearly 40 years ago he had gone as a young farm steward—so long ago it seemed like a dream.

On the way home he visited his newest kindergarten at Darmstadt in the shelter of the Oberwald Mountains, rich in cherry orchards and vineyards.

'We have more children than we know what to do with,' was the encouraging report of the young directrice, Ida Seele.

Home again at Keilhau, Friedrich found the friendly house in a buzz of excitement. Elise, hearing that her friend Luise had at last been freed of her many responsibilities, had persuaded her to join the community, her encouragement echoed by Albertine, Middendorff's wife.

'You are obviously devoted to children,' they wrote to her, 'And are therefore ideally suited to this life. It will be lonely for you now at Osterode. Now that you are free don't lose a minute, you will love it here.'

Friedrich was tired after his travellings. It was at these homecomings too that he missed Henrietta most poignantly. She had always been there to greet him, to listen eagerly to the news of his journey, to encourage or even to criticise. Now there was no one, despite the warmth of the friendship between him and Middendorff, despite Barop's steady good humour and wise counsel. At night when they had gone to bed, Friedrich would sit alone and watch the stars, as he had once watched them with Henrietta. Still more dimly in his lonely mind was the image of Lotte, whose youngest daughter was even now on her way to join them at Keilhau.

*   *   *

The Midsummer of 1845 was particularly hot and sultry. As the mailcoach in which Luise was travelling towards Keilhau reached the head of the Schala valley, in which Keilhau lay, the clouds were building up alarmingly, the summits of the hills on either side shrouded in mist and the thunder already rolling in the distance.

'I'll not go on any further tonight,' said the driver. 'The horses will never get through the pass in this weather. You ladies will have to spend the night the best you can in the coach I'm afraid. It's a miserable prospect, I fear, but probably more comfortable than the shepherds' hut which you gentlemen will have to share with the groom and me over there'—he pointed to a rough shack by the wayside. 'There's blankets enough for us all and the coach cushions should make a fair rest for the ladies.'

They scarcely had time to make their arrangements before the storm broke in all its fury. The rain lashed down and the wind blew so fiercely that it seemed that the whole coach might be overturned at any minute. The horses, tethered to the fence beside the hut where the men were sheltering, neighed and whinneyed with fright as the lightning flashed across the valley and the thunder crashed and echoed from hilltop to hilltop.

Luise, normally not a nervous woman, was unable to stop herself shivering; the might of the storm was so tremendous, heightened as it was by the mountains and their solitary situation. When the thunder rolled away into the distance she tried to sleep but the rain beat a tattoo on the roof of the coach and she was cramped in uncomfortably with the other women—an elderly lady travelling to visit her daughter and two young girls going to Leipzig to finish their education, giggling and whispering or weeping with terror in each others' arms.

Luise eventually fell into an exhausted sleep from which she was aroused some three hours later by the sun shining through the windows of the coach onto her face. She was stiff and aching with her uncomfortable night and could hardly straighten her legs to climb down to the sodden road.

The storm had passed and the sun was shining, if only momentarily through a gap in the clouds, but the sky was still dark on the horizon with the promise of more rain to come.

'I'll not go on today.' The coachman was adamant. 'The road will be bogged down after this rain and we'll never get through ... apart from the danger of an avalanche. With your permission, ladies and gentlemen, I propose to turn back to where you can get a meal and decent lodgings and we can proceed by this or another route tomorrow, according to the weather.'

'I *can't* go back!' Luise cried. For weeks she had been eagerly looking forward to this new life, growing more impatient with the slow passage of time. Now she was nearly at her destination and being told to turn back!

'Where are you bound then?' The old coachman was concerned. 'Keilhau? Well, it's only a mile or two on, but I can't take you, really I can't. I would if it were possible but we'll only get stuck and maybe even lose the horses.'

'If you won't take me I'll walk!' Luise was determined. The coachmen and the other passengers tried to dissuade her, but she would have none of them. 'I'll walk!' she repeated. 'You can keep my luggage and bring it on when the roads have improved. I'm not a horse with four legs to slide in the mud. The road is straight, I believe, right through the valley, so there's no fear of my losing myself.'

Uneasy though they were at the thought, there was no dissuading such a determined young woman and before mid-day, as the coach turned and moved off in the opposite direction, Luise, with a small hand case, her shawl about her shoulders and wearing her strongest shoes, set off along the valley road alone.

The sky was still dark; the Schala valley wound away before her, the summits of the hills on either side still wrapped in heavy thunder clouds. The strange, stormy light seemed to intensify the green of the grass, the starry white blossom of banks of wild carrot flecking the wayside like snow.

Keilhau lay at the end of the valley. Luise's excitement dispelled any qualms she may have had on the journey, which was long and lonely. By the time the red roofs of the old farmhouse came into sight round the bend in the road her feet were sore, her hair dishevelled by the chill wind now blowing behind the storm, but she was elated.

At the door of the 'Lower House,' as Christian Froebel called the home he and his wife shared with their married daughter Emilie, Luise was welcomed with loving tenderness by all her old friends from Osterode, particularly by Elise, her devoted confidante since childhood. The girls had not met for many years but time seemed to melt away on their re-union and they were soon talking excitedly without any feeling of shyness or strangeness, as if they had never been apart.

After changing her damp clothing and refreshed by hot milk and slices of new farm bread and cheese, Elise took Luise to the main building at the other end of Theodor's carefully planned gardens. Barop was there with Middendorff, and their children and other teachers who worked at the boys school which now flourished at Keilhau.

'But where is *Der Oheim?*' Luise could not contain her impatience. Here she was at Keilhau and had met every one but the one she longed to see most of all... Der Oheim... Friedrich Froebel, the beloved uncle of her babyhood at Osterode and the inspiration of her new-born ambition to become a teacher.

Friedrich had spent the day at Blankenburg, where his kindergarten, despite its aesthetic success, was always in financial difficulties. He had forgotten that this was the day when Luise was expected. He returned to Keilhau at dusk on a sultry evening which had still not seen the last of the thunder. Luise, still tired from her long walk, wandered out into the warm, still garden after supper. The air was fresh from the rain and heavy with the scent of the lime trees. As she stood looking down the hill from the terrace she saw a tall figure hurrying up the path towards her.

'*Der Oheim!*' she whispered to herself, frightened now that she was about to meet him. As he drew nearer she realised with a shock that he was no longer young. Still upright and strong in his steps, but his shoulders had a slight stoop and his black hair, falling to his collar after the custom of the time, was flecked with grey. However, his thin, eager face had lost none of its sensitivity: it was still the face of a man whose spirit had defied the years and their sorrows.

He looked up then and saw her standing there. In the half-light of the stormy evening he saw a young woman, with fair hair pulled away from her face into a coil at the nape of her neck, a slim, neat, quiet woman, a sweet solemnity in her smile as she moved towards him, her hands held out in greeting. He had forgotten Luise, the child of long ago, and saw now only what his heart yearned to see... in the magic twilight it was Lotte, her mother, not Luise, who moved towards him through the scented garden, across the years, out of the darkness of death, Lotte as she was when he last saw her in the orchard at Osterode so long ago.

He took Luise's hands in his own.

'It has been so long... so *long!*' he said as he held her firm young hands in his... and the spell broke and he cursed himself for a foolish old man.

'Luise! My dear! Welcome to Keilhau.'

She in her turn, not understanding, was embarrassed by the warmth and emotion of his greeting. Later she told Elise: 'He seemed to know me... yet we have not met since I was a child... hardly more than a baby.'

Elise laughed. 'Take no notice!' she said. 'Der Oheim is a darling, but he's the most absent-minded man in the world. He probably mistook you for someone else.'

Certainly when they next met, Friedrich gave no sign of the strangeness of his first greeting and treated Luise as he did all the Keilhau community, with a detached good humour.

He listened attentively while Luise tried to explain her long desire to make teaching her career and the reasons why she had had to postpone her training so long.

'First one thing, then another,' she said. 'It seemed that I would never fulfil my ambitions and then suddenly the opportunity came... and here I am. I only hope it is not too late. You know I am already turned 30?'

Friedrich laughed: 'Only the young can be shocked by their age! Do you know that I am over 60? More than twice your age! Yet I know that it is *never* too late . . . they think I am mad here.'

'Oh no!' Luise was shocked.

'Yes, they do!' he laughed again. 'You haven't seen me playing with the village children. I am teaching them, but strangers call it playing. "Look at the old fool!" they say. "He's in his second childhood!" And now even Barop thinks I am mad because I care more for the teaching of young women, the mothers of tomorrow, than for his boys' school. He can run the boys' school without me . . . and I have so little time left to do all that is to be done.'

CHAPTER ELEVEN

Luise did not see Friedrich again for some days. He did not live in the school buildings but had lodgings in the village, whereas she had been given a room at the Lower House, with Christian's family, and the days passed happily in the companionship of Elise, Albertine and Emilie, with whom she joined in tasks about the house or simple work in the school, which she was able to do without experience. She took the youngest children for walks, showed them the wild flowers and the birds, helped them to gather posies and make daisy-chains, to build little houses with twigs, and to collect feathers and leaves to make into pictures.

It was while she was on one of the meadowland expeditions with half a dozen of the littlest boys that she met Der Oheim again. He had his usual retinue of village children with him and as they walked they were playing a singing-game, the tiniest ones skipping ahead of him and tumbling about his feet like puppies.

He saw her over the brow of the hill before they actually met, and once again his eyes deceived his mind, because he wanted them to, and the years rolled away so that it was Lotte who stood there, fair-haired and sunburned amongst the long-stemmed daisies and the poppies.

'I am old... *old*,' he told himself as he looked at his hands, which were crumpled and papery. He remembered how proud he had been of his strong, lean hands, as smooth and brown as stones. 'Old!... And yet when I look at her I cannot believe it... she is the image of her mother.'

When they met, the children joined laughingly together and chased each other through the bracken which divided the meadow from the hillside.

'I'm so glad I met you!.' Friedrich took her hand. 'I have a young woman who has come to study whom I'm sure will be delighted in your company. Her name is Anna Hesse and she is about your age. I am sure you will like her and there is much you can teach each other. She is already well-grounded in my kindergarten methods but she has not your experience of life.'

Friedrich was right, Luise and Anna were instantly attracted to each other. Anna came from Annaberg; she was a tall and lively girl with a sweet disposition and a sense of humour. She gave Luise her notes to read and would faithfully repeat the lectures which Der Oheim gave to his pupils in the upper rooms of his lodgings but which Luise was sometimes prevented from attending because of her duties at the house and the school.

'He never stops teaching us!' Anna told her. 'Even when he is just sitting in the room with us, even during meals, or while we are out walking. I know he stays up half the night writing his own notes and letters because he leaves no other time for himself.'

'Don't you think Der Oheim works too hard?' Luise asked Albertine.

'His life is his work and his work life,' the older woman told her.

'But he must not *kill* himself!' Luise was passionate in her anxiety.

Albertine was surprised at her intensity. 'You care so much for him?'

Luise blushed, dismayed that her feelings should be so transparent. 'Surely we all care for him?' Embarrassed, she turned the conversation away, and picked up a little book lying on the table by Albertine, Friedrich's *Songs for Mothers and Babies*. 'What a pretty little book!' she said, turning its pages.

'It's a wonderful book,' Albertine agreed, 'but more money has gone into the making of it than will ever come out again. 'Come here...' she took Luise by the hand and led her to the window. 'Look... these buildings, our school, the roofs are leaking, the equipment is old, we need more books, better accommodation, more teachers... Always we need money. It's always been that way. Even now the three of them are arguing about money.' She pointed to the courtyard, where Friedrich with Barop and Middendorff were walking up and down in earnest conversation. 'Wilhelm told me this morning that Der Oheim wants money to open another kindergarten, in Marienberg, and the others do not think it justified when there is so much to be done here.'

Friedrich argued in vain with his friends. Even Wilhelm, his truest and most sympathetic companion, would not give an inch.

'It's no good, Friedrich,' he said. 'We cannot pay our way *here*. We cannot possibly afford to subsidise any other efforts.'

Friedrich went back to the village dispirited. The peasant woman where he lodged tried to cheer him up. 'I'll cook you a fine supper,' she said. 'The schnitzel you love and a strudel tart to follow.' The charm of his personality had already enslaved her and she would do anything for him.

He thanked her but he had little appetite and when she brought the meal and served it elegantly on his best linen and with his best silver, he only toyed with it. She watched him anxiously and to please her he helped himself to another serving of her buttered vegetables, using the old silver spoon which had been part of the manse plate when he was a boy at Oberweissbach. Feeling its weight in his hand he suddenly brought the spoon down on the table with such a bang that the poor woman was startled and thought he had been taken ill, but he quickly dispelled her fears by bursting into a peal of laughter.

'Your excellent meal has inspired me!' he cried. 'Tonight I must make a journey, but I shall need your husband's help. Firstly, though, I must do justice to this splendid meal...' and whereas before he had pecked halfheartedly, he reloaded his plate and ate with relish.

Later that night, when the moon was rising above the pines, Friedrich was on the road to Erfurt, in company with the lodging-keeper, wheeling a barrow. On the barrow stood the Froebel plate chest, the contents of which he pawned next day to his great advantage.

He left almost immediately afterwards for Marienberg in the Erzebirge mountains, with their timber forests and saltmines, a prosperous district of growing towns and thriving industries. His reception was cordial, for his reputation had already gone before him and a young woman called Auguste Steiner had already laid the ground work for a new Kindergarten. This made a total of nine and already plans were in the making for at least as many more in towns all over the Thüringen Wald. As he journeyed home to Keilhau, Friedrich felt serene and satisfied and strangely excited. He would not have admitted, even to himself, that a lot of that excitement was the prospect of seeing Luise again. He had brought her a present, as he had for all the womenfolk of the household, but for Luise, in addition to a little embroidered needlebook, he had written some verses. He was rather shocked at himself for doing so, and would have torn them up had he the time to have written others and repacked the little present, which was for her birthday as well as his homecoming.

Keilhau welcomed Der Oheim back with all the old differences over money forgotten. The story of his journey with the barrow taking the silver to the pawnbroker in Erfurt had been told with tears and laughter. Now the house was decorated in honour of his return, with masses of daffodils from the hillside woods, trails of young ivy and bluebells.

He did not give Luise her present immediately and when he did he told her solemnly. 'You must not open it now... this is my homecoming, but tomorrow is your birthday and this is your birthday present.'

They walked back to the village together with Elise. Luise knew that another celebration in honour of her birthday awaited her at her lodgings, where her room had been decorated with posies of spring flowers and there were little presents from every member of the family. They had already bidden Friedrich goodnight and he had gone on alone to his house a short distance along the road. While Elise was admiring her presents, set out ready for the morning on a little flower-decked table by her bed, each wrapped in gay paper and ribbons by the children of the house, Luise took the opportunity to slip into a corner and open the present she had been longing to see ever since Friedrich had given it to her. It was still several hours short of midnight, so she was defying his command to wait, but she could not contain her curiosity any longer. She undid the wrappings and found the exquisite little needlecase worked on velvet in the form of a pansy flower. As she opened it the verses he had written with shy embarrassment fell to the floor. In his thin, neat handwriting she read them, her hand trembling with the delight and surprise of this tender and personal greeting...

You asked me once 'Is it too late?'
I ask *you* now the same,
Within the autumn of my life
To know the spring again?
You asked me once 'Is it too late?'
And sad, I must reply
That all October's beauty bright
Cannot recall July.

Luise read the verses again, oblivious of Elise's chatter about her presents and the evening's party. They were simple, sad and unskilful, the words a boy might write to a girl, and yet Der Oheim had written them for *her*. It made her heart beat faster and her cheeks flush.

She hardly heard Elise, who had moved to her side.

'You know, Luise, I think Der Oheim was disappointed when we left him alone just now. I think he would have liked to spend the rest of the evening with us. Why don't we ask him? It is still early and it is sad for him to be alone on the day of his homecoming.'

Luise would not have dared to have suggested such a thing herself, but emboldened by Elise's encouragement she hastily thrust her present and the verses into her pocket and agreed to the suggestion that while she called Der Oheim to join them, Elise would prepare a simple meal for them. Before she left she took some of the flowers from her table that he might have them to cheer his room too.

She found him alone in the upper room of his lodgings which he used as a study. He had already lit the candle and was settling down to read the letters that had accumulated during his absence. When he looked up and saw her standing in the doorway he was amazed, even distressed, to find that his heart leapt at the sight of her.

'Thank you!' She could say no more to him, but moved by an emotion stronger than her shyness, she dropped on her knees beside his chair. 'Thank you so much.'

'It was presumptuous of me,' he said. 'Forgive me! I am a foolish old man.' He took her hand in his. 'Luise, there is something I must tell you. You were so young you would never have known, and your mother surely never told you, that she and I loved each other dearly when we were children. Your mother was the sweetest, purest woman that ever lived and I will love her all the days of my life, as we must always love those who shared our youth and its magic. You know that I married, and I loved my wife dearly—even now, eight years after her death, he could not speak of Henrietta without emotion. 'But your mother was part of a brief boyhood happiness, which I still look back on as the golden days of my young life. When I saw you two years ago, when you first came to Keilhau, I thought for a moment, in my foolishness, that I had died and it was your mother who had come back to me, out of time, out of life. Do you think that I am mad?'

'Oh, no!' Luise's eyes were filled with tears as she looked up at him.

'And now, Luise, you have come into my life when I am very old.'

'You are not old!' she was childishly adamant.

'I *am* old... and no one knows so more than I. You must not let me be foolish. If I do anything, or say anything that offends you, you must scold me.'

'But I *love* you!' The words had slipped from her before she realised it.

'Dear child!' He took her face in his hands and tilted her chin. 'You do not know what you mean... but I treasure your words.'

'I have brought you these.' She laid her posy in his lap and he took it in his hands. The flowers were anemones and violets, so young and small and fresh in his hands which were old and tired...

*   *   *

In the summer that followed, Friedrich travelled widely, to Hamburg, to Hanover, to Bremen, visiting new kindergartens, one of which was to be run by Middendorff's daughter, Alwine. Before he left he asked Luise if she would care for an arum lily which he cherished and which he feared might die if not watered regularly. She readily agreed; any little service she could do for him satisfied the strange attraction which he held for her... so much older than she was, yet so charming, so compelling, that she found herself blushing like a girl when ever he spoke to her.

He wrote to her from Bremen in August, after she had told him that his lily had bloomed again.

'This will prove that I am anxious to express my warm thanks for your thoughtful care for my arum. A human being who—like the lily—enjoyed such faithful daily care would also surely feel like blossoming twice over and thus show his gratitude by breathing out his thanks into the air! I am glad my arum has proved grateful.' His letter continued to urge her to consider a teaching career, 'how much pleasure and gratitude would be in store for you if you decided to devote your talents to the guidance of young children, of whom you are so fond.'

Luise, still uncertain that she was capable of such work, decided to make a short visit to Osterode to seek the advice of her older brothers, two of whom still lived there. Friedrich wrote to her again, this time sending her copies of some articles which had appeared on his work during his visit to Quetz. 'Your affectionate, poetic nature would be so satisfied to see the unspoken thanks in the unsophisticated faces of little children,' he wrote, and concluded 'Since my return to Keilhau our lily has opened another bud, to my great delight, thus reminding me of the gentle care it received at your hands and serving as the bearer of a new greeting from you.'

During the winter, Luise, having finally decided that she could find a career in teaching, joined Alwine Middendorff in serious study at Keilhau. Alwine, who was already running the Hamburg kindergarten and had returned for a few weeks of extra instruction, proved the more apt pupil, but both young women entered with enthusiasm into Friedrich's animated lectures, often delivered impromptu when he was inspired by some event in everyday life.

On one occasion, when they were working in his sitting room, he drew their attention to the frosty patterns on the window-pane, the ice flowers drawn with a delicate tracery of fronds and feathers.

'There are better still on the wash-house windows' he cried with the eagerness of a boy and immediately led them out to explain their science and the spiritual significance of their inexplicable beauty.

'See how ordered and even they are!' he told them. 'Symmetrical and balanced... nature is never untidy!'

Sometimes master and pupils walked in the bright winter sunshine to the top of the hill beyond the outhouses of Keilhau. The crisp snow sparkled in the sun and the branches of the fir trees were frosted with silver ice-lace.

Despite his age, Friedrich found he often had to slow his steps to accommodate the young women, who laughingly begged him not to go so fast as they were out of breath... and he could outplay them too in the games they organised for the village children as part of their instruction.

It was a bitter winter, and fuel was as short as money in the Keilhau farmhouse, where nothing was ever lavish. Alwine and Luise frequently had to share Friedrich's study to prepare their notes as it was the only room in their part of the house which had a fire.

On one such occasion, when Luise and Friedrich were alone, they were disturbed by a shy tap on the door. When she opened it she was surprised to see one of the village children standing outside—a little boy who was a regular participant in their games.

'I've come to see Der Oheim.' he said.

'Der Oheim is busy,' Luise told him... but Friedrich had come up behind her and beckoned the boy into the room.

'I expect you have come for a story?' he asked and the little boy nodded eagerly. Putting his own work aside, Friedrich took the child on his knee and reached for a book from which he read and pointed to the pictures, to the young visitor's great delight.

An hour or so later, when the little boy had left, well satisfied, Luise dared to express her surprise that he should interrupt his work for so trivial an interlude. Friedrich looked at her wisely. 'My dear,' he said. 'Who am I to say what is trivial? That child may become a far more distinguished man than I am.'

At Christmas it was decided that there should be a special series of meetings in various parts of Thüringia. Friedrich was unable to keep the festival at Keilhau, much as he would have liked to do so. However, he promised to return to the farmhouse to keep New Year's Eve with the household, but as usual he was busy up to the last moment in business in Sonnenburg. It was late afternoon before he realised that the last day of the Old Year was more than half over and he was still a considerable distance from home. There was only one way to keep his promise and that was to walk. He set off over the hills, trudging through deep snow, sometimes losing the path and buffeted by a bitter wind but determined that the new year at Keilhau should not be seen in without him.

Meanwhile, at the farmhouse the festivities were already in full swing. The rooms were decorated with fir branches and holly, garlands of paper roses hung from the ceilings and a bright log-fire glowed in the huge hearth. The children played games, there was singing, dancing and music.

Just before midnight, Middendorff called for silence. 'The old year is dying.' he said. 'Let us pause a moment in our merriment to pray a little... for our families, for each other, for ourselves, for the great cause in which we all believe. God bless us and keep us... every one... and most of all may He bless our beloved founder, Friedrich Froebel, who sadly is not with us tonight'...

As he spoke there was a flurry round the doorway and standing in the entrance was Friedrich, stooping to pass his height through the archway of the door, his shoulders encrusted with snow, snow in his hair, on his eyebrows, but laughing and holding out his arms to them all.

'My beloved children!' he cried 'I am home! A happy new year to you all!' and as he spoke the bell of the village church in the valley began to ring its new-year peal, and the room was filled with greetings and laughter. A table covered with his belated Christmas gifts had been waiting for him and as he opened the little presents, something from every one of them, even the youngest children, he told them happily of the success of his journeys and the growing strength of the kindergarten movement all over Germany.

Success, however, did not bring money. Friedrich still owned a furnished house at Blankenburg, called the Powder Mill. Desperate for more funds to aid his travelling and not daring to ask for more from the school at Keilhau, he decided to sell this furniture, which left him without any real home of his own. He lived frugally in his small lodgings in the village, managing as best he could with very few comforts.

With the end of winter he decided to move on again—this time to the heights of the Thüringen district and particularly to the area around Schalkau.

Luise was distressed at the thought of him going away again.

'Do you think it is wise?' she asked. 'These journeys are so strenuous and the weather is still cold. You will overtax yourself, I'm sure.'

'Then you must come with me and help me!'

She was astonished and delighted.

'Come with you! There's nothing I would like better! But what will the others think?'

'They will think it very noble and self-sacrificing of you to give your strength and energy to help an old man on his journey!'

So Luise and Friedrich set off together on what became a triumphant progress. The weather remained harsh and there was still snow on the ground when they made their return journey just before Easter, after several weeks of successful talks and visits to schools all over the area. It was decided to make the journey by sledge as the snow was too thick for a carriage. As they passed through the woods above Sonnenburg the sledge, which had been making heavy progress over rough ground, lurched and hit a rock and the occupants were tossed out into the snow. As she fell Luise was thrown against Friedrich and they landed together, bruised and breathless but unharmed at the foot of a fir-tree, with the driver swearing at the tangle of the horses' harness and sweating to right his sledge, which was comparitively undamaged.

Friedrich struggled to his feet in the snow and turned to help Luise. As he did so he saw, as he had done so often before, not the young woman who was his pupil but her mother, Lotte, as she once lay in the woods at Stadt Ilm on that thundery summer day over 50 years ago. His eyes filled with tears that were not caused by the bitter chill of the wind and he could hardly speak when Luise anxiously enquired if he was alright.

'It is so cold,' he told her, 'so cold... and I was dreaming of summer.'

She did not understand him...

CHAPTER TWELVE

One public meeting followed another, more travelling, more demonstrations. In May 1848 the biggest ever of these was planned to take place at Rudelstadt. Children who were to take part came from villages all over the neighbourhood and the whole event demanded immaculate organisation. Those attending included many government representatives as well as teachers and others interested in education. There were long debates and discussions, not always in agreement, but the final result was one of overwhelming success. The event's fame spread far beyond the district in which it was held, and letters and messages of congratulation flowed in from all over Germany.

Overwhelmed, Friedrich wrote to Luise: 'They have raised an old man's hopes and faith in the great possibilities of human nature. I have lived through the chill of indifference and hostility while urging men to take new responsibilities and to undertake new work for the sake of our children. It seems that a better day is about to dawn!'

Meanwhile, Middendorff too had achieved considerable acclaim for a book on Kindergartens, dedicated to the German government. In it he had the enthusiastic co-operation of Friedrich, who, when he was not travelling and lecturing, would spend days, and nights too—for he seemed to require less and less sleep as he grew older—working with his friend on a book born out of the dream they had created long ago, when they were young men. When the book was printed it was Friedrich, less tied to the duties of the school at Keilhau than Middendorff, who would frequently walk over the hills to Saalfeld to the printer to work on the proof corrections.

The book was launched into the most receptive atmosphere—best of all in Saxony and Meiningen, where a meeting of teachers urged the government to make the support of Kindergartens obligatory in every parish as the best possible foundation of any educational system.

Another result of the Rudolstadt demonstration was an invitation to Friedrich to spend the next winter in Dresden, during which he would be paid a salary to give lectures on his methods. Adolf Frankenburg, one of his own old pupils, was running his own kindergarten in the city and put the school at Freidrich's disposal for demonstration purposes.

Luise, meanwhile, had accepted a post as governess to a family at Rendsberg, feeling that she needed more practical experience away from the sheltered life of Keilhau, happy though it might be.

At Christmas, Luise, with Middendorff's daughter Alwine, now the successful and much-loved directrice of a kindergarten at Hamburg, were reunited with Friedrich at a friend's house in Bergedorf.

During the weeks at Dresden, fully occupied with the preparation and delivery of his lectures, Friedrich had schooled himself not to think of Luise more than in the terms of a trusted colleague with whom he shared his hopes and plans, but he knew in his heart that he was deluding himself. He found himself looking forward eagerly to her letters, reading them over and over again, and when he was alone in the evenings his thoughts, drifting into dreams, would play their old trick of mixing the past with the present, until the image of Luise and Lotte, her mother, became as one.

The Christmas meeting was therefore one full of expectation and excitement; Friedrich's success had given him new life and it seemed impossible to believe that this vigorous, lively man was nearing 70. He was already full of new plans to establish a training college for young women and had even selected a situation for its establishment, a country house at Marienthal, not far from Liebenstein. Friedrich had visited Liebenstein during his travels and had been captivated by its charms. Owing to its mineral springs the town, on the south westerly slope of the Thüringen Wald, had become widely known as a spa. Overshadowed on the north east by the Schlossberg and to the south by wooded heights, both crowned by medieval castles, it was a fairytale setting and as such appealed to the romantic in Friedrich, which had never died. In addition the house on which he had set his heart was owned by his old acquaintance, the Duke of Meiningen; their earlier differences mellowed with the years and there seemed no reason why he should not secure the lease with reasonable ease.

'All is ready,' he told Luise and Alwine. 'The prospectus is printed and I have already a number of pupils enrolled.'

Luise was alarmed: 'But say you do not get this house you want?'

'I shall get it,' assured Friedrich, but as the weeks rolled by and he received no answer from the Duke, even his confidence was shaken.

His lodgings in Liebenstein were the home of the matron of the Baths, a kindly woman, Frau Minne Muller. When he confided his dilemma to her she laughed good-naturedly. 'You're a dreamer and no mistake! A college, a prospectus and students already enrolled and nowhere to house them! Never mind, I think I can help you ... if you're not too fussy! My relatives have a large farmhouse just outside the town which is much too big for their needs. I am sure they could let you use a few rooms, if that would be any good, to tide you over until you get something settled?'

It was all that Friedrich wanted. He still had his heart set on Marienthal, but for all his dreaminess he was practical enough to realise that he could not wait any longer if he was to retain the goodwill of his potential pupils. So in the midsummer of 1849 Friedrich moved in to his 'Training College,' part of which was a disused cowshed which he himself had laboriously white-washed. But he was not alone—he had written eagerly to Luise: 'Everything is ready and awaits your coming. Even the birds are singing a hymn of praise to welcome us!'

Luise arrived a few weeks later, having given up her post as governess and bringing with her a young great-niece of Friedrich's, a girl called Henriette Breymann who had offered to take care of the housekeeping.

It was Keilhau in the early days all over again, but this time it was Luise instead of Henrietta who worked with him, planning, dreaming, even actually labouring on the redecorating and furnishing of their temporary and rather primitive headquarters.

The activity at the farmhouse aroused a great deal of curiosity among their neighbours and the townspeople, and especially the visitors, many of whom came to take the spa waters.

Among these was the Baroness von Marenholtz Bulow, an influential and wealthy woman, the second wife of a member of the Privy Council in Brunswick. Her only child, Alfred, had died young after a long illness which she believed to have been brought on by the severity of his education. She had two step-daughters for whom she had great affection, but still grieved for the son who had never reached maturity. She was drawn to the spa not for her health's sake, as were most of the visitors, but by her lively curiosity in the news that at Bad Liebenstein there was an old man who said that children could learn *and* be happy... and whose new system of education was spreading across all Germany.

The Baths were the centre of social activity in the town and no one knew more of the town's affairs than the matron, Minne Muller.

'Of *course* I know him!' she told the Baroness.

'It is Herr Froebel—he used to lodge with me! They call him "The Playmaster." Some of the visitors say he is mad because he plays games with the village children... But he is *not* mad, Madam.' Frau Muller continued earnestly: 'I get to know people in my job here and I can judge character. Herr Froebel is a wise man and a good one. If there were more like him, your poor little Alfred might have been with us still.'

The Baroness lost no time in visiting the farmhouse to which she had been directed by Frau Muller. As she approached the house she was rather surprised to see that the garden in front of the building was crowded with people. Drawing nearer she realised with still greater amazement that they were all dancing... at least they were moving. She paused in her astonishment for now she could see clearly that the group was composed entirely of young women playing some sort of simple ball-game with great seriousness. Among them, more serious but just as energetic as any of them, was an elderly man, tall, slightly stooped, his long dark hair streaked with grey and his black cloak flying behind him like the wings of a dark angel. As she entered the gate, the game stopped and the man drew away from his companions to greet her.

The Baroness, her long, dark frock sweeping the grass behind her, advanced majestically towards him and, dropping in a low curtsy, held out her hand.

'I have, I believe, the honour to greet "The Playmaster"?'

Friedrich caught the smile in her eyes and returned it.

'They call me that, Madam.'

'I am the Baroness von Marenhotlz Bulow. I have heard of your work, I still have much to learn, but if what I hear is true I shall pledge myself to your cause.'

*   *   *

The Baroness was true to her words. After a long stay at Liebenstein she devoted the rest of her life to the establishment of kindergartens all over Europe and in Britain.

'She is a wonderful woman,' Friedrich told Luise. 'She has imagination, culture and a sense of humour, rare bed-fellows in anyone's character, particularly a woman's!'

'Shame on you!,' Luise scolded him. 'You who are so devoted to the cause of women's higher education.'

'Education does not necessarily mean a sense of humour,' Friedrich smiled at her. 'You, my dear, frequently show that you have very little sense of humour when I tease you!'

'That is because I mind so much that you should think me stupid.'

'I never think you are stupid!'

'Well, *young* then.'

'I *know,* you *are* young, to my sorrow...'

She looked at him questioningly.

'To your sorrow? Do you wish I were old then?'

'Older... because it would be easier for me. Yet if you were you could not do what I want you to do—to carry on when I am gone.'

'Friedrich!' she was distressed, surprised, confused. 'I couldn't do *that*. What am I? I have only worked with you a few years. What do I know really of your great plan? I am only a beginner. Barop, Middendorff, so many others, are much more fitted than I am...and you must not talk of it, you are still comparitively young, and so vigorous! You have many, many years ahead of you!'

'Luise, my dear.' He put his hand on her fair head. 'I am *not* young...in a few years I shall be 70. That is man's allotted span; any time after that is borrowed time. Middendorff is younger than I am, I know, so is Barop, but not *so* young. You are only 34; you have, with God's blessing, half your life ahead of you, maybe much more.'

'But Friedrich!'

He would not be interrupted. Now at last he had found the courage to say what he had wanted to say for nearly five years, since Luise had first come to Keilhau.

'Would you marry me, Luise, knowing I am an old man? I promise I would not embarrass you in any way.' He placed his hand on her shoulder. 'Young women need young men and I could not give you what you deserve, but I would be greatly honoured and I would love dearly above all for you to take my name to bear it onwards, after I have gone, to carry on our work.' He took her hand in his and held it lightly, the young, smooth hand in his accentuated to him the pathetic and obvious difference in their ages.

'Well?' he questioned calmly, for she had not replied. When she looked up at him he saw she was crying silently, the tears running freely down her cheeks.

'Luise! What is the matter? Have I distressed you? Please forgive me! You must not be afraid to refuse me...I shall not be offended, I realise all too well that this is a ridiculous, preposterous proposal!'

She was still speechless, trying to control her tears. When at last she did speak he could not believe what he heard.

'I *love* you, Friedrich! I told you years ago but you did not believe me. But you have not said that you love *me*...I could not bear a marriage without love!'

He looked at her sadly 'My dear, there is no one love, you will learn that. There is love of country, love of one's work, there is love between mother and child, between man and woman, and not between only *one* man and *one* woman. I loved your mother, I loved Henrietta. Love never stands still but grows and changes...and now I love you. Does that satisfy you?'

She looked up at him and saw that his eyes that returned her gaze were deep and sincere, as she had always known them: eyes that still had youth in their depths, even passion.

'They will laugh at us!' she told him but she was laughing herself as she said it and he knew that she did not mind what they said, or how they laughed, as long as they were together.

When he left for Hamburg late in the autumn of 1849, on another lecture tour, Friedrich made Luise the directrice of the Training College which already had a large number of students. The Baroness, true to her promise, had used her influence on their behalf and it now seemed only a matter of time before they could move into the house at Marienthal.

In Hamburg, Friedrich saw the opening of the first 'Town Kindergarten' in addition to many private Kindergartens already flourishing, despite the noisy opposition of a few dissenters, the worst of whom was a virulent writer called Folsing.

He came back to Liebenstein briefly at Christmas, just in time for the the Kindergarten children's festival. His engagement to Luise was still a secret as she was still afraid that the difference in their ages might have an adverse affect on their cause.

On one of the days just after Christmas, Friedrich and Luise drove by sledge to Marienthal to settle final details for their move there in the spring. When New Year's Eve came, and he had to leave again for Hamburg, he told Luise: 'Soon we will be together for good.'

On his way back just before Easter he visited Keilhau to tell them the news that he and Luise were to be married. To his relief he received nothing but enthusiasm in reaction, with only a warning word from the business-like Barop, who questioned him soundly on his financial position to leave a widow well provided for.

During his stay at Keilhau he also visited Blankenburg, where he had once worked so long and with such self-sacrificing effort. The little town welcomed him warmly and the Town Council eagerly offered him the title of honorary citizen.

'I cannot accept, but I would like you to confer the honour on my future wife.' he told them, but they refused. 'He is senile,' the Mayor told the Town Council, and the ladies of the town tut-tutted when they saw the young woman by his side, for Luise had joined him at Blankenburg.

With the first awakening of spring, Friedrich and Luise moved to Marienthal, but for him it was only a brief respite from more travelling. It was not until high summer that he could return to the college, now fully established in its new home. Every doorway was garlanded with archways of greenery to welcome him, summer flowers glowed in every room, and the children from the kindergarten which Luise had opened as a demonstration school sang to welcome him.

Luise was painfully aware of the expression of weariness on his face. 'Oh I shall quickly recover in this beautiful place,' was his cheerful answer. 'City life has worn me out but here in the country, with you, I shall soon be well again.'

And he was right. Within days he was his old self, full of plans for the future, busy with the work of the present. His morning lectures, as well as the first in the afternoon, were generally given out of doors, sometimes taking the form of a walk in which he would draw on everything they passed by on the wayside to illustrate his points—a strata on the rocks, a tuft of moss or some other plant struggling for life on a barren stone.

'See,' he would tell the young women who were his students, 'see how nature has the courage and strength to overcome all difficulties, and yet is always beautiful!'

Almost every evening, groups of children would arrive at the house from the neighbouring village of Schweina, often accompanied by curious strangers who had heard of the strange old man at Marienthal. One evening a mother came with her little boy, they were visitors staying at the Baths at Liebenstein and she was anxious to see how her little one, a painfully shy child who stammered and shunned the company of other children, would re-act to the persuasive Playmaster, of whom she had heard from the Baths matron.

The other children were happily engaged in a singing-game in a circle on the lawn. His mother tried to encourage the little boy to join in, but he hung back reluctantly, his lower lip drooping in the threat of tears. Friedrich approached them and, greeting the mother, dropped on one knee beside the child tilting his chin and smiling at him.

'Look what I have for you,' he told him and took from his pocket a small wooden box, the toy he called his 'second gift' or occupation, consisting of wooden shapes swinging on strings. Soon the little fellow was absorbed in the spinning toy, and when another little boy came to join him he did not cry and run away but began to play with him, laughing delightedly as the shapes bobbed and twisted.

'It's miraculous,' said his mother. 'Never before have I seen him play with another child.'

Incidents such as this were legion. Friedrich's genius with children sometimes surprising himself, seeming even to increase with the years. The gifts, the bricks and boxes for building, the spinning toy, the other occupations such as paper-cutting and weaving and the making of models, seemed to content and delight the day's generation of children as much as they had little Hans and Pieter von Holzhausen nearly 50 years ago in Frankfurt when Friedrich had been their tutor after he left the Model School of Herr Gruner.

The other simple amusements at Marienthal, which made life so delightful, included part-singing in which the community was inspired by a young man called Stangenberger, who even persuaded the children and their teachers to give a concert at the village church. The course of training for these young teachers was six months and so by the end of the year one group of students had left to take appointments in other kindergartens and new ones had enrolled.

Although she had agreed to their marriage, Luise was still hesitant to carry her agreement into practice. She had no doubt at all about her own feelings but she was still afraid that the great difference in their ages might damage Friedrich's reputation at a time when it was going from strength to strength. Nevertheless, they were happy, working together every day, sharing their pleasures, their problems and their dreams of the future.

As the spring came round again Friedrich urged Luise again to put her fears aside and make their marriage possible.

'Time is so short... so precious,' he told her 'we dare not wait any longer.'

She was stirred by his urgency and wrote to her brother at Osterode: 'His age does not trouble me at all. In my eyes he is the greatest, the best and the dearest of men and I only marvel how he can possibly care for a woman so much beneath his level in every respect. My one anxiety has been to make sure that the rather unusual step of marriage at his age will not do harm to his work in the world.'

On July 9th 1851 they were marrried quietly, the ceremony being held in the little village church at Schweina, where the vicar, their friend the Pastor Ruckett, blessed their union. Friedrich was 69, Luise 36. Afterwards their old friends from Keilhau and the staff at Marienthal joined together in a joyous celebration, the only cloud over which was the absence of Christian, who had died the previous January at the age of 81.

It had been agreed by both Friedrich and Luise that they should not go away after their wedding. Both were so bound up in the life at Marienthal that it would have seemed absurd to leave it at this moment of great happiness. Their only concession to the occasion was to take a little time off from their usual duties to walk alone together in the surrounding countryside, at its most beautiful in the lush days of midsummer.

On the Sunday after their wedding they drove in carts with some of their friends, who were still visiting, to the neighbouring estate of the Duke of Coburg. On the way home, drowsy with the long day in the open air and sunshine, Friedrich and Luise, travelling together in the leading cart, were unabashed in their delight in each other, his arm round her waist and her head on his shoulder. Glancing sideways at him she was astonished to see how the moonlight had softened the lines of age on his face, showing only his lean, fine profile, the thin, aquiline nose and high cheek-bones.

He turned to catch her looking at him.

'Are you examining your old husband, and wondering why you married him?'

She smiled gently at him: 'I am trying to learn every line of your face so that I can see it at night even while I am sleeping, because I cannot bear to be separated from you even in my dreams!'

His hand covered hers, and he could not speak for love of her, so late into his life and yet so precious because she was—and yet was not—the same love as the love of his youth, because she had something of Henrietta in her gentle wisdom. He had heard it said that a man might love many women but all of them would have some quality in common. With the women who had brought happiness into his life, that quality was gentleness and a quiet serenity which soothed his own restless spirit, calmed his impatience, and consoled his disappointment.

He looked up at the stars—the same stars that had shone down on him the night he had fallen on his knees in wonder and praise on the hillside outside Grottingen. Luise followed his gaze and asked him to name the constellations for her—the Plough, the Great Bear, the constant northern star blinking coldly above the pines.

Thereafter the stars became an added pleasure which they shared, and during the rest of the summer a star-map lay constantly spread upon the table near their open window to provide happy hours after dusk scanning the heavens.

The number of pupils was large that summer. Earlier in the year Friedrich had been summoned to the neighbouring country seat of the Altenstein, where the reigning ducal family spent the summer months. The Duchess received him warmly and begged him to allow her daughter Augusta to receive tuition by his kindergarten method. Friedrich had delegated this task to Luise, who visited the castle twice a week to teach the little princess, then eight years old. This happy association led to a great gala day when the kindergarten children from the neighbouring villages were invited to a fête in the castle gardens, playing singing-games and dancing, joined by the princess and admired by their parents, including the Duke and Duchess.

Schoolmasters from all over the district were constant visitors to the house at Marienthal. In their company and stimulated by their youth, for mostly they were young men, Friedrich sometimes felt he was living again the happy days of debate and argument at Jena and Gottingen.

To the children Friedrich was always the 'Playmaster,' one day a little fellow called Josef was found by Luise standing patiently outside Friedrich's study door, a posy of drooping flowers clutched in a grubby hand.

'The Playmaster is busy,' Luise told the child, 'you must not disturb him now.'

But Friedrich had already heard his visitor. 'Let him come in,' he said, and the boy ran to him, thrusting the weary flowers, many of which were garden weeds, into his hands. Friedrich took the little boy's hand in his and kissed it. He handed the posy to Luise: 'Look after my flowers, liebschen' he said, 'and my weeds, for I have learned from them both.'

Friedrich's patience and gentleness constantly amazed Luise. She, who loved her work and the children, still found herself sometimes tired and impatient, but with him it never seemed to be so. The poor children from the village received his greatest care and consideration. He never found fault with their untidiness but would quietly draw out his own pocket comb and comb their hair for them, tidying their clothes, wiping their grubby hands and faces with a little sponge he kept in his study for this purpose. Usually his attentions had good effect and they began to take more pride in themselves, particularly when he took pains to point out to them the attraction of clean, bright things, whether they be bright balls or beads or the clean colours of a flower.

The summer moved happily on towards harvest time. Early in August, Friedrich and Luise took the advantage of a quiet Sunday to make the short journey to Liebenstein from Marienthal to spend the afternoon with the Baroness von Bulow. The journey to town was by a quiet road, twisting downhill through pine woods, in places so dense that it was as dark as night despite the brightness of the noonday sun above. They arrived at Liebenstein refreshed and looking forward to a happy afternoon for the Baroness was an excellent hostess and a vivacious companion.

She greeted them warmly. 'We'll have tea in the garden,' she said. 'It is such a beautiful afternoon it seems a shame to waste a moment indoors.'

Her garden was particularly lovely. The roses were still prolific and their scent and the scent of the lavender hung sweetly in the warm air. She led them to a shaded seat under a tree.

'And I have your favourite tea' she told Friedrich laughing. 'Cucumber sandwiches.'

'He shouldn't have them' smiled Luise. 'They give him indigestion and he complains all the rest of the day that he shouldn't have eaten them.'

'It's one of the many ways my body reminds me it is old,' said Friedrich. 'When I was a boy I could eat cucumbers like apples. They never gave me indigestion then. Nevertheless, whatever Luise says I shall have some of your cucumber sandwiches today.'

'I have another guest coming shortly,' the Baroness told them. 'You will like him I know. He is extremely interested in our cause and was most anxious to meet you.'

The visitor arrived just as the Baroness's housekeeper had started to lay the tea on the garden table. He was a stout little man, pleasant of appearance but at this moment appearing distressed and out of breath.

'Fritz!' cried the Baroness, 'You shouldn't hurry so in this hot weather! It is extremely bad for you at your age and you know I always *expect* you to be late!'

'Late? Am I late?' The little man seemed pre-occupied and was obviously unconscious of his lateness.

'Of course you are late,' scolded the Baroness good naturedly. 'We were just about to take tea without you, but I'll forgive you, as I always do. Now sit down do and calm yourself. You make me feel hot, seeing you puffing and panting. Also, you have not yet met Herr Froebel and his wife.'

'Herr Froebel!' The visitor seemed even more distressed. 'Frau Froebel! I am honoured to greet you, despite the sad circumstances of our meeting.'

'Sad circumstances?' The Baroness was alarmed. 'Fritz! What is the matter? We know of no bad news.'

'You have not heard then?'

'Heard? For heavens sake man, don't speak in riddles!' The Baroness could be forthright when she chose. 'If you have bad news and we must know it, for pity's sake tell us and put us out of our misery.'

'I would it were not I who had to bring such tidings to you on such a day, but all Berlin is talking of it...the Education Minister, von Raumer, issued a decree yesterday prohibiting all kindergartens in Prussia. The government is made up of mad men, inefficient, tyrannical, they seek a scapegoat for their shortcomings and choose to sacrifice the innocent. In this way Prussia will one day destroy itself...see if I am not right!'

Friedrich had not moved. His expression was unchanged but he was breathless, his heart was beating as fast as if he was climbing a mountain, and his lungs could not keep pace with it. It was as if an iron band constricted his chest, a sharp pain in his breast-bone adding to the illusion.

Luise had risen quickly and rushed to his side.

'Friedrich! You are ill!'

'No,' he said. 'I'm alright.' The feeling had passed. 'It is the heat, and the ill news I have just heard.'

The Baroness was furious. 'It is outrageous!' she cried. 'Why, only a few days ago Herr Borman of the School Council wrote praising our work. Such hypocrisy! Such double-dealing! It is despicable.'

Friedrich had recovered. He turned calmly to her.

'Don't disturb yourself,' he said. 'Such opposition throws us back on our principles. I lived through just such a storm in Switzerland long ago and we came out of that victorious.'

'I do not know how you can be so patient!,' said the Baroness. 'I cannot share your confidence. These madmen that govern us now will stop at nothing.'

On the way home in the early evening Friedrich took Luise's hand as the carriage rolled along the hill-road back to Marienthal.

'You were wonderful this afternoon,' he said. 'I was the one who failed, and I should know better. I have had long experience of such things, whereas you are new to these hardships and disappointments. I would have forgiven you if you had taken our sad news badly.'

'I was too concerned for you to care about anything else,' said Luise. 'You were ill! I'm sure you were! Are you alright now? *Really* alright?'

'Of course!' He squeezed her hand re-assuringly. 'Old hearts don't take shocks so well, and I did feel a little faint for a moment, with the heat of the afternoon and my distress, but it soon passed and now I am ready to fight on ... with you to help me, liebschen! You are young and vigorous, you will make up for the strength that I lack.'

'Of course I will fight on with you!' Luise, reassured that he had recovered from his indisposition was filled with hope and enthusiasm.

'I am sure all this is a terrible mistake...a misunderstanding,' she said. 'How else is it possible that a government should wish to prohibit a work of pure benevolence and humanity? I have seen what miracles you can work. You give only happiness to those who follow you. Surely there is no sin in happiness?'

'To those who are unhappy there is no greater sin.' Friedrich told her. 'My dear, you are still very unwise in the ways of the world, but I love you for it!'

*   *   *

The weeks that followed were a time of vigorous activity. Friedrich forwarded copies of every book or pamphlet he had ever written to the Minister of Education, along with a request for a thorough investigation of his work at Marienthal and Liebenstein. But a Minister of State is infallible and the only answer to his appeal was that the decree would not be withdrawn and all Kindergartens were to be closed.

Friedrich received this answer early in September.

'Whatever do we do now?' Luise asked him despondently.

'I shall invite anyone interested in our work to visit us here. We will hold a congress later this month; then they shall see my work for themselves and pass judgement on it. There is no law yet against my holding a congress.'

The congress was fixed for three days from September 27 to September 29. A large number of people, both men and women, including teachers and ministers of religion, town councillors and others accepted the invitation, although to do so was to lay themselves open to criticism and censure in thus showing allegiance to an outlawed cause. Their enthusiasm was unanimous and heartening and at their suggestion it was decided that a literary effort should be made in the form of a kindergarten journal.

The only refusal to attend the congress came from the official government educational department. This rejection distressed Friedrich, if anything even more than the actual ban on his work. The first might be a passing political mood, the second was an obvious and deliberate decision not to give him even a chance to defend himself and his system.

'The Baroness was right,' he told Luise. 'We are governed by madmen... my heart bleeds for Prussia, our fatherland, in the hands of such infidels. Even Napoleon could have done no worse for us had he been victorious.'

As the autumn days shortened into winter the news was as dark as the long evenings and as chill as the winds that blew down on Marienthal from the icy hillsides above.

'I feel there is only one course open to us,' Friedrich told Luise at the end of November. 'We must leave Germany...'

'Leave Germany!' Luise was startled. 'But Friedrich, wherever could we go? You cannot start again... it's too hard, too cruel! Even I could not find the strength to do that.'

'You could!' Friedrich was undismayed by her pessimism. 'And so could I. We will go to America.'

'America!'

'Yes... to the New World! I believe it is a haven for all those who are persecuted for their love of liberty, their progressive ideas.'

'But Friedrich? How?'

'Your brother in Philadelphia,' he reminded her. 'He would help us... We must write to him.'

In the weeks before Christmas, Friedrich spent most of his days working on a detailed plan for the opening of a training college and Kindergarten in Philadelphia. They posted the letter to Luise's brother on Christmas Eve, and their festivities took on a more hopeful note. New Year's Day being really jubilant now that they had something to look forward to, something on which to pin their faith.

The spring of 1852 was one of unequalled beauty. The winter snows melted early and by March the daffodils were already setting the woods alight with banks of gold which caught the sunlight through the still bare branches of the trees. Friedrich and Luise would leave Marienthal in the evenings for gentle walks along paths where the violets grew so thickly that all the ground seemed purple with their flowers.

'Do you suppose that there will be springs like this in America?' Luise still feared the enormity of the step that they were about to take.

'Of course!' Friedrich had shed his years with the excitement of new hope. 'As beautiful and more beautiful! Your brother, you know, has already written much of the great beauty of his new country. Luise—take heart! We *will* be happy, in our work and in each other. And we will be free!'

'You have more courage than I.' Luise would not be entirely comforted, but she was cheered by his optimism, for in the weeks after the first news of the ban on kindergartens he had aged suddenly and frighteningly. Now it seemed that much of his old vigour had returned.

They reached a turn in the path where the trees cleared and the hillside dropped away beneath them, revealing acres of fir tops now beginning to take on the grey mistiness of evening. The sky was crystal-clear, blue faded to the pink of an early sunset with streaks of darker clouds confusing the hill lines on the horizon until the beauty of earth and heaven became one.

Ever since he was a boy Friedrich had never looked on such scenes without emotion which frequently embarrassed him. A man never shed tears without embarrassment and on many occasions the tears had flowed unchecked down his cheeks. Through the years, in off-guard moments, mostly at night when he woke from sleep and, waking, he had come face to face again with the old terror of his boyhood . . . the reality of death. 'I *must* die!' he would tell himself. 'One day, inevitably I must die. It will happen to me too, as it must to us all, the last breath . . . the darkness . . . the nothingness!' Religious beliefs so easy in the comfort of day would be hard to maintain in the face of this terror by night, and his throat would contract with fear. He would take his own hand in the darkness and feel its firm strength, knowing that the flesh would rot and crumble from the bones.

Most of all he feared the darkness . . . not to see, not even to feel. In student days he had confided these fears to others, who even found comfort in their belief that death was an extinction.

To suffer no more . . . to be no more, they said . . . but he would rather suffer anything than not to *be*.

Middendorff's faith was simple. Deeply religious, he believed with almost childlike faith in a material heaven, not completely that of gold pavements and harp-playing angels, but not far from it: a place of everlasting joy and happiness but definitely a *place*. To Friedrich its promise of idleness was unattractive. They could talk with scholarly detachment, even humour, of their beliefs and hopes but it was only in these dark moments in the night that Friedrich really came to terms with himself about the inevitable. As a boy he had wept: his stomach had churned and ached physically with his fear. As a young man he met it with the optimism of a distant prospect. In middle age he was consoled that there were still many years to come. But now there was no such consolation; already his allotted span was drawing to its close. Yet he told himself men lived to be 80, even 100, but even as he took this comfort he knew he was fooling himself and waited for the fear to grip him

Yet strangely it was not there any more. Like a novice swimmer who cannot believe that he can float, he tried to sink his thoughts to the level of panic that they once reached so easily, but they would not be sunk. There was still regret and sadness... he thought of Luise... what would she do when the time came for her to go on alone? But there was no terror, no panic.

As he stood on the hillside in that late March evening he had the strange sense of detachment, as if he was looking at himself from without, looking at an old man knowing himself still to be young. All around him was the beauty of the earth and sky which moved him to tears... the country sounds of the rooks, making their bedtime circles above their nests in the tall elms surrounding the house, and the echo of the cowbells as the herds moved down the hillsides to their night pastures.

Luise was looking out across the valley, in profile her likeness to Lotte cutting across the years. He tried again to frighten himself, afraid to trust the conquering of a lifelong fear but he could not even quicken his own heartbeats. Lotte was dead... Henrietta was dead... his brother Christoph so long ago, his brother Christian only last year. It might not be for ten years, or even fifteen, but ten springs could fly, he knew, in a twinkling and their passing be inevitable.

All he could feel was an overwhelming sense of peace, of timelessness and security. The vast arc of the sky seemed to draw his vision upwards. 'I will lift up mine eyes to the hills.' The words of the psalm came to his lips and he realised he had spoken them aloud. Luise turned to him, smiled and took his hand.

They walked back slowly through the darkening woods where owls were already calling and the path was so dark that at times they stumbled and held each other, laughing like children.

CHAPTER THIRTEEN

The days were so full of plans and activity that even in the lengthening laughing light of Spring they seemed scarcely long enough for all that had to be done. Luise's brother had replied enthusiastically to their enquiries. He was already making further investigations to see whether the proposal to move to Philadelphia was a practical possibility.

Despite the government ban on their work the devoted women who had run kindergartens all over eastern Germany and further afield kept in constant touch with their founder.

Every mail brought letters from Zoblitz, Lunen, Dresden, Gratz, Marienberg, Gera or Hamburg, where Alwine, Middendorff's daughter risked everything by continuing classes in her own home. At Erfurt too, for some miraculous reason or oversight, the kindergarten had been spared, possibly because many of its pupils were drawn from the families of the town councillors, who were so pleased with their children's progress that they did not want it to be interrupted.

In early April another letter arrived, from Gotha, inviting Friedrich to address a conference to be held there under the chairmanship of Theodor Hoffmann at the end of the month. It was a great opportunity, a great honour, and Friedrich insisted that he must accept, although Luise was disturbed by the thought of the long and tiring journey, the strain of so great a public function, and the hostility which he might encounter in view of the political opposition.

In any case, a more personal event had to be considered before the journey was made to Gotha. On April 21st, Friedrich would be 70. For weeks the household at Marienthal, both pupils and students—for he had managed to keep a nucleus together despite the official ban—had planned a celebration worthy of their adored Playmaster. There were scufflings and laughter as the children hid their handmade presents whenever he came into a room and caught them unawares. So many were the whispered conferences that had he not have been well aware of what they were about, he might have feared an insurrection.

Middendorff arrived from Keilhau a few days before the event and Friedrich, entering into the spirit of the affair, pretended to have no idea as to why his old friend should have chosen to make the journey at this time. He was persuaded to go to bed early on the birthday eve and eventually agreed, although he enjoyed teasing them that he was not the least tired: he knew they

215

wanted him out of the way while they got on with their business in his honour.

He was awakened by the sun shining on his pillow and the sweet sound of children's voices singing a part-song outside his bedroom door. When he rose and put on his robe and went to greet them he found that they had not wasted a moment of the night, for the whole house was decorated with wreathes and garlands, young ivy and blackthorn, hawthorn and trails of bryony, every corner banked with daffodils and posies of violets and celandines.

After breakfast the children urged him into the garden, where they had arranged a masque in his honour—a simple story told in verse and song, telling of kindergarten life and pursuits. The festivities continued all day and were joined in the evening by the villagers and their children. There was laughter and dancing under the trees and plenty to eat and drink, with Friedrich wandering among his guests, receiving little gifts and giving them in return, a plant or a posy, a gingerbread cake, a little woven mat made laboriously by a child's untrained fingers, a little poem, blotched and written with difficulty by an eight-year-old, but presented with pride.

As the shadows lengthened and dusk dimmed the further outlines of the garden, Friedrich felt tired, not only with the physical strain of the day, for he had risen early, but with the emotion, the overbrimming happiness of having about him so many whom he knew and loved and whom it seemed, miraculously, loved him. The boy who had often craved affection in vain in his childhood now received it in abundance on the brink of his old age. The children danced about his feet, tumbling over each other in their efforts to be the ones who might hold his hands. The adults clasped him warmly about the shoulder, shook his hand, patted him on the back.

When it was all over he sank down, tired but happy, in his chair by the window and said to Luise: 'I still do not really understand it. What have I done? I have failed ... our ways are *verboten* here. We are outlawed, yet these good people treat me as if I had succeeded.'

'You *have* succeeded,' said Luise as she bent to kiss his head. 'You have succeeded in your heart and in the hearts and minds of all those who love you and believe in you.'

*   *   *

At Whitsun they left for Gotha. Now that the railway linked all the principal towns in Germany, there was no question of the long and arduous journeys by carriage or on horseback which Friedrich had made in his youth. While recognising that at his age travel in such a way would be out of the question, he could not help feeling a slight pang of regret when he recalled those far-off days when he and Christoph had set off along the hill-roads on horseback with only the scent of the pines in their nostrils and the only sound that of the horse's hooves on the stones and their heavy breathing on the steep ascents. Now a journey meant hours in a stuffy railway carriage over-draped and furnished, as if it were feared that a little light and air might prove too much for the passengers. The sulphorous fumes of the engine drifted in through the window and everything you touched was black with soot and smuts.

Nevertheless, to reach Gotha from Marienthal Friedrich and Luise had to travel by road to Wutha, the nearest station. To do this they hired a carriage, setting off early as they were uncertain of the times of the trains. It was an enchanted morning in May.

At Wutha they found the train due in an hour and spent the time drinking chocolate in a cafe near the station. When they finally boarded the train Friedrich was disturbed to find that he was already feeling rather tired, and the journey had scarcely begun. He said nothing to Luise for fear of alarming her: since his sudden illness last year at Liebenstein she was quick to become anxious.

The rest in the train revived him, despite the stuffiness of the carriage and the vibration. When they eventually pulled in to Gotha station he was feeling refreshed and more ready to face the ordeal ahead.

The congress chairman, Herr Hoffman, was at the station to greet them and they immediately travelled by carriage to the conference hall. Luise was shown to a seat in the visitors' gallery while Hoffman and Friedrich proceeded to the main body of the hall, where the delegates were already assembled.

As they entered the entire assembly rose to its feet as one and stood in silence broken only when Hoffman, as chairman, announced 'I have great pleasure in introducing our guest speaker... Dr Friedrich Froebel.' His words were hardly finished before they were drowned in a great outburst of cheering and applause. Friedrich felt his eyes pricking and filling with tears, the assembly before him blurring into a shapeless form of dark and light as the sun shone through the high windows on to the sea of faces. When the applause subsided he had regained his composure and was able to thank them for their greeting.

He spoke simply, hardly needing to refer to his notes because he was so sure of his thoughts—the crystal-clear dreams which had taken on the substance of reality and which had so filled his life that he was at one with them.

'In all things there lives and reigns an eternal law. Education should lead and guide man to clearness concerning himself and in himself, to peace with nature and to unity with God. Hence it should lift him to a knowledge of himself and of mankind, to a knowledge of God and of nature, and to the pure and holy life to which such knowledge leads.

The Kingdom of God is the kingdom of unity, of love, of peace, of law, of perception of the inner essence which underlies outer manifestations. It is the kingdom of social union, of trustfulness, of belief, of hope...'

He did not realise that he had spoken for an hour, during which the assembly had sat absorbed and silent. When at last he sat down the delegates rose again but this time their reception made their earlier enthusiasm cool by comparison. They cheered, they clapped, threw their programmes in the air, even left their seats and swarmed up the aisles to the platform to offer their hands in congratulation, so that the stewards had to call for order.

Luise, watching, wept openly, the tears running unchecked down her cheeks, splashing on to the white frills of her blouse. Friedrich himself, also no longer able to control his emotion, stood to acknowledge the acclamation. His handkerchief went to his eyes and his hand trembled, clutching the arm of his chair with a firmness that hurt, as if this might, in its slight pain, convince him that this was not a dream from which there might be a harsh awakening to disappointment.

When at last he was able to speak through the noise he said little but to thank them, adding with difficulty, for the words came slowly through his emotion. 'If you believe in me, as you appear to believe... If you believe in the future destiny of men, to walk in freedom, independence and happiness which is born of wisdom, open the gates of knowledge to little children. We cherish the plants of our gardens, the crops of our fields, yet a little child is surely worthy of much more care than these? Soon I must leave these tender beginnings to others to cultivate. I implore you, do not let the cold winds of pride, power and despotism destroy them. I am only the gardener, given a little time. To you I hand the keys of the garden of little children, to you and those who come after you. Do not betray my trust.'

He sat down, and now the strain of the emotional situation was too much for him. He bowed his head in his hands and could not face their response, which burst with spontaneous enthusiasm from everyone in the hall.

*   *   *

When later he had to fight his way through a mob of cheering delegates, held back by a laughing Herr Hoffmann and the stewards, to join Luise at the entrance, he found her joyful but cautious.

'You must come away quickly,' she told him. 'Already they say that messages have been sent to the Town Hall to report this meeting... to the extreme your speech could be considered treasonable. Come away at once.'

They drove with the carriage blinds down, despite the warm sunshine of the afternoon, to the friend's house where they had been invited to visit and refresh themselves. When they arrived Luise was relieved to hear that, as far as could be ascertained, official re-action was one of displeasure but there was no rumour of any definite action.

'I do not think you should speak again though,' their host warned Friedrich. 'You have already endangered yourself.'

'There is another meeting tonight,' he said.

'Don't go,' Luise begged him. 'Say you are tired.'

'I cannot disappoint them.' 'It is not their disappointment that I fear,' she said, 'but disaster, not only to us, but to our work. Don't go, Friedrich, please, I beg you.'

Reluctantly he agreed, because he loved her, and because, although he would not have told her, he was desperately tired.

After a late lunch, a message having been sent to the conference that Dr Froebel would not attend the later session, they sat in the garden with their host, the headmaster of a large boys' school in Gotha which had already incorporated the theme of Friedrich's system in its curriculum. The afternoon was warm, and the beds of wallflowers that surrounded the lawns were breathing their sugary fragrance into the air.

'All earth's joy is here,' said Friedrich. 'This sunshine, and blue sky, the grass and flowers, the trees and birds, God's creatures and those I love around me.' He fondled the ears of his host's collie dog, which had laid its head on his knee, and with the other hand took Luise's hand in his. 'I think this must be the happiest day of my life...'

*   *   *

They left later in the afternoon, reaching Wutha an hour or more before sundown. The carriage was waiting, and they were soon driving along the mountain road towards Marienthal. It was a clear evening, and the sun was still high in the sky when they reached the crest of the hill from which a path led to one of their favourite walks. 'Der Glöckli' Luise called it, for the shape of the little hill seen from their bedroom window looked exactly like a bell.

'Stop a while,' Friedrich called to the driver. 'I would like to get out for a few moments and stretch my legs.'

'Aren't you tired?' Luise was anxious again.

'Nonsense!' said Friedrich 'I *am* tired of sitting! A little exercise will do me good... make me sleep better. Come on, let's walk up the slope of Der Glöckli together... or will it be too much for *you*?'

She laughed. 'You are a wilful, wayward old man!' and he laughed with her for she only called him an old man when he felt most young.

They left the driver happy to doze over his pipe in the warm evening and set off together up the path. Friedrich was annoyed that he had to stop so often. He knew that his breathlessness could so easily turn to pain, the pain that sometimes gripped his chest and paralysed him.

They reached the summit, only some two hundred yards of fairly steep slope, just as the sun was dropping behind the pines to the west. The sky was scarlet, deepening to mauve and grey above them, and the first stars were shining. Below the valley was already hidden by mist and darkness.

They sat on a flat stone, the evening air already beginning to chill, and the sheep which cropped the close grass moved nearer to them, reassured that they would come to no harm from these intruders. A light flickered in a farmhouse far below as the farm wife took a lamp to her window, or went out to lock up her hens for the night. An owl hooted and was answered somewhere in the woods on the far side of the hill.

'When I die I want no memorial but my name here,' said Friedrich. 'Just carve it on this flat stone... with the birds and the sheep for company. My spirit, if it has a home, could find it here, on our hill, watching over you and all that we have cherished together.'

'Friedrich, you talk too much of dying!' Luise begged him with her eyes. 'This is a happy day. You are still young. There are years before us. Years of work, years of happiness. Do not talk of death tonight!'

He spoke of death just to test himself that he had really lost that fear and found that it was still so, but he did not want to upset Luise, so instead he wrapped her cloak more closely about her shoulders and said; 'It is you who will be dying... of pneumonia... if we stay here any longer... come, the coachman will have gone to sleep, and the horses walked home without us,' and with the stride of a man half his age he led her down the hill back to the road.

Marienthal welcomed him back with enthusiasm, which in its small way equalled that of Gotha but was warmer and more intimate because it was the love and praise of friends. Middendorff was there and Albertine, the Baroness and hosts of children.

They returned to Keilhau, and the blossoms of cherry and plum succeeded the apples in the pink and white snow of the spring countryside, and the house was always busy and cheerful with the comings and goings of visitors. Friedrich was still convinced that he should nevertheless pull up these deep and firm roots in his beloved Thüringia for greater freedom and opportunity in the new world.

The roses opened and it was June, with long, light warm evenings and the nightingales singing. Still Friedrich tried to persuade Luise, who loved her home, that there were other springs as beautiful, although far away.

As Midsummer Day drew near, and the children were planning a pageant to celebrate, Friedrich made one more effort to change her mind. 'We can only stand still here,' he said 'and to stand still for so long is to slip backwards. In America we can progress. There will be no bigotry, no prejudice.'

'America is a new country, and new countries change rapidly,' she said. 'How do you know that there are not men there as there are here, who will oppose your ideas because they hinder their ambitions for power? And it will be worse, because there you would be a foreigner. And what will happen if you leave Germany? Your ideas will die here, and then we shall be lost in both worlds... the old and the new.'

She would not be persuaded.

He lay awake long after she had gone to sleep that night. He lay in the dark listening to her breathing, watching a star which shone through the top pane of his window. Perhaps he was wrong to want to leave Germany... perhaps he should stay here. In his heart he knew it was what he really wanted to do, although his duty urged him to adventure on wider horizons. He wanted to stay where Lotte lay in the little churchyard at Osterode, where Henrietta slept at the foot of the Kirschberg in Keilhau, the country of high hills, deep forests and tall pines, of valleys filled with singing streams.

As he lay thinking his body became aware of sensation that was stronger than his thoughts. It was at first as if the bedclothes were too heavy... then it progressed to a tightness in the chest which grew from a dull constriction to a pain. He told himself to be calm, although the sense of breathlessness that came with the pain alarmed him and a cold sweat broke out on his forehead. Luise was still asleep and he willed himself against the overwhelming urge to wake her, to have her comfort, to hear her tell him all was well and that this would pass as other bad times had passed. But this time it did not pass but grew stronger. Unable to stop himself he cried out. She was awake in a second and beside him, lighting the lamp, holding his hand, desperately asking him what was the matter. Between the grip of the pain he tried to tell her.

She went to the bedroom door and cried out and within minutes Middendorff was there, alert and distressed.

'Get a doctor!' cried Luise. 'Friedrich is very ill.'

The pain receded a little until it was a coldness that, while it lacked the savagery of his earlier agony, was almost worse in its numbing ache.

The doctor came, surprisingly quickly it seemed, for Friedrich remembered that he lived at the other end of the village and it was already past midnight. He stood at the foot of the bed after he had made his examination and whispered, so that Friedrich strained to hear what he was saying but could not because the numbness seemed to have made him deaf. He could see Luise, childlike in her white nightdress, a robe hastily thrown across her shoulders... Or was it Lotte? It must be Lotte, and why was she here in his bedroom at Stadt Ilm? It *was* Stadt Ilm he knew, because he could smell the roses in Uncles Hoffman's summer garden.

'Grossmutter!' he cried out as the pain gripped him again. 'Grossmutter!'

The watchers were puzzled and looked at each other in distress and dismay, but he saw the one he sought, the little old dumpy figure hurrying into the room with a candle to comfort the boy who cried out to her in his nightmare.

The ache in his chest was because he had run too fast up the hill, trying to catch Christoph, whose legs were so much longer than his. He threw himself down on the short, warm grass and Christoph was beside him: Christoph tall and browned by the sun, a boy of eighteen with his little brother, pushing clover down his neck and tickling him. The tickling turned to pain again, and he was struggling to get away through trees that crossed against him, barring his way in a forest that was denser than anything he had ever known. Behind the trees he could see Lotte... It *was* Lotte this time, her fair hair in plaits as it was when they were children and her sunburnt arms held out to him.

The trees were thinning and the sun was coming out, so bright now that it hurt his eyes. He put his hand out to keep out the brightness, but it increased until the light seemed to be inside his head, bursting into brighter lights, spinning like a million brilliant stars. There was pain, but it was the pain of birth, not death, a gripping and tearing which reached a peak and then fell away, and as it fell from him he knew that it was over. The pain had gone for ever; now there was only a weightlessness, a strange unreality which frightened him but did not hurt any more... and the spinning suns in his head had settled into one cool brightness that was the light of the summer sky.

'I am dead,' he thought, 'but I can still smell the roses.'

*   *   *

Luise had watched beside him to the end. His hand had gripped hers in his agony until she too had nearly cried out at the pain that was physical as well as mental. And now it was over. Albertine had sent her away while she and the other women did what had to be done.

The night was already lightening into dawn when they came to her as she sat alone in the room which had been her's and Friedrich's.

'It is morning,' said Middendorff. 'Go upstairs. Luise, my dear, the doctor has left you a draught. Take it and try to sleep.

The lamp was still burning, Luise rose from where she was sitting, she pulled the heavy curtains aside to let in the grey light of the morning where somewhere a blackbird was singing. As she stood at the window looking out she began to cry—deep soundless sobs shook her as she held the rough stuff of the curtain against her.

Middendorff took her in his arms.

'Luise... my dear!'

Through her sobs she spoke, choking back the tears so that she could say what she must say to save her heart from breaking.

'If only I had been able to give him a child! He loved children so much, and yet he had no children of his own.'

Middendorff took her hand gently from where it lay across her burning eyes.

'Luise,' he chided gently. 'Luise... what are you saying? He had thousands of children. More his than any father could call his own... and generations of children yet unborn!'

The sun had risen above the trees on the slope of the hill, and the first pale shafts of light fell across the garden, casting the long shadow of the dawn. Middendorff turned off the lamp and, taking Luise gently by the arm, led her from the room.

END

POSTSCRIPT

In the year of Froebel's death the college at Marienthal moved back to its old home at Keilhau under the supervision of Wilhelm Middendorff, assisted by Luise Froebel. In 1853, shortly before his death (in November), Middendorff was enthusiastically received when he lectured on Froebelian methods to the Congress at Salzungen. The Keilhau institution was then taken over by Johannes Barop, but closed in the following year, when Luise Froebel went to Dresden to assist in the training college and kindergarten of Dr Bruno Marquardt. Later in the same year she became directrice of the Public Free Kindergarten and Training College in Hamburg, a position she held until her death.

The Baroness von Marenholtz Bulow, true to her promise, undertook a long series of missionary journeys to spread the cause of the kindergarten system. In 1854 the first kindergarten in England was opened at Hampstead, followed shortly after by another in Fitzroy Square.

In the next 20 years kindergartens were also opened in Ireland, Switzerland, Russia, Canada, America and Italy.

Langethal died in 1879, at the age of 87, and in 1882 the centenary of Froebel's birth was celebrated by the erection of a monument at Blankenburg, where he had established his first kindergarten, by the Baroness von Marenholtz Bulow.

In 1874 a group of enthusiasts in the kindergarten movement inaugurated the Froebel Society in London, with examinations for teachers to be certified proficient in the principles and practices of the kindergarten. In the same year one of the teachers trained at Keilhau became principal of the first Kindergarten Training Department at Stockwell College.

A friend and pupil of Baroness von Marenholtz Bulow, Madame Marie Michaelis, became the first principal of the Froebel Educational Institute, a training college for teachers in West Kensington. This moved to Grove House, Roehampton, in 1920, where it is now known as the Froebel Institute College. It is part of the Roehampton Institute of Higher Education, with an established international reputation for pioneering and developing Froebel's educational ideas and philosophies, particularly in the realm of teacher training, and its own demonstration school, Ibstock Place.

Apart from those who can be described as Froebel teachers the methods which Friedrich Froebel pioneered are used all over the world in the teaching of young children, being regarded as 'modern' and progressive by many who